THE LITERATURE OF IRELAND

One of Ireland's foremost literary and cultural historians, Terence Brown's command of the intellectual and cultural currents running through the Irish literary canon is second to none, and he has been enormously influential in shaping the field of Irish studies. These essays reflect the key themes of Brown's distinguished career, most crucially his critical engagement with the post-colonial model of Irish cultural and literary history currently dominant in Irish Studies. With essays on major figures such as Yeats, MacNeice, Joyce and Beckett, as well as contemporary authors including Seamus Heaney, Derek Mahon, Michael Longley, Paul Muldoon and Brian Friel, this volume is a major contribution to scholarship, directing scholars and students to new approaches to twentieth-century Irish cultural and literary history.

TERENCE BROWN is Fellow Emeritus and former Professor of Anglo-Irish Literature at Trinity College, Dublin.

D1056728

THE LITERATURE OF IRELAND: CRITICISM AND CULTURE

TERENCE BROWN

CAMBRIDGE
UNIVERSITY PRESS

CAMBRIDGE UNIVERSITY PRESS
Cambridge, New York, Melbourne, Madrid, Cape Town, Singapore,
São Paulo, Delhi, Dubai, Tokyo

Cambridge University Press
The Edinburgh Building, Cambridge CB2 8RU, UK

Published in the United States of America by Cambridge University Press, New York

www.cambridge.org
Information on this title: www.cambridge.org/9780521136525

First published 2010

Printed in the United Kingdom at the University Press, Cambridge

A catalogue record for this publication is available from the British Library

Library of Congress Cataloguing in Publication data
Brown, Terence, 1944–
The literature of Ireland : criticism and culture / Terence Brown.
p.   cm.
Includes bibliographical references and index.
ISBN 978-0-521-11823-1 – ISBN 978-0-521-13652-5 (pbk.)
1. English literature–Irish authors–History and criticism.
2. Literature and society–Ireland.   3. Ireland–In literature.   I. Title.
PR8718.B765   2010
820.9'9417–dc22
2010008751

ISBN 978-0-521-11823-1 Hardback
ISBN 978-0-521-13652-5 Paperback

For Michael and Carolyn

Contents

Acknowledgements

The essays reprinted in this book (with some minor changes) appeared as follows. I am indebted to the publishers and/or editors who in each case kindly gave permission to reprint.

'The Literary Revival: Historical Perspectives', in M. H. Mutran and L. P. Z. Izarra (eds.), *Kaleidoscopic Views of Ireland* (Sao Paulo: Humanitas, 2003), pp. 11–25.

'Joyce's Magic Lantern', *James Joyce Quarterly*, 28, 1 (Spring/Summer 1991), 791–8.

'Music: The Cultural Issue', in R. Pine (ed.), *Music In Ireland: 1848–1998* (Cork: The Mercier Press, 1998), pp. 37–45.

'Shakespeare and the Irish Self', in P. Kuch and J. A. Robson (eds.), *Irelands in the Asia-Pacific* (Gerrard's Cross: Colin Smythe Ltd, 2004), pp. 3–17.

'Irish Literature and the Great War' appeared as 'Writing the War', in J. Horne (ed.), *Our War: Ireland and the Great War* (Dublin: Royal Irish Academy and RTÉ, 2008), pp. 235–46 (Courtesy of RTÉ Libraries and Archives).

'Ireland, Modernism and the 1930s', in P. Coughlan and A. Davis (eds.), *Modernism and Ireland* (Cork University Press, 1995), pp. 24–42.

'Two Post-Modern Novelists: Samuel Beckett and Flann O'Brien', in J. W. Foster (ed.), *The Cambridge Companion to the Irish Novel* (Cambridge University Press, 2006), pp. 205–22.

'Kavanagh: Religious Poet', in K. R. Collins, J. Liddy and E. Wall (eds.), *Patrick Kavanagh: Midlands Conference Papers* (Omaha, NE: Creighton University Press, 1995), pp. 462–70.

'MacNeice's Irelands: MacNeice's Islands', in V. Newey and A. Thompson (eds.), *Literature and Nationalism* (Liverpool University Press, 1991), pp. 225–38.

'Louis MacNeice and the Second World War', in K. Devine (ed.), *Modern Irish Writers and the Wars* (Gerrard's Cross: Colin Smythe Ltd, 1999), pp. 53–63.

'MacNeice and the Puritan Tradition', in K. Devine and A. Peacock (eds.), *Louis MacNeice and His Influence* (Gerrard's Cross: Colin Smythe Ltd, 1998), pp. 208–18.

'John Hewitt and Memory: A Reflection', in H. Mutran and L. P. Z. Izarra (eds.), *Irish Studies and Brazil* (Sao Paulo: Humanitas, 2005), pp. 175–84.

'Michael Longley and the Irish Poetic Tradition', in A. Peacock and K. Devine (eds.), *The Poetry of Michael Longley* (Gerrard's Cross: Colin Smythe Ltd, 2000), pp. 1–12.

'Seamus Heaney: The Witnessing Eye and the Speaking Tongue' appeared as 'The Witnessing Eye and the Speaking Tongue', in E. Andrews (ed.), *Seamus Heaney: A Collection of Critical Essays* (Basingstoke and London: Macmillan, 1992), pp. 182–92.

'Derek Mahon: The Poet and Painting', *Irish University Review*, 24, 1 (Spring/Summer 1994), 39–50.

'Telling Tales: Kennelly's *Cromwell*, Muldoon's "The More a Man Has, the More a Man Wants"', in M. Kenneally (ed.), *Poety in Contemporary Irish Literature* (Gerrard's Cross: Colin Smythe Ltd, 1995), pp. 144–57.

'Redeeming the Time', in J. Acheson (ed.), *The British and Irish Novel* (Basingstoke and London: Macmillan, 1991), pp. 159–73.

'Have We a Context?: Transition, Self and Society in the Theatre of Brian Friel', in A. Peacock (ed.), *The Achievement of Brian Friel* (Gerrard's Cross: Colin Smythe Ltd, 1993), pp. 190–201.

'Butler and Nationalism', in C. Agee (ed.), *Unfinished Business: Essays on Hubert Butler* (Belfast: Irish Pages, 2003), pp. 11–25.

'The Irish Dylan Thomas: Versions and Influences', *Irish Studies Review*, 17, 1 (February 2009), pp. 45–54.

'Modernism and Revolution: Re-Reading Yeats's "Easter 1916"' was delivered as the Parnell Lecture at Magdalene College, Cambridge, November 2007. I am grateful to Professor Eamon Duffy for permission to print it here.

I am especially grateful to Dr Ray Ryan of Cambridge University Press, who suggested I might compile this collection and had faith in it.

Introduction

In the second volume of *The Cambridge History of Irish Literature* (2006), edited by Margaret Kelleher and Philip O'Leary, the critic Colin Graham wrote as follows of a study of the poet Louis MacNeice that I published in Dublin in the mid-1970s:

> By the time of Terence Brown's *Louis MacNeice: Sceptical Vision* in 1975, the sceptical-liberal version of MacNeice which Brown is interested in is entwined with MacNeice's often sardonic but affectionate relationship with Ireland. In reading MacNeice as something of a stranger in his own land, and as a man of personal and individualist integrity at a time of ideological extremity (in the 1930s in Britain), Brown claims a role for literary heritage in the maintenance of a neutral or, at least, a 'sceptical' vision when regarding the conflict in the North. Because it is one of the first substantial pieces of literary criticism in Ireland to undertake a rewriting of 'Northern' literature of the period immediately preceding the Troubles, Brown's book is absolutely crucial to the development of literary historiography from the 1970s on. Through its quiet polemic about the role of the writer (which effectively argues – by exemplary reading – that literature will always be political yet rise above dogma because it is literature), Brown's book marks out some of the key concepts by which both contemporary and past Irish writers are now understood.[1]

It was gratifying, undoubtedly, to have a work of one's own so favourably mentioned in as authoritative a scholarly production as a Cambridge University Press *History*, but I must admit that my pleasure on having that book identified as 'crucial' to Irish literary historiography since the 1970s was mingled with considerable surprise. For the book in question was not written, as I remember it, with the kind of concepts in mind that Graham discerns as governing its 'quiet polemic', and in as much as they can be derived from what I began to write over four decades ago, that must be reckoned as an example of the way contexts can generate literary and critical meanings of which an author may have been unaware.

The book to which Graham so generously refers began as a doctoral thesis presented to Trinity College, Dublin, in 1970. The thesis and the volume publication certainly addressed the issue of the poet's political attitudes in 1930s Britain, but only, I thought then, as an aspect of a more fundamental religious and philosophic scepticism that I argued was a defining force in MacNeice's poetic imagination. The thesis and the resulting book were, I thought, attempts to answer the question whether scepticism could be a creative energy in poetry, notwithstanding a general sense that poetry involves commitment and beliefs. The issue of poetry and belief was in the 1960s a matter of some considerable critical discussion in relation to such poets as W. B. Yeats and T. S. Eliot and the fact that I was myself undergoing a crisis of religious faith in my postgraduate years added personal urgency to the work I was doing on MacNeice (agnostic son of a devout Christian clergyman father). Even though the research and writing were done as the Troubles broke out and intensified as I transformed thesis into publishable book, my focus remained on the MacNeice whose work spoke to the religious and philosophic efficacy for poetry (and, by extension, for living itself) of self-conscious, creative disbelief. I did not think of my work as a contribution to Irish literary history, or to what later came to be known as Irish Studies. Indeed, the introductory biographical chapter of *Sceptical Vision* (which explored among other things the poet's formative Northern Irish background) was only added at a late stage in the writing at the suggestion of a London publisher who then declined to publish on commercial grounds; MacNeice in the 1970s was little regarded in England.

I labour these points, in what I fear must seem a self-regarding fashion, because I think they suggest significant things about the way the institution of criticism and literary history has developed in Ireland since the 1970s, things that bear on the essays (all written since 1990) I have chosen to reprint (occasionally in slightly amended form) in this volume.

Sceptical Vision got written because the topic was suggested to me in 1967 by the poet-academic Brendan Kennelly and because I became absorbed in studying Louis MacNeice by the questions about poetry and belief referred to above. The fact that the kind of sensibility I helped to define as characteristically expressed in MacNeice's poetry could later help to place him as an enabling, exemplary presence in Irish literary history was an unintended consequence of my work, and one made likely by the Troubles. Which is to say that although I did not in 1975 primarily think of my book as a work of Irish literary criticism about a Northern poet (an essay published later in the same year tried to do that), but a work of criticism about a poet, the times allowed it to be seen in the former way, the way Colin Graham in fact chooses to do.

Reading Graham's remarks about my book and thinking about why they surprised me, helpfully reminded me that criticism can be an existential encounter with ways of seeing the world and being in it. This does not necessarily mean that such encounters cannot be seen as contributions to the construction of a field or an institution like a literary history or, indeed, an Irish Studies bibliography. I have accordingly included in this book some essays which engage with Irish writings in this way: I adduce as examples the essay on Kavanagh as religious poet (which is concerned with how belief functions as an energising force in his poetry as scepticism did in MacNeice's) and the essay on John Hewitt and memory (a reflection on how memory is a compositional principle in his verse).

One could, of course, see how essays of this type could be reckoned to contribute to general discourses of one kind or another (on Irish poetry and religious faith, for example, or Irish writing and memory); in this collection, however, they stand as occasions when the critic seeks to engage with the phenomenon of poetic consciousness considered in its own right. Most of the other essays in the book can more readily be seen as contributions of one kind or another to Irish literary history, to cultural history or to the burgeoning contemporary field of Irish Studies. I hope, nonetheless, that all of them remain true to the critical imperative of engaging with literature as literature even as various historical and critical contexts, within which literary creativity can be situated, suggest themselves as analytically fruitful.

It may be in order here to address in terms of personal memoir how this commitment to literary phenomenology was formed in my case and has remained, I hope, vital, in a body of work which has been marked over three decades by its involvement with history (an involvement that is obvious in this collection). And in allowing the impulse towards memoir some free rein in the academic arena, I hope I may be indulged as I further consider how and why that commitment was joined in my case with a commitment to historical critique in a period when the latter involved matters of considerable contention.

The education I received at Magee University College, Derry, and subsequently at Trinity College, Dublin (the course bore the impressive title 'Moderatorship in English Language and Literature'), was markedly historicist in tenor. It ranged from the literature of Anglo-Saxon England to Ginsberg's *Howl*. Reading lists for specific elements of the course intimidated by their inclusive extent, and the overall structure enforced a sense of historical development. One did not get to read the major novels of the English tradition until one had read quite deeply in Elizabethan and Jacobean prose. Joyce and other modern Irish writers (taught in the third year of the four-year course) were preceded by a year-long first-year course in nineteenth-century Anglo-Irish literature. It would have been difficult not to have understood that 'English' in the University of Dublin was a historical discipline, in the sense that it was predicated on the concept of a literary history slowly accumulating, with its major and minor works forming a rich continuum, well worth studying. The first-year course in Anglo-Irish literature in my own experience was especially significant in this respect. I read the works (or at least a proportion of them) on that extensive reading list, from Maria Edgeworth to Somerville and Ross, from Thomas Moore to Samuel Ferguson and early Yeats, at the window of a room in Magee College, overlooking the river Foyle in Derry (Magee prepared Honours candidates for the first two years of the Trinity College courses). For a young man for the first time gaining a sense of an Irish life lived beyond Belfast and the unionist community of its north-Down environs, the fact that the college's library contained a whole roomful of Anglo-Irish authors was an advancement in learning indeed, and one bearing a distinctive historical message. Ireland had a literature in the English language and I was holding it in my hands, for many of the works I was able to borrow from the library and take to my room were first editions or at least handsome nineteenth-century productions, three-decker novels or presentation copies. In some instances I had to blow away the dust of the decades. History was real.

From the vantage point of 2009, what is striking is how much of what was then termed Anglo-Irish literature Trinity English included. Equally striking is how little its inclusion was seen to raise problems about what its presence in a course called English Language and Literature actually meant (a course on the history of the English language barely mentioned Hiberno-English). Its presence in the course probably owned something to the insistence of the Marxist critic in the department, the Northern Irishman J. K. Walton (Shakespearian textual critic and admirer of Arnold Kettle) and to the foresightedness of the Head of Department, Professor Philip Edwards (Renaissance scholar), who had been to the fore in the construction of the course I was fortunate to take. As an Englishman in Ireland, he had had the vision to see that Anglo-Irish literature must be a key element in an undergraduate education in an English department in Ireland and not just a money-spinner at graduate level as it had tended to be before his arrival in 1960. When he left in 1966, he had in fact been planning with the writer Frank O'Connor to establish a course in Irish Studies in Trinity. The project had foundered for lack of financial support and Edwards's departure and O'Connor's untimely death in 1968 meant that the college did not manage to make their vision of such a course actual until 2007, almost forty years later.[2]

In our current jargon, 1960s English at Trinity was under-theorised (literary theory in as much as it was mentioned at all meant a book by the American critics Austin Warren and René Wellek). So if the inclusion of Anglo-Irish literature and of a quite comprehensive course in American literature in the fourth year were not deemed in any way problematic alongside the major and minor works of the English literary canon, this was probably because, with one or two exceptions, most of the faculty were literary historians of settled historicist outlook for whom methodological issues did not seem at all pressing. One young lecturer, the late Geoffrey Thurley, did bring a Leavisite intensity to the explication of poetry, especially to that of T. S. Eliot, and the poet Brendan Kennelly bore witness in vivid lectures to the imaginative power of romantic art, but in the main, the department seemed basically untroubled by the kinds of theoretical issues that were beginning to disturb English departments elsewhere in the English-speaking world.

So my intellectual formation (to dignify what was often an undergraduate anxiety to second-guess the examiners) through the study of English Language and Literature certainly predisposed me to value historical perspectives in the life of the mind. In my case this sense of things was joined by a developing specific awareness that my own country possessed a valid English-language literary tradition (the presence of an Irish language tradition was not highlighted at any point, although the Irish Studies course proposed by Edwards would have been bilingual in content, in the way the current course is). This predisposition and national inflection has remained central to my academic preoccupations, as I hope is evident from this collection of essays.

However, there was another aspect of my intellectual experience in the 1960s that had a significant effect on my academic development and on such sensibility as I possess. The crisis of religious faith, referred to above, that I underwent in my undergraduate and graduate years was crucially involved with questions about text and history. These were questions that in many ways anticipated the hermeneutic disputes that invaded 'English' in the 1970s and 1980s as a consequence of the general 'theoretical turn' in the discipline, but which, for a Christian believer as I was in my early twenties, were of inescapable existential import. Let me explain.

As the elder surviving son of evangelical Christian missionaries, who had both spent the grim years of the Second World War in Japanese-occupied inland China, I was raised to consider the Holy Bible as the inerrant, infallible Word of God, Whose scriptural communication with his Christian children should be made the basis of daily reading, reflection, interpretation and prayer. The truths of salvation were to be found within its pages, open directly to the honestly searching spirit, without the mediation of any church, priest, minister or pastor. The act of reading was accordingly an awesome yet intimately familial one when the text was sacred. The ethos of a Northern Irish School where evangelical convictions were a pervasive presence had further confirmed family values. However, the 1960s in the English-speaking world were a decade when even the most cloistered Christian would have been aware that dependence on Scripture as an infallible source of revelation was fraught with intellectual difficulties. The immense popularity of Bishop John Robinson's little book of 1963, *Honest to God* (over a million copies sold), had put the cat among the pigeons in the English-speaking Protestant world, as it made very public the kind of historicised readings of Scripture and especially of the Gospels that had been the basis of theological disputation in the schools of theology for more than a hundred years. For a few years speculative theology became quite fashionable, with paperbacks rolling off the presses on such lively subjects as the death of God, the secular city and religionless Christianity[3] (that oxymoron drawing on the Lutheran martyr to Nazism, Dietrich Bonhoeffer), but for a reader like myself life issues were at stake. Could one continue to commit oneself to the Christian life when the historical sources of the faith were so open to historical question, with Form Criticism the dominant force in the academy that inferred a radical scepticism about the Gospels' 'historicity'? As I read for my examinations and thesis, I also immersed myself in the contemporary debate about Christian origins and the possibility of religious revelation in texts so evidently constructions of believing communities with their life situations and needs. Looking back on one book I read at that time, I note that I underlined the following bleak sentence in an essay that sought to contract Form Criticism's findings: 'In other words, the Gospels are *both* the material rehandled *and* the evidence for the rehandling',[4] introducing me to the kind of hemeneutic circle that later in literary theory texts would similarly induce the vertiginous sense of an *aporia*.

The writings of the German-American Paul Tillich were among the most influential among the works of popular theology of the period that broadcast in such works as *The Courage to Be* the need to reinterpret the Gospel message as a call to feel 'ultimate concern' and to be aware that life possessed 'depth', in a way that seemed to rob Scripture of any propositional content. Yet it was the writings and ideas of Rudolf Bultmann, which called for the demythologising of the New Testament world-view (with its concepts of Virgin Birth, Incarnation, substitionary atonement, resurrection, assumption into Heaven and promise of a second coming; the substance of the historic Christian creeds, indeed), that I found the most disturbing and challenging. His radical doubts about the historicity of the New Testament texts, and his urging that the essential *kerygma* (declaration, preaching) of the early church must be encountered by the reader of these mysterious works when their mythological way of speaking had been fully admitted, resonated with my own attempts as a student of literature to understand how myth functioned in some of the key Modernist works (three decades later as I struggled with Yeats's *A Vision* as a key work of the poet's maturity, my earlier theological readings about image, myth and religious symbol proved their critical use[5]). More significantly, they gave me to feel that religio-literary meanings, although products of historical circumstances and expressed in terms of particular world-views, could transcend the conditions of their production (a formulation that I know sounds hopelessly inadequate when one thinks, for example, of the Gospel of St John). That sense has remained with me in my literary–historical work, though the belief that the New Testament documents are some kind of special divine revelation has not (my problem was basic enough: once one accepted the dubiety of Christian sources and that what the Gospels contained was the 'preaching' of the early church couched in terms of mythic consciousness, what reason could be given for believing that Christianity was a revealed religion with a special claim upon us to believe its implicit truth claims about reality, whatever one makes of the ethic it advocates).

Given these kinds of concerns (and they had significant personal implications in terms of family traditions and friendships), it should not surprise that two books of literary criticism that deeply impressed me at that period of my life were J. Hillis Miller's *The Disappearance of God: Five Victorian Writers* (1963) and *Poets of Reality* (1965). The former explored how nineteenth-century writers had reacted to their own crises of faith in the era of metaphysical reductionism, while the latter examined how key twentieth-century English-language writers (predominately poets) had sought to deal with the impoverishment of imagination and spirit that modernity represented for them. These were subjects embraced by the critic-son of a distinguished American Baptist in a way that spoke directly to my own questioning preoccupations. That they did so through a compelling synthesis of New Critical attention to verbal detail with the Geneva School's belief that literature opened a door to another's consciousness (Miller was at that time heavily influenced by the work of George Poulet) had direct impact on my own attempt to encounter the world of MacNeice's poetry and other writings as a phenomenon of consciousness.

In his subsequent career, of course, Miller was to heed the voice of the 'deconstructive angel', becoming in the 1970s one of the most ingenious and influential of those who sponsored a critical turn in the North American academy that made of Derridean insight a critical *praxis*. Developments in Ireland, I reckon, disallowed the kind of disengagement from history that deconstruction could encourage when insight and subversive critique became the basis of pedagogy and, sometimes, glib learned response. For the years 1968 to 1975 were those in which the Irish question (suppurating since the 1920s) reopened as a violently inflamed wound. History was not dusty books in a library, however fascinating, nor a matter of mere textuality to be experienced as a site of *aporia*, but dreadful occurrences in streets one knew. Events such as Bloody Sunday and Bloody Friday in 1972, the Dublin and Monaghan Bombings in 1974 during the Ulster Workers' Strike of that year, were shaking historic foundations. Minerva's owl was certainly on twilit wing. Who knew what night could bring? Crises of faith became crises of politics.

As a product of the British educational system, of the post-war welfare state, recipient of a university scholarship courtesy of the Butler Education Act (which was made applicable to British subjects in Northern Ireland in 1947), I had naturally greeted the election of Harold Wilson's Labour Government in the United Kingdom in 1964 with enthusiasm (Wilson promised social reform in 'the white heat of the technological revolution'). Labour traditions with roots in English Methodism and in Welsh nonconformism had historically given to the British Left a certain evangelical aura (the preacher and the prophet could share a platform). Labour seemed the natural home for those raised to believe the Gospel had a social dimension. And in my own field of English Studies, the writings of Richard Hoggart and of the Welsh Marxist Raymond Williams offered a rich cultural analysis of British society and its intellectual and social inheritance that supplied ideological grist to the mill of political hope. So it seemed possible in 1969 to 1970 (with James Callaghan as Home Secretary) that disaster could be averted in Northern Ireland through genuine reform. That it was in fact a Tory Government under Ted Heath that negotiated with the Irish Government the Sunningdale Agreement of 1973 (which would largely be replicated by the Good Friday Agreement of 1998 a generation later) was surprising. That it was Wilson's second government that allowed it to fail in the summer of 1974 was not only surprising but utterly shocking. I still remember how unnerved I was by the querulous impotence of the Northern Ireland Secretary of State, Merlyn Rees, in face of the Ulster Workers' Council direct-action assault on the agreement, and how astonished I was by Wilson's ill-judged speech on the crisis, in which he had seemed to damn the whole northern Protestant community as a bunch of 'spongers' on the British state. It was hard not to sense that he was governed by a colonial mindset with Northern Ireland as troublesome a colony as the Rhodesia that had given him so much grief during his several premierships.

As it happened, in the month leading up to that momentous period in May 1974 I had been giving a lot of thought to the question of the province's status in the United Kingdom and in the island of Ireland. With support from the Arts Council of Northern Ireland, I was researching and writing a book on the course of poetry in the north of Ireland since the seventeenth century (the pioneering work and conversation of the socialist poet of Methodist background, John Hewitt, had encouraged me in my efforts and Raymond Williams's book *The Country and the City* was an example of what such a survey could achieve). By grim chance I had been reading in the National Library in Dublin poems about the Nazi blitz on Belfast in the Second World War, when the dome of the building shook with the impact of one of the murderous bombs that loyalist terrorists placed in the city on 17 May, during the massive Workers' Strike north of the border (which brought down the power-sharing executive at Stormont established under the terms of the Sunningdale Agreement). The aftershocks of those events could not but affect what I wrote later that year as the conclusion to what was published as *Northern Voices: Poets from Ulster* in 1975 (the book included an essay on Louis MacNeice as an Anglo-Irishman, adverted to above, shifting the focus from my book-length study). My conclusion began: 'Chapter one of this study was entitled "Poetry in a Colony", considering as it did the North as part of colonised Ireland. Perhaps the entire volume might properly have borne that title, for many of the problems and thematic concerns that I have examined in the work of the various poets are those resulting from the province's status as a British colony in an island that has attempted to break that country's hold.'[6] I refer also to 'the colonial predicament', 'colonial domination', and invoke in a final sentence as counter-weight to these 'the quality of a free form of life, an independent pattern of living'.[7] Looking back on this now, I am struck by the stark fashion in which I deploy the term 'colony' and by how little I interrogate it. I can only plead in mitigation that the times were frighteningly dangerous and that British inaction in Northern Ireland seemed like a prelude to full-scale civil war (we now know Wilson contemplated the ultimate inaction, precipitate withdrawal). Since then, as will be seen in this book, I have tended to use the term more sparingly, preferring to see the Irish experience of the twentieth century as bound up with the collapse of European imperialism following the Great War, and the country's complex relationship with Britain as only partially illuminated by the colonial/post-colonial model of that relationship that has come to dominate the field of Irish Studies (in chapter 1 of this volume I address this development in more detail). Ironically, it was the publication of *Northern Voices* that, in a sense, created the conditions for my beginning to think more comparatively about this issue.

In 1977 the historian F. S. L. Lyons, who had noted the cultural history elements of my study of the northern poets, invited me to contribute a volume on the post-independence period to a series on Irish socio-cultural history to be published by William Collins Ltd (who had published the paperback edition of his own magisterial *Ireland Since the Famine*, in 1973), of which he would be the general editor. After a good deal of trepidation I set to work, unaware that I would be the only member of the assembled team (historians almost to a man, if memory serves) who would complete the assignment. My *Ireland: A Social and Cultural History, 1922–79* appeared as a stand-alone work in paperback, to little notice, it must be said, in 1981 (subsequently it has been the most-cited of my works).

The preparation of this work involved not only extensive researches in the literary and cultural archives but an attempt to grasp the overall shape of independent Ireland's historical experience. Such Irish social histories and anthropological studies as then existed proved locally helpful, but it was Clifford Geertz's essay 'After the Revolution: The Fate of Nationalism in the New States' (included in his *The Interpretation of Cultures*, 1975), with its international perspectives, that proved most enabling. I was most struck by his contention that new states formed with nationalist underpinning in the twentieth century were driven by two impulses that he termed 'essentialism' and 'epochalism'. The former involved states answering the question 'Who are we?' by employing 'symbolic forms drawn from local traditions', while the latter stimulated the new states to discern and adapt to 'the outlines of the history of our time and what one takes to be the overall direction and significance of that history'.[8] Geertz saw this not simply as a kind of 'cultural dialectic, a logistic of abstract ideas, but a historical process as concrete as industrialization and as tangible as war'.[9] In many ways the Irish Free State and the republic which succeeded it in 1949 offered a laboratory in which to test Geertz's theory, with some of the kind of 'thick description' that he encouraged elsewhere in his book as the purpose of anthropological study. In my book I sought to supply that to the degree that current research allowed, while being governed by the broad outlines of his general thesis.

I doubt I could have managed to conceptualise twentieth-century Irish history to the degree that I did in my book without Geertz as an organising presence. However, as I wrote I was aware of complicating factors, especially that an intimate if often uncomfortable propinquity exists between Ireland and Britain and that partition politically connects the two islands, whatever view one takes of it. In the post-independence period, the essentialist impulse found expression in Irish Ireland ideology and its expressive practice in a reactive response to what were thought to be alien English influences (which were often crudely vilified as pagan excrescences on native purity), while the attempt to discern the wider movement of history tended to aspire to European and North American vistas that could seem to render nugatory how much Ireland was affected by the United Kingdom's international decisions. Both tended to expunge from awareness how the United Kingdom itself was not a static unchanging phenomenon in the twentieth century and how often what happens in one island can affect the other. Accordingly, in the volume of essays I published in 1988 (all of which were composed in that decade of ongoing political and economic crises) as *Ireland's Literature: Selected Essays*, I was at pains to include entries that dealt in detail with literary relations between our two islands and to indicate how the Irish Literary Revival (the fulcrum in the book's historiography) could be considered as 'a part of the history of Victorian Britain' as well as an aspect of the 'rich and scarcely harvested field of Irish Victorian life and thought'.[10]

The essays included in this volume all, as stated earlier, date from 1990 onwards, and many of them derive from the period when I was at work on a critical biography of W. B. Yeats (published in 1999) and thereafter on a revised and extended version of *Ireland: A Social and Cultural History* (published 2004). Both these works, I believe, reflected my settled sense, expressed again in this new volume, that the study of the literature, culture and society of Ireland often requires an awareness of developments in the neighbouring island. The Yeats biography demanded an awareness of the poet's near bi-location as Dubliner and Londoner throughout much of his life, while the new version of *Ireland* had to address British policy in Ireland in the 1990s as two states arranged a version of shared governance for Northern Ireland. So in what follows I take it as indicative of that pre-occupation that Louis MacNeice figures significantly in essays that assess the nature of his Irish identity, his experience as a Londoner (a role many Irish men and women have adopted to varying degrees over the centuries) during the Second World War, and how his work can be read as a contri-bution to English and British culture. (An essay remains to be written on how Heaney has impacted, probably to a greater degree, on the culture of Ireland's nearest neighbour, though his 'passport's green'.) Other essays consider how English literature and literary developments in Britain have affected the course of Irish writing from Yeats to Michael Longley, while studies of literary texts by writers from the north of Ireland indicate that a region as site of contestation highlights the complexity of socio-cultural relations in our islands. A final essay on Dylan Thomas and Ireland allows issues of region and nation, centre and periphery, to be considered in a less fraught context. In all of this, Hugh Kearney's pan-optic book *The British Isles: A History of Four Nations*, in its two manifestations (1989, 2006) has been an inspiration.

It was of course in the 1990s that the colonial/post-colonial model of British/Irish relations took firm hold in the discipline of Irish Literary and Cultural Studies. And Declan Kiberd's *Inventing Ireland: The Literature of the Modern Nation* (1995), with its energy and panache, made its pre-suppositions seem necessary, even normative, in Irish Studies as a whole. Yet a key aspect of that deservedly influential work (its controlling sense that England remained a kind of constant in history, with Ireland gener-ating its own creative hybridity in vibrant response) has tended in work by critics less gifted, less *engagé* than Kiberd to be taken as axiomatic; the result is sometimes an almost Manichean moralism of fixed critical certi-tude. Perhaps some of the essays in this book may be read as my demurral with regard to this development.

The force field of post-colonial interpretations of Ireland's experience can, of course, generate compelling readings of the past and present, especially when it affects the mind of a major writer. The essay on the drama of Brian Friel, in this volume, I think, makes that clear. But as a critical paradigm the model can occlude not only the complexity of sameness and difference (in this volume war emerges as a zone of such often bitter entanglements) but the specificity of Irish realities. The short essay on Joyce included here, I suggest, indicates how precisely calibrated these can be in the hands of a master.

Mention of Joyce naturally introduces the subject of the Irish Modernism to which he so signally contributed. That the critic can credibly deploy the term 'Irish Modernism' is a further indicator of significant change in recent years in the critical field. The phenomena of international Modernism and of post-modernity in the last two decades have, as I discuss in following pages, increasingly been subjected to analyses that explore national provenances as well as transnational defining characteristics. A number of the essays in this book are included as my contribution to this academic topic. That this element of my book comprises historical reflection and an extended formal reading of Yeats's poem 'Easter 1916', may indicate that the useful cast of mind Colin Graham discerned at work in my study of MacNeice, published over three decades ago, still affects the work I try to do as a literary and cultural historian. I can only hope it does.

NOTES

1 C. Graham, 'Literary Historiography, 1890–2000', in M. Kelleher and P. O'Leary (eds.), *The Cambridge History of Irish Literature,* Vol. II: *1890–2000* (Cambridge University Press, 2006), p. 585.

2 For Edwards's account of his efforts to establish Irish Studies in Trinity in the 1960s, see P. Edwards, 'Frank O'Connor at Trinity', in M. Sheehy (ed.), *Michael/Frank: Studies on Frank O'Connor* (Dublin: Gill and Macmillan; London: Macmillan, 1969), pp. 129–36.

3 For a lively, journalistic account of this, see V. Mehta, *The New Theologian* (Harmondsworth: Penguin Books, 1965).

4 R. P. C. Hanson, 'The Enterprise of Emancipating Christian Belief from History', in A. Hanson, *Vindications: Essays on the Historical Foundations of Christianity* (London: SCM Press Ltd, 1966), p. 39.

5 See in particular E. J. Tinsley, 'Parable, Allegory and Mysticism', in Hanson, *Vindications,* pp. 153–92.

6 T. Brown, *Northern Voices: Poets from Ulster* (Dublin: Gill and Macmillan, 1975). p. 214.

7 *Ibid.,* p. 221.

8 C. Geertz cited in T. Brown, *Ireland: A Social and Cultural History, 1922–79* (Glasgow: William Collins and Sons, Ltd, 1981), p. 181.

9 *Ibid.,* p. 182.

10 T. Brown, *Ireland's Literature: Selected Essays* (Mullingar: Liliput Press; Totowa, NJ: Barnes and Noble, 1988), p. viii.

CHAPTER I

The Literary Revival: historical perspectives

At the sixth Annual Conference of the Canadian Association for Irish Studies held in Montreal in March, 1973, Seamus Deane delivered a lecture entitled 'The Literary Myths of the Revival: A Case for Their Abandonment'. This was less than three years after the founding meeting of the International Association for the Study of Anglo-Irish literature, now IASIL, in the summer of 1970 at Trinity College, Dublin. At that Dublin meeting, the Northern Troubles, in their earliest phase, scarcely registered. No one seemed surprised. By 1973 with Bloody Sunday in Derry, Bloody Friday in Belfast, with internment poisoning the communities in Northern Ireland and the Provisional IRA in the midst of a bombing campaign, it would by contrast have seemed surprising if a meeting dedicated to Irish Studies had not heard something bearing on the developing Irish imbroglio. Deane, with severe passion (I remember the tone precisely in the grand 'colonial' chamber in McGill University's Great Hall, in a city that knew its own kind of ethnic and linguistic divisions), spoke of 'our present delapidated situation' that had 'borne in upon us more fiercely than ever the fact that discontinuity, the discontinuity that is ineluctably an inheritance of a colonial history, is more truly the signal feature of our condition'.[1] Deane's lecture, which was published in 1977, set literary historians the task of unmasking what he thought were the disabling Yeatsian myths of the Irish literary revival, which had for too long enjoyed the status of literal truth. For, he asserted, 'Perhaps the most seductive of all Yeats's historical fictions is that he gave dignity and coherence to the Irish Protestant Ascendancy tradition'.[2] The Yeats imaginary was not even an historical interpretation of the past, but an aesthetic strategy. Deane argued:

The aesthetic heritage with which we still struggle clearly harbors the desire to obliterate or render nugatory the problems of class, economics, bureaucratic systems and the like, concentrating instead on the essences of self, nationhood, community and Zeitgeist. If there is any politics to be associated with such an aesthetic, it is the politics of Fascism. It is again surprising that this clear implication should pass almost unnoticed in the body of contemporary Irish writing and in the scattered conviction many writers still retain about the so-called autonomy of the imagination.[3]

What Deane called for in his lecture was for a literary history to be written in Ireland that took account of the things that historians proper should address – 'the problems of class, economics, bureaucratic systems and the like' – adding his own demand that that history should be read as 'colonial'.

Deane's was a minatory performance, made the more telling in the almost complete absence of social and cultural histories of nineteenth- and twentieth-century Ireland extant at that date and by the very limited amount of literary criticism or literary history written by Irish scholars in Irish universities since partition and the founding of the Irish state. For in 1973, something it is difficult to imagine now, there were almost no monographs on Irish writers by resident Irish scholars (other than Daniel Corkery's *Synge and Anglo-Irish Literature,* 1931) and few thematic or general works of reflection. Classics such as Jeffares and Henn on Yeats, and Mercier on the Irish comic tradition, had been penned by Irishmen who had made academic careers abroad. Some of the best critical works were in fact by writers, with Frank O'Connor's *The Backward Look* (1967) an early plea for Irish Studies.

At the beginning of the 1970s, historians had in fact begun to lay the groundwork for the kind of socio-cultural and political account of the Irish Literary Revival, that Deane had called for. In November 1970 in the journal *20th Century Studies* (produced at the University of Kent at Canterbury), the historian L. P. Curtis, Jr, published an excellent article entitled 'The Anglo-Irish Predicament', which anatomised the caste Deane believed to have been successfully mythologised by Yeats. It remains a very valuable contribution as a study in the decline and fall of a complex social and cultural formation, brought low by five forces: 'agrarianism, clericalism, egalitarianism, Celticism, and urbanism'. By the end of the Great War, Curtis argues, Anglo-Ireland was finished:

By rejecting so much of the new cultural nationalism as well as the old political nationalism and by denying the Irishman's fitness for self-government in the name of Anglo-Saxon superiority, the Anglo-Irish gentry engendered a much more emotional and therefore lethal response from those whom they dismissed as separatists and self-seekers. To return to the arboreal metaphor, the Anglo-Irish tree crashed in the first strong wind after the war because it was attacked from without and diseased from within.[4]

In 1971 F. S. L. Lyons, then Professor of History at the University of Kent, published his magisterial *Ireland Since the Famine* with its groundbreaking chapter 'The Battle of Two Civilisations'. Roy Foster, in *Modern Ireland* (1988), has encouraged us to see how Lyons's chapter presents the ideological confrontations inscribed in the cultural debates of the Literary Revival rather too much on their own terms;[5] but as a contribution to our sense of the period it remains a key text. It takes to heart what Curtis, Jr, had indisputably established – that Anglo-Ireland as a social–cultural formation was collapsing between 1880 and 1920 – and he reads the Anglo-Irish efforts by Yeats and his confederates as an attempt to envisage a cultural synthesis in a future Ireland to which they could contribute much of value. But where Deane found their machinations offensive, Lyons afforded the luminaries of the Revival sympathy and admiration as cultural politicians of a high order. As historian, nonetheless, he knew their fate had been sealed:

Although nothing can take from the quality of their achievement, those who made it possible were in the long run losers in the battle of two civilisations. Even by 1903, more clearly by 1907, beyond any conceivable doubt by 1913, it had become evident that their movement could not succeed on their terms, only on terms which seemed to them humiliating and dishonourable. The truth was that their initiative … was founded on a false assumption, an assumption easily enough made in the silence that followed the fall of Parnell. It was the assumption that in art, as in society, collaboration between the classes, religions, and races would fill the political vacuum. But in reality there was no vacuum. The political issue – the separation from Britain – remained the central issue and everything else would continue to be judged according to whether it added or subtracted from the national demand.[6]

If a taxonomy of accounts of the Irish Literary Revival were to be assembled, Lyons's would be a persuasive political entry, which has been complicated by further work but not really superseded. What subsequent political studies have added to Lyons is the concept of colonialism, which Deane adverted to in Montreal in 1973, and of course an awareness of Modernism as informing context. These later accounts work with the socio-political parameters identified by Lyons, without always acknowledging his contribution in the field, setting them explicitly in the context of colonialism or in that of international Modernism, to which Irish writing in English made such a significant contribution, or in both.

In the 'colonial' reading of the Revival, writers, and particularly Yeats, are to be understood as colonial agents seeking cultural power for themselves and their caste at the very moment when the Ascendancy's actual political influence was on the wane and the British state was preparing to abandon them. Lyons had seen the Revival writers as Irish men and women of a distinctive kind with something valuable to contribute to Ireland as a whole. In stringent versions of the 'colonial' reading of the Revival enterprise, the main movers are defined and limited by their imperial role, indeed, they are almost dismissed. As Gerry Smyth succinctly states of Yeats in his *Decolonisation and Criticism: The Construction of Irish Literature* (1998), (exaggerating it must be said the demographic crisis of Anglo-Ireland in the late Victorian period): 'As self-appointed spokesman for the dwindling Anglo-Irish Protestant population of Ireland, Yeats's task … was to invent a history and an identity which would guarantee Anglo-Irish inclusion in, if not domination of, a restored Irish nation.'[7] In David Cairns and Shaun Richards's Gramscian terms in *Writing Ireland: Colonialism, Nationalism and Culture* of 1988, in their case in fact citing Lyons: 'What complicated the early twentieth-century struggles for hegemony in Ireland, however, was the colonial dimension, for as Lyons has stated, "the dominant culture was the English culture – other cultures had no option but to relate closely to it".'[8] In this sternly binary context, they identify 'Celticism' as 'One form of discourse through which engagement with the metropolitan power was invited – on terms which advantaged the metropolitan vis-à-vis colonial culture'.[9]

A good deal of energy has been expended since 1973 in studying the construction of Celticism in nineteenth-century Ireland as an aspect of the Revival project. Matthew Arnold's 'On the Study of Celtic Literature' of 1865–6 has been a much visited text. In this work scholars and critics have drawn on John V. Kelleher's seminal 1950 article, issued as a pamphlet by the American Committee for Irish Studies in 1971, 'Matthew Arnold and the Celtic Revival'. There he saw the identification of 'the Celtic genius' in Arnold's work as the stimulus for 'the fanciest hogwash ever manufactured in Ireland. In scores of slim green volumes the discovery of popular Celtic mysticism was celebrated.'[10] Kelleher exonerated Yeats and indeed AE, Lady Gregory and Synge from perpetrating this fatuity, arguing indeed that Yeats to his credit 'never wrote a perfect Celtic Revival poem or play'.[11] Other scholars have not been so discriminating or so forbearing. For them the construction of Celticism is seen to be a Revival strategy, in which Yeats played a major part, which allowed Irish culture to be represented in terms that involved complicity with the imperialism that is taken to underpin Arnold's treatise. So conventional has this line of argument become that in 1996 Marjorie Howes, in her *Yeats's Nations, Gender, Class and Irishness*, announced in her introduction: 'Thus chapters 1 and 2 do not focus on the question of whether or not Yeats's early Celtic nationalism was complicit with British imperialism and Anglo-Irish domination. They ask what shape that complicity took, what heuristic value it has, and how particular conceptions of gender and class functioned within it.'[12]

The basic argument is simply outlined. In associating the Celt (and by implication the Irish, though Arnold's work is largely focused on the very limited number of Welsh texts which he knew in English) with sensibility, the lyric cry, with a lack of architectonics in brief melancholic utterances, with 'natural magic', the English poet/critic had paid the Irish a backhanded compliment. They were called to Celticise the English whose Saxon natures needed an infusion of Celtic spirit, just as their Hebraic and puritan consciences required the sweetness and light of Hellenic humanism to help keep anarchy at bay (Arnold's lectures, which became the treatise, were delivered in the decade in which he was also delivering the lectures that would become *Culture and Anarchy* in 1869). They were not suited to self-government. Celticism, therefore, finding expression in poems by a genius like Yeats or by the kind of poetaster Joyce satirises in 'A Little Cloud' in *Dubliners*, reinforces a deceptively benign English view of Ireland which in fact serves the interests of a British Imperialism disinclined to grant Ireland even Home Rule. And when the gender implications of Arnold's theories are drawn out – with critics noting how he follows Renan in gendering the Celtic race as feminine and examining how Arnold's sense of the Celts as given to transports of excitable exaltation parallels Victorian stereotypes about women – then the case that Celticism is a regressive phenomenon is apparently open and shut.

So dominant is the political and colonial paradigm in contemporary Irish Studies that any attempt to interrogate it or to complicate it unduly is likely to be dismissed as itself complicit in some way with regressive forces. Terry Eagleton, it is true, could write unequivocally in 1995 (in his book *Heathcliff and the Great Hunger*) that 'the enlightened wing of the Anglo-Irish remains an object-lesson … in … *rapprochement*, and one whose magnanimous spirit Irish history has yet to surpass';[13] but Emer Nolan's observations in *James Joyce and Nationalism* (1995) that a post-colonial reading of Joyce's *Finnegans Wake*, in its vision of the post-imperial, sets the nation the admittedly difficult task of distinguishing 'between those who are complicit with neo-colonialism and those who are not, whether they be former natives or former settlers'[14] suggests a more exacting critical climate.

Nonetheless, I think it worth remarking that the emphasis on political and post-colonial readings of the Irish Literary Revival and of the Revival's role in international Modernism has tended rather to occlude other kinds of study since the 1970s. Among these might be the biographical–psychological and the literary-historical. The phenomenon of Celticism, and Yeats construction of it, can offer a test case in this regard.

A biographical/psychological analysis in the literary–historical context of Yeats's relationship to Celticism crucially involves a study of his occultism, which must take us to the London of the 1880s and 1890s rather than to a set of lectures delivered two and three decades earlier. Indeed, in passing, I am dubious that a line of influence between Arnold's lectures and Yeats's construction of his own peculiar version of the Celtic can be easily drawn. It was not in fact until June 1898 that Yeats published his essay in *Cosmopolis* on 'The Celtic Element in Literature', towards the end of a decade when the poet had been trooping frequently with 'things discovered in the deep', more driven by his reading of Blake, his engagement with *ritual* magic and his effort to establish the rubrics of an Order of Celtic Mysteries to be situated on an island in Lough Key, County Roscommon, than by an Arnoldian worship of 'natural magic'. Yeats's 1898 essay was probably attributable to the fact that since 1896, with his French as poor as it was, he had been able to read Ernest Renan's *La poésie des races celtiques*, which appeared in William G. Hutchinson's English translation in that year (Yeats quotes loosely from that translation on the opening page of his essay, somewhat disingenuously announcing 'I must repeat the well-known sentences'[15]). Of course Yeats's purpose in the essay is to distinguish from Arnoldian Celticism the possibility that the new century may see a renaissance of spirituality presaged in the symbolist movement in literature. And that new force would not carry modernity back to a distinctive Celtic world-view but would recreate 'the ancient religion of the world'.[16] This religion would be marked, Yeats believed, by an anti-positivist, anti-commercial vision; it would be without 'our thoughts of weights and measure … our own strait limits'[17] and would offer something of the 'supreme ritual' of the ancients, celebrated because they lived nearer 'to ancient chaos'[18] than the inhabitants of a modern suburb. Whatever the author of *Culture and Anarchy* hoped for from the study of Celtic literature, it was scarcely an approach to ancient chaos, which Yeats names 'every man's desire'.

The psychological, emotional and intellectual dynamic of Yeats's occultism in the 1980s and 1990s, in which Celtic mysteries played a part, was rooted, I am convinced, more in his sense that materialist modernity

had desacralised the world, than in a political unconscious that sought
surrogates for a diminishing caste hegemony. Yeats is more the successor
of Blake and Swedenborg, than a Celticist of the Arnoldian type, one
whose religion is a defiance of 'single vision and Newton's sleep'. Here
I think Roy Foster, in his British Academy lecture 'Protestant Magic'[19]
and indeed in his magisterial biography of the poet, tilts the balance of
explanation rather too firmly Irishwards in his account of Yeats's occultism.
He argues early in his biography that

> WBY ... might be located in a particular tradition of Irish Protestant interest in
> the occult, which stretched back through Sheridan le Fanu and Charles Maturin,
> took in WBY's contemporary Bram Stoker and carried forward to Elizabeth
> Bowen: all figures from the increasingly marginalized Irish Protestant middle
> class, from families with strong clerical associations, declining fortunes and a
> tenuous hold on landed authority. An interest in the occult might be seen on one
> level as a strategy for coping with contemporary threats ..., and on another as a
> search for psychic control.[20]

Foster hedges his bets here, with that 'devil in the detail' phrase 'on
one level'. But even later, when he considers other 'levels' of explanation to
account for Yeats's occultism, he is magnetically drawn back to Irish politics. 'The uses of occultism are manifold', we are told, but by the end of two
paragraphs in which we move from the Golden Dawn as compensation for
the drabness of his home life, as confirmation of a literary tradition that
included Blake and even Tennyson, and as a way of asserting himself with
Maud Gonne, we arrive at what most fully interests the historian author,
Yeats as politician using magic to gain a purchase on Irish nationalism: 'All
in all, occultism had a particularly Irish relevance ... and when millen-
arian hopes of nationalist revolution developed at the end of the decade,
occult divination came into its own. In some areas of nationalist activity
WBY's position was ambiguous and his commitment suspect; occultism
combined with Irishness, however, might not only confer political credibility but weave a lover's spell.'[21]

Such a reading of Yeatsian occultism, I would argue, underestimates
the significance of new work in British Victorian Studies that has allowed
us to see other kinds of 'relevance' than the Irish and locally political in
esoteric preoccupations. I am thinking especially of socio-cultural studies
of Victorian scientific and professional discourse, and of occultism and
spiritualism as counter discourses in that context and especially of feminist interventions in that field of study. I highlight Janet Oppenheim's
*The Other World: Spiritualism and Psychical Research in England, 1850–
1914* (1985), Diana Basham's *The Trial of Women: Feminism and the Occult*

Sciences in Victorian Literature (1992) and Alex Owen's *The Darkened Room: Women, Power and Spiritualism in Later Nineteenth-Century England* (1989). All this work offers a different context in which to situate Yeatsian occultism, in which Celticism is an element, from the explicitly Irish to which Foster and others seem so inexorably drawn. This body of work has allowed Elizabeth Cullingford, myself indeed, David Pierce and Marjorie Howes[22] to represent Yeats's engagement with magic as imbricated with social forces at work in British and Irish society that involved changing power relations between the sexes, in which women were asserting themselves, and opposition to the institutionalisation of knowledge in predominately male professional preserves. In this context Yeats sought to tap into the powers generated by an esoteric order, the Golden Dawn, in which complex gender exchanges and collaborations were at work (casting in doubt the integrity and the valency of the individual subject) in order to resacralise the world, to create what he thought of as a magical personality, a living community.[23] This could act as a transformative agent in a materialist society. Such a personality, Yeats believed, could in fact be a nation and not just a magical order, if the nation was properly induced by magic to become akin to a mystical order (Howes in *Yeats's Nations* writes with particular insight about the ways in which Yeats thought of the Irish Literary Theatre and of the Abbey in such ambitious magical terms). But what seems clear to me in all of this is that the fundamental Yeatsian purpose was not just rooted in a desire for cultural power for his declining caste in Ireland, nor was it primarily an expression of that caste's terminal insecurity. Rather it involved an exorbitant ambition. For he sedulously hoped that Ireland could be induced to become a new kind of society, one brought into being by occult powers which ritual magic and a ritual theatre could generate. Had England, in fact, seemed a viable location for such an experiment in metaphysical revolution, he would have sited his theatre there (indeed for a time at the turn of the century he seriously considered that possibility). He wished to transform Ireland because he wished to transform the world. A biographical, psychological account of Yeats as Revival writer must take account of this extra-Irish dimension.

Leon Surette, in his book *The Birth of Modernism: Ezra Pound, T. S. Eliot, W. B. Yeats and the Occult* (1994), has allowed us to see how Modernism, even in so apparently materialist a writer as Ezra Pound, had its esoteric agendas as it sought to respond to the crisis presented by contemporary civilisation. Yeats, it is clear from this study, was only one of the most floridly ostentatious of early twentieth-century artists who hoped art could perform such miracles on a global scale. Scholars of Ireland's contribution to Modernism have tended to ignore this essentially spiritual, putatively universal, religious dimension of Modernism, as they have been inclined to emphasise political rather than more general literary historical issues in their analyses of it. And the explanations offered by scholars and critics of Irish literature as to why writers of the Revival period made so signal a contribution to Modernism are primarily political and socio-cultural in tenor. Eagleton's chapter 'The Archaic Avant-Garde', in his *Heathcliff and the Great Hunger* (1995), is a representative text as it draws together a good deal of fairly recent thinking of the political–cultural kind about Ireland and Modernism.

Eagleton's central point in this essay is that 'The Revivalists … combine tradition and modernity, but largely under the sway of the former.'[24] In so doing, they exemplify the characteristics of what Declan Kiberd celebrates in his *Irish Classics* (2000) as the radical conservatism of major Irish writers since the seventeenth century. Eagleton draws on Perry Anderson's Marxist analysis of Modernism to suggest that Ireland in the Revival period met conditions likely to produce that phenomenon: 'the existence of an artistic *ancien régime,* often in societies still under sway of an aristocracy; the impact upon this traditional society of breathtakingly new technologies; and the imaginative closeness of social revolution'.[25] But where he is most interesting is where he considers how nationalism is conducive to formal attributes in literature that make it Modernist in technique. He is especially insightful in drawing analogies between nationalism's sense of non-linear time and the elisions of historical time which are offered in the classic Modernist texts. It is no accident, as he has it, that a country whose nineteenth-century sense of historic time was so close to mythic repetition should produce works where past and present intermingle in defiance of mere progression. And he is perceptive, too, on how a country where experience itself has been so fragmentary, apparently beyond the stabilising powers of fictional realism, should find expression in a literature where the fragment is ubiquitous. But his argument throughout, like Foster's on the significance of occultism in Yeats, is weighted towards Irish political explanations of a very complex matter (though it should be said Eagleton has a greater sense of the crisis of British society in the period than does Foster in his biography – a feature of that work is how English society is mostly rendered as a given, unaffected by change between the 1880s and the eve of the Second World War, while Irish society is treated to a considerable degree as a construct of various power interests). In order to address how complex the phenomenon of Irish Revival writing in fact is in relation to international

Modernism, we may ponder an illuminating specific issue: the key role played by translation as an activity in making Revival literature akin to that of Modernist writing in its eschewal of realism. This essentially literary historical focus may offer its own insights in addition to or in contrast with those supplied by narrowly political–cultural perspectives.

Nationalism in nineteenth-century Ireland naturally stimulated acts of translation; for the sense of depth in history so essential to national *amour propre* meant drawing on Gaelic antiquity. Literary production conducted in the context of national feeling accordingly revived and translated texts to allow them to exist once more in the timeless spirituality of the nation's continuous being. 'The best that has come out of Ireland in my time', Yeats reverentially announces when he introduces Lady Gregory's *Cuchulain of Muitehemne* in 1902, investing her book with timeless, classic status at the very moment of publication and making it an act of impersonal artifice. And the fact that so many of the writings of the Revival period involve translation and versions – from Standish O'Grady's *Bardic History of Ireland* (1878, 1880), through Douglas Hyde's *The Love Songs of Connacht* (1893) to the very curious process of double translation George Moore afflicted upon his 1903 collection of stories, *The Untilled Field* (from English to Irish and then back to English) – highlights how much of the writing of the period aspires to the impersonality of translation. This is because the spirit of the nation, assumed to be present in redactions, versions, editions, translations, is vested with a spiritual power greater than the individual can muster himself or herself. This 'religious' truth which allows the construction of an objective, impersonal work to be superior to the work of individual vision accounts for the prevailing ambition in the period to write a sacred book of the people.

It was the translation impulse bred of the nationalist climate (combined with folkloric and anthropological impulses, which also meant actual and figurative translation) that, it can be argued, made so much Irish writing of the period seem to flout the canons of realism. For works of translation, and the literary fabrications which sought to emulate their impersonal quality (such as Yeats's *The Secret Rose*) as obviously made things, drew attention to the fact that a literary artifact is not to be reckoned an apparent reflection of a contemporary social world or of a recoverable historicity, in the manner of realist texts. Rather, they advertised how writing obeys its own internal laws of narrative structure, employing as it does juxtapositions, temporal and contextual elisions, reiterated motifs and conventional descriptions of locales and personae. Translation therefore broke the canons of literary realism as well as undermining the romantic notion of a text as an expressive phenomenon rooted in the unitary organic self of an originary creator. So the paucity of realism in the literature of the Revival period (or disdain for it by influential opinion-formers) may indeed be attributable, as Eagleton and others have argued, to the fragmentary nature of Irish experience with which a stabilising form could not deal. It can also be attributed, I am suggesting in literary–historical terms, to a literary fashion for translation generated by national feeling (in a broad sense this obviously had a political basis), which affected Unionist, Home Ruler and separatist alike.

There is a further way in which the literary impulse to produce translations, bred of a nationalist climate, meant that Irish writing of the period exhibited characteristics that suggest Modernist aesthetics. For of course Irish Nationalism, like nationalism in general, had its occult aspects. It sought to summon from the past in its acts of translation the spirit of the nation and to let a modernising society feel spiritual kinship with the heroic denizens of mythological time. Avatars were to be called from the vasty deep. Cuchulain could stalk through the Post Office because Standish O'Grady discovered prehistory in a library. In this fabricated spirituality in which translation played such a part, Irish writers were producing texts that anticipated and indeed, as is clear in the case of Yeats, could be entered into the canon of Modernist writings. For in that canon are significant acts of translation that share some of the occult ambition implicit in nationalist invocation of spirits. Stan Smith in fact has written illuminatingly (in his book *The Origins of Modernism: Eliot, Pound, Yeats and the Rhetorics of Renewal*) of Pound, Eliot and Yeats that 'translation is not just one of several activities for modernist writers. It is, rather, a key to all their activities.'[26] So as he analyses Pound's 'translations' from the Chinese in *Cathay*, he notes how 'in the many meditations between Li Po and Pound, a wholly imaginary "intellectual and emotional complex", has been created, transcending cultures and histories, which is entirely contemporary: the *illusion* of unmediated rapport with the dead'. In this transaction, akin to that of Eliot in relation to tradition in *The Waste Land*,

real time is an eternal present where all that is truly living coexists. Literature provides privileged access to it, for literature offers the subjective interior of dead lives as if we were living them for the first time. It is a kind of spiritual possession, and indeed the vocabulary of mediumship recurs in the theorising of the Modernists.[27]

Smith highlights how past subjectivities seem to become contemporaries in Poundian theory and practice. His insistence that works of the past come to us in the 'translations' of *Cathay* as illusions of an unmediated presence is crucial, for it permits us to reckon with the way in which Modernist texts and translations stimulated by Irish Nationalist feeling in the Revival period ('Revival' as a term has its spiritual and spiritualist connotations) share a fabricated sense of possession. So, it can be argued that it was the translation impulse in the context of nationalist feeling which meant that Irish writers produced texts that shared the occult religious ambition and the spiritualist implications of key Modernist texts like *Cathay* and *The Waste Land*. This, I stress, is a literary–historical thesis, not of course lacking in political consciousness, but one emphasising the 'literary' in that term. After three decades in which the 'historical' has meant social, political and cultural analyses of a high order, it may be necessary, I am suggesting, to redress the balance somewhat towards a renewed literary history, in the interests of more nuanced accounts of texts and their multiple contexts.

NOTES

1 S. Deane, 'The Literary Myths Of the Revival: A Case For Their Abandonment', in J. Ronsley (ed.), *Myth and Reality in Irish Literature* (Waterloo, Ontario: Wilfred Laurier University Press, 1977), pp. 325–6.
2 *Ibid.*, p. 317.
3 *Ibid.*, p. 322.
4 L. P. Curtis, Jr, 'The Anglo-Irish Predicament', *20th Century Studies* (November 1970), 62.
5 R. F. Foster, *Modern Ireland, 1600–1972* (London: Allen Lane, 1988), pp. 455–6.
6 F. S. L. Lyons, *Ireland Since the Famine* (Glasgow: William Collins Ltd, 1973), pp. 245–6.
7 G. Smyth, *Decolonisation and Criticism: The Construction of Irish Literature* (London and Sterling, VA: Pluto Press, 1998), p. 73.
8 D. Cairns and S. Richards, *Writing Ireland: Colonialism, Nationalism and Culture* (Manchester University Press, 1988), pp. 89–90.
9 *Ibid.*, p. 90.
10 J. V. Kelleher, *Matthew Arnold and the Celtic Revival* (University of Chicago, 1971), p. 214.
11 *Ibid.*, p 213.
12 M. Howes, *Yeats's Nations: Gender, Class and Irishness* (Cambridge University Press, 1998), pp. 5–6.
13 T. Eagleton, *Heathcliff and the Great Hunger: Studies in Irish Culture* (London and New York: Verso, 1995), p. 271.
14 E. Nolan, *James Joyce and Nationalism* (London and New York: Routledge, 1995), p. 161.

15 W. B. Yeats, *Essays and Introductions* (London and Basingstoke: Macmillan, 1961), p. 173.
16 *Ibid.*, p. 176.
17 *Ibid.*, p. 178.
18 *Ibid.*
19 R. Foster, 'Protestant Magic: W. B. Yeats and the Spell of Irish History', *Proceedings of the British Academy*, 75 (1989).
20 R. Foster, *W. B. Yeats: A Life*, Vol. I: *The Apprentice Mage* (Oxford University Press, 1997), p. 50.
21 *Ibid.*, pp. 106–7.
22 See Howes, *Yeats's Nations*, E. Cullingford, *Gender and History in Yeats's Love Poetry* (Cambridge University Press, 1993), David Pierce, *Yeats's Worlds: Ireland, England and the Poetic Imagination* (New Haven and London: Yale University Press, 1995) and T. Brown, *The Life of W. B. Yeats*, (Oxford: Blackwell, 1999).
23 See Brown, *W. B.Yeats*, pp. 116–18.
24 Eagleton, *Heathcliff and the Great Hunger*, p. 315.
25 *Ibid.*, p. 297.
26 S. Smith, *The Origins of Modernism; Eliot, Pound, Yeats and the Rhetoric of Renewal* (London: Harvester Wheatsheaf, 1994), p. 6.
27 *Ibid.*, p. 5.

CHAPTER 2

Joyce's magic lantern

Pope Leo XIII published his poem *Ars Photographica* in 1867, recognising
a new era when the light of the sun would allow marvels of realistic representation far beyond anything the pencil had hitherto achieved. Ironically,
the future Holy Father chose to celebrate this augury of a new age in one
of the languages of the ancients. But in English his poem might run:

> Drawn by the sun's bright pencil,
> How well, O glistening stencil,
> You express the brow's fine grace,
> Eye's sparkle, and beauty of face.
> O marvelous might of mind,
> New prodigy! A design
> Beyond the contrival
> Of Apelles, Nature's rival.[1]

It was Apelles, the fourth-century Greek painter, whose artful grapes were
so realistic that the birds are reputed to have pecked them. Photography,
it is implied, will perform even greater mimetic miracles in the future.
And the light of the sun is the source of this new art.

This poem is the only item of ecclesiastical history which the mock-
synod conducted around a Mr Kernan's bed in Joyce's 'Grace' in *Dubliners*
in fact manages to get right. All other matter in this catechetic class conducted for the benefit of the unfortunate Mr Kernan is a litany of what
Hugh Kenner has been pleased to identify as Irish fact,[2] in which prejudice and half-remembered detail achieve the condition of mythology.
Why Joyce should have allowed Martin Cunningham in the story to
remember the detail of the Papal poem aright is something scholarship
has ignored. The Pope's poem and its subject, the creation of realistic and
deceptive images, may perhaps have more relevance to the text than has
yet been allowed.

'Grace' of course begins in darkness, the darkness of the unconscious,
drunken Mr Kernan who has fallen down the stairs of a public house,

badly injuring his tongue in the process. A former Protestant and apparently an irredeemable drinker, his cradle-Catholic friends, in the narrative, take the chance afforded by his convalescence at home to urge him
to join them in a retreat in a city centre Jesuit church, where he can start
on the road to reform.

Light, that radiant gift of the sun, eulogised in Apelles's poem certainly plays its part in 'Grace'. The 'man' (all we know of Mr Kernan at
the beginning of the tale) makes, we are told, 'light of his accident' as
he responds to the constable in the premises where he has suffered his
undignified injury; Mr Fogarty as he enters Mr Kernan's bedroom comes
'forward into the light'; Pope Leo, Mr Cunningham avers, 'was one of the
lights of the age' and imagines, quite incorrectly, that his motto was *'Lux*
upon Lux – Light upon Light'. As the assembled guests about Mr Kernan's
bed ponder the mysteries of Holy Church, 'the light music of whisky
falling into glasses made an agreeable interlude', a pleasing play on the
homophonic nature of the word left unexploited in the first usage in the
text. Furthermore, in Mr Cunningham's version of the liturgical fate that
awaits the penitents at the retreat in Gardiner Street, all they will have
to do is 'stand up with lighted candles in [their] hands and renew [their]
baptismal vows'. When they finally get there, 'The light of the lamps of
the church' falls upon 'an assembly of black clothes and white collars,
relieved here and there by tweeds, on dark mottled pillars of green marble and on lugubrious canvasses'.[3] There is, too, in the dim religious light
appropriate to piety the 'distant speck of red light' cast by the sanctuary
lamp, which brings irreverently to mind, when Father Purdon enters the
pulpit, the red-light district in the city with its notorious Purdon Street.
And of course the Gospel text Father Purdon chooses for his comfortable
sermon for *"the children of this world"* invokes *"the children of light"*.

In the wonderfully comic theological and ecclesiastical seminar conducted on Mr Kernan's behalf by his friends around his bed, much is
made of the heroic career of John MacHale, Archbishop of Tuam. And
indeed many of the religious and educational details of this story might
bring to mind the biography and opinions of that redoubtable cleric. Mr
Power's allusion to his time in the penny-a-week school reminds us that
MacHale himself began life in a hedge school in his native County Mayo.
Mr Kernan's reply, 'There was many a good man went to the penny-a-
week school with a sod of turf under his oxter … The old system was
the best: plain honest education. None of your modern trumpery', also
reminds us that MacHale opposed the national schools in Ireland on the
grounds that they were insufficiently Catholic and opposed the education

together of Catholics and Protestants. The ex-Protestant Mr Kernan, in offering the opinions he does here, is circumspectly and uncharacteristically, identifying himself in the company (by which in his weakened state he seems somewhat intimidated) with MacHale's conservative and rurally based Irish faith (his wife after all could believe in the banshee as well as the Holy Ghost, if put to it). But there were aspects of Irish Catholicism (about which we are told he was fond of 'giving side-thrusts') that as a former Protestant he could not stomach. And Mayo played a crucial role in these.

The year is 1879. On 3 June an agent of the government in Ireland sent a report to Dublin Castle (where we remember from *Ulysses* Mr Martin Cunningham would later work) of a public meeting in a small County Mayo village on 1 June. In this he describes how on that day about three hundred men marched to the village, and an assembly of about fifteen hundred persons was addressed in the most seditious of terms. A principal object of attack for the stout supporters of land reform (for that was the purpose of the occasion) was the local parish priest, one Father Cavanagh, who had, it seems, opposed them tooth and nail. One of the agitators, a man named O'Kane, spoke as follows on that threatening day:

Father Cavanagh had made a wanton attack upon him who wished to see his Country free. It was said they were fenians – if that means haters of British rule they were all fenians. Did father Cavanagh wish to be reconciled with British Rule? Who made their Country a desert? Would they be reconciled? (Three cheers for the Zulus.) They should wait for their opportunity. England was as hostile as of old.[4]

The meeting concluded with a resolution that the tenants of the district should hold out 'against their tyrant landlords'. Revolutionary feeling was obviously running high in this small Mayo village, as it was in various parts of the country, in a spring and early summer of heavy rains and general dearth (Parnell spoke on land reform to a large crowd in Westport, County Mayo, on 8 June, and the Land League was founded four months later). And the authority of the local parish priest was being outspokenly challenged.

Within seven weeks Knock, County Mayo (for that was where the march and meeting took place), was to become the object of more than Dublin Castle's attention. On 21 August 1879, around the time of the Feast of the Assumption, the Blessed Virgin Mary, accompanied by St Joseph and, it seemed, St John the Evangelist, appeared to the wonder of at least fifteen witnesses at the church in Knock, where the Very Reverend Archdeacon Bartholomew A. Cavanagh served as parish priest.

No more was heard from the O'Kanes of the district. Immediately Knock became the focus of pious pilgrimage and miraculous cure. His Grace the Archbishop, MacHale himself, was required, so great was the popular response, to institute an inquiry into the extraordinary events in Knock, at which depositions from the several witnesses were taken. These were swiftly seized upon by the local and national press and were soon in more permanent form. One John MacPhilpin of Tuam, editor of the local newspaper, prepared and edited his *The Apparitions and Miracles at Knock: Also The Official Depositions of the Eye-Witnesses,* which was published in Dublin in 1880. This is an interesting Victorian document in its own right, apart altogether from the sensational nature of its subject matter.

MacPhilpin was an early believer in the authenticity of the apparitions at Knock, even as he realised that 'very few learned Catholics yet give credit to the events that have been narrated'.[5] His pamphlet is therefore an earnest attempt to meet the objections of the sceptical. It operates in an intriguing area between the faithful believer's pious assumptions and the Victorian educated man's awareness of the claims of science and developments in technology. His major concern is to prove that the apparitions could not have been stage-managed by any other than a celestial agency. And his concentration on this aspect of his argument is very telling, for it suggests that almost from the start, even in Ireland, serious doubt was cast on the origin of the phenomena that had made Knock an object of pious and sceptical attention in many countries. Perhaps there were even those who hinted that Father Cavanagh himself had a hand in things to distract his parishioners from the inflammatory oratory to which they had so recently been subjected.[6] Certainly MacPhilpin associates the most recent events at Knock with the more general political excitement of Mayo in the year 1879, in a passage touched by some sense of relief that a distraction from material concerns has made itself felt in Mayo:

A wonderful centre of religious excitement, and a great incentive to faith, has suddenly started into form and favour in South Mayo. For the past twelve months the west of Ireland has been the trysting-place of all who have laboured for the improvement of the condition of the small farmers living on Irish soil. The eyes of all in England, and of friends and foes to the cause of the people at home and abroad, have been turned to the west of Ireland. It is here that a flame of political and social excitement has been fanned which is spreading at present over the entire land, embracing, it may be said, the four provinces. The west at the present moment presents an extraordinary attraction of a higher kind to not alone natives in Ireland, but to all Catholics in these kingdoms, as well as to their brethren on the continents of Europe and America.[7]

MacPhilpin is concerned accordingly to defend that 'attraction of a higher kind' (a formulation to which we shall return) against the inroads of Victorian scepticism, and he is gratified that 'the multitudes who flock to the chapel, or Catholic church at Knock, from the surrounding districts are quite as numerous as those that formed the monster meetings which for the past nine months have been held in the counties Mayo, Galway, and Sligo'.[8] His argument hinges on matters of light.

MacPhilpin knew that many interesting visual effects could be achieved by the manipulation of light and that the Victorian world was fascinated by these. He outlined the possibilities that scepticism might prefer to account for the apparitions, considering the effects of reflected light: some kind of magic lantern proceeding, the effect of phosphorous or of electric or magnetic currents or of natural gustations from the earth below, arising, perhaps, from a stratification of coal or petroleum some thirty or fifty feet beneath the surface. Each of these he sets aside with much display of scientific expertise in which his knowledge of light and visual effects is studiously exhibited. MacPhilpin must, one imagines, have known that magic lantern effects were increasingly popular aids to piety in much of Victorian Britain.[9] In these photographs religious statuary was used to supply images of religious and biblical figures. Consequently, although he swiftly dismisses the notion that the images on the gable wall of the church in Knock (where the apparitions had been seen for several hours from twenty minutes after sunset on that wet August evening) had their source in a magic lantern, he is anxious in his remarks on the depositions (as David Berman has shown)[10] to underplay those moments in the witnesses' accounts where comparisons with statuary occur. The trouble is that when he wishes to dismiss the idea that phosphorous might have been used by some illusionist, he is driven to supply evidence that would tend to suggest that the images had a photographic origin:

Phosphoric light is ever fitful and fluctuating, like the light of a reflected moon on the disturbed surface of a rippling lake. It is never even, nor at rest. But in the Apparition there was no rippling, or ever and constant changing of light. The figures and likenesses that were seen were settled; they presented an accurate outline, and were constant and continuous in their pose for two hours and a half.[11]

One notices here how the writer seems to slip unconsciously into a language more appropriate to the description of a photographic image than a heavenly visitant, as he negotiates the troubled space between faith and Victorian scientific knowledge and technology. It is as if he has read Pope Leo's poem on the magical realism of photography and is both intrigued

and fearful in his pamphlet of what tricks might be effected by it and
how knowledge of its powers could be used to undermine belief in the
Knock apparitions which in 1880 still seemed dubious even to many of
the devout. Through his text and the record of the depositions, one is
struck indeed by how the words 'image', 'statue', 'apparitions', 'light' supply a lexicon of faith and doubt.

Mr Kernan in 'Grace' (whose wife, for all her belief in the Sacred Heart
after a quarter of a century of marriage to her ex-Protestant husband, had
'few illusions left') knows where he stands on these matters. He will agree
to go on retreat with his friends, even admitting the possibility of auricu-
lar confession (anathema to most Irish Protestants), but he bars candles.

He shook his head with farcical gravity.
– Listen to that! said his wife.
– I bar the candles, said Mr Kernan, conscious of having created an effect on his
   audience and continuing to shake his head to and fro. I bar the magic-lantern
   business.
   Everyone laughed heartily.
– There's a nice Catholic for you! said his wife.
– No candles! repeated Mr Kernan obdurately.

Mr Kernan retains a proper low church horror (the Church of Ireland
in which he was most probably christened was resolutely low church in
liturgical matters) for Romish sacerdotalism, and the man who enjoys
side-thrusts at his adopted creed knows that the Knock apparitions were
a hoax, a trick of light, a magic lantern show. The laughter of his wife
and friends suggests that they know precisely to what he refers, and their
opinion of his vulgar and ridiculous Protestant offence to Our Lady is
freely expressed in their hilarity.

For all the comedy of this scene, one suspects that Joyce shares
Mr Kernan's scepticism about church shrines such as that at Knock in
this tale with its reference to the diocese of Tuam, to a poem on photography, and with its allusions to light, to statuary and its mention of
illusion. And the reference to Knock in Mr Kernan's sceptical prohib-
ition of the worst excesses (in his view) of Catholic superstition has a
distinct relevance in this story, which concludes its portrait of Dublin
religious life with a sermon in which Father Purdon combines religious
obligation with sound business sense. For this is a story in which Christ's
revolutionary message to the wretched of the earth is rendered anodyne
in a series of self-satisfied platitudes. And perhaps in Knock, the revolutionary energies of the momentous year of 1879 were to some degree, in

Joyce's opinion, misdirected into a cult of the Virgin that had its origins in chicanery.

Certainly from the first the economic potential of the sacred visitation was not lost on commentators, in a fashion which would have pleased Joyce's materially minded Father Purdon. Indeed MacPhilpin's curious pamphlet is made even more curious by his decision to include in it not only the depositions and his own refutations of sceptical interpretations of events there, but a kind of tourist gazetteer of the region's potential. When he wrote about the west affording 'an extraordinary attraction' of a higher kind than the social agitation of the year of 1879, he falls unself-consciously into the idiom of tourism which is so much a part of the topographical sections of his pamphlet. There is, it must be said, something of an impression therein that the Blessed Virgin Mary has chosen wisely in appearing at a village which 'is distant about five miles from Claremorris, which is favourably situate on the great North-Western Railway'.[12] In MacPhilpin's oddly patronising description of the region, we have in fact an example of just that combination of material interest with complacent spirituality that Joyce so sharply satirised in 'Grace' in the person of the egregious Father Purdon. I do not think it fanciful to imagine that Joyce had Knock and a manufactured cult in mind when he wrote this story of religion conducted in 'a businesslike way'.[13] Here, to conclude, is Mr MacPhilpin on the attractions of Knock and environs:

Tourists or travellers coming to Knock must pass through either of the two towns, Claremorris or Ballyhaunis, which are points at the extreme ends of the base of the irregular triangle, of which the village of Knock forms the vertex. The Chapel of the Apparition must be reached by car, either from Claremorris or Ballyhaunis – the former is five miles distant, the latter is six and a half. In excursion trips the fare, either from Dublin or Athlone, to these towns is the same, and at Claremorris a number of cars are usually at call, ready for all comers. The accommodation, too, is fair considering the extent of the town, and the means of the inhabitants. The people have been by strangers pronounced civil and obliging. There are in the town two hotels, in which good accommodation can be had, besides private apartments, where families can find themselves at home.[14]

Even Mr Kernan, if he could get over his silly prejudices, might not feel so very much out of place on such a pilgrimage, after he had washed the pot, of course, under Father Purdon's gentle instruction at the retreat in Gardiner Street.

NOTES

1 The translation is by R. M. Adams in his *Surface and Symbol* (New York: Oxford University Press, 1962), p. 179. See also the prose translation by R. Boyle, S. J., 'Swiftian Allegory and Dantean Parody in Joyce's "Grace"', *James Joyce Quaterly*, 7 (Fall 1969), 16–17.

2 H. Kenner, *A Colder Eye: The Modern Irish Writers* (New York: Alfred A. Knopf, 1983), p, 3.

3 Joyce is possibly suggesting here in this odd use of black and white and colour descriptive details a contrast between photography and the painter's canvas. All quotations from 'Grace' are taken from J. Joyce, *Dubliners* (London: Penguin Books, 1992).

4 Quoted in D. Berman, 'The Knock Apparition: Some New Evidence', *New Humanist*, 102 (December 1987), 8. I am grateful to my colleague Professor David Berman of the Department of Philosophy, Trinity College, Dublin, who brought this article to my attention and who made available other materials on the Knock apparitions.

5 J. MacPhilpin, *The Apparitions and Miracles at Knock: Also The Official Depositions of the Eye-Witnesses* (Dublin: M. H. Gill and Son, 1880), p. 23.

6 MacPhilpin's pamphlet does in fact contain evidence that Father Cavanagh was a suspect from the beginning. He includes in his text an article from the London *Daily Telegraph*, which, under the caption 'A Mayo Lourdes', contains the following observations, in which the Archdeacon's probity is celebrated in terms that suggest it has recently been impugned: 'Archdeacon Cavanagh is reputed along all the country side as a man of simple piety, gentle manners, and a modest and retiring disposition. This character is justified by his appearance; he at once makes a favourable impression, and is about the last man in the world whom a stranger would look upon and suspect of anything but straightforward, honest conduct.' MacPhilpin, *Apparitions and Miracles*, p. 58.

7 *Ibid.*, pp. 6–7.

8 *Ibid.*

9 Magic lantern slides also played their part in para-politics in Ireland. The historian Gearóid Ó Tuathaigh tells me that slides which recalled Parnell's famously undignified exit by window from Kitty O'Shea's bedroom were employed in the moral campaign to discredit him as leader of the Irish Parliamentary Party following Captain O'Shea's divorce action.

10 See D. Berman, 'Papal Visit Resurrects Ireland's Knock Legend', *The Freethinker* (October 1979), n.p.

11 MacPhilpin, *Apparitions and Miracles*, p. 26

12 *Ibid.*

13 Joyce as a loyal Parnellite would have been aware that the forces aligned against the incipient Land League in 1879 (which it seems included Father Cavanagh, whatever his role in the matter of the apparitions) were much the same as those which turned on Parnell and destroyed him. Furthermore

Parnell had made a strategic alliance against landlordism with the O'Kanes of the Irish world under the leadership of the Land League's Mayo-born Michael Davitt. So a twenty-year vista of Irish history is opened up by this reference to a magic lantern in 'Grace' and to the apparitions at Knock which it contains, a vista of conservative and revolutionary landmarks that were all too familiar to Joyce himself.

14 MacPhilpin, *Apparitions and Miracles*, p. 16.

CHAPTER 3

Music: the cultural issue

In 'The Dead', James Joyce's wonderfully composed short story, the musical world of turn-of-the-century Dublin is evoked with the author's characteristically exacting sense of social and cultural detail. Music is a principal topic of conversation at the Misses Morkans' annual Christmas soirée for their friends and pupils at the music school they run together, and it plays a crucial part in the meaning of the tale itself. As well it might in Edwardian Dublin, where a musical career was one of the few open to a respectable unmarried woman.

Gabriel Conroy, the Misses Morkans' nephew, is to give the after-dinner speech at this culinary and musical feast at his aunts' rented home in Usher's Island. He judges that his audience would respond most enthusiastically not to a quotation from the 'difficult' Victorian poet Robert Browning, but to something they would recognise, 'some quotation from Shakespeare or from the Melodies'. As a *soi-disant* intellectual, he fears that the culture of his aunts and their friends and pupils is essentially middle-brow and conventional. He knows that the *Irish Melodies* of Thomas Moore are wholly familiar to them and vested with the same unexceptionable respectability that the Victorian and Edwardian middle classes, even in Ireland, curiously allowed the Bard of Avon.

Joyce in *Dubliners* makes Moore's *Melodies* a ubiquitous musical presence, along with Balfe's romantic opera *The Bohemian Girl*. It is, for example, the plangent notes of the *Song of Fionnuola* ('Silent, Oh Moyle, be the roar of thy water') that are sounded in 'Two Gallants' with great symbolic import (a nation wronged awaiting rebirth), that grim tale of male exploitation of woman; and 'The Dead' itself may get its title from one of the *Melodies,* 'Oh, Ye Dead!' Yet there is a profound irony in this latter appropriation of one of Moore's poetic effusions, which were inspired by Edward Bunting's famous collection of Irish airs. For it is not any of the sweet, sentiment-infused musical suasions of Moore's Regency confections which steal the show at the Misses Morkans' party, nor indeed

Aunt Julia singing 'Arrayed for the Bridal' from Bellini's *I Puritani*, despite Freddie Malin's intoxicated enthusiasm, but a tenor performing a west of Ireland version of the Child ballad 'The Lass of Lochroyan'. The song 'The Lass of Aughrim', 'which seemed to be in the old Irish tonality', transfixes its audience as they prepare to depart, with its tale of seduction, betrayal and heartfelt grief. The melody and the starkly brutal words of the ballad sound a note of unignorable passion at the end of an evening when Gabriel, in his cliché-ridden speech, has set the seal of unexceptionable bourgeois *pietas* on a representively Irish occasion.

The hostesses and their guests at the Christmas party in 'The Dead' can, it must be said, be asked to rise to such representative status, since in their several persons and their familial inheritances they reflect much of the social and cultural history of nineteenth- and early twentieth-century Ireland. For we learn in the tale that the Misses Morkan are the daughters of a man who kept a starch mill in Back Lane. Gabriel, his grandson, tells the dinner table a comic tale at his expense (he calls him, with mingled humour, social self-consciousness and probably some embarrassment, a 'glue-boiler'). The family home had been in Stoney Batter, across the river from where Gabriel's mother, the dead Ellen Morkan, had gone to her marriage with the impressively named T. J. Conroy of the Port and Docks Board. From Stoney Batter and a starch factory in the liberties to the middle-class and Protestant world of the Port and Docks Board, in which powerful Dublin institution her husband had clearly achieved considerable respectability, was a journey of some major social and cultural distance. It had begun a familial trajectory that helped to propel her son Gabriel, by way of a university education, into the lower reaches of a literary life as a college teacher and a reviewer on a national daily, with a house in Monkstown no less, and her other pretentiously named son Constantine (an archangel and emperor for progeny), into the Church as a curate in Balbriggan, some sixteen miles to the north of the city.

Gabriel in Joyce's story, however, is regrettably ignorant of the historical associations of a Back Lane business address.[1] For it was there in 1792 that the Catholic Association (dubbed the 'Back Lane Parliament' by its enemies) had met to demand relief from the Penal Laws. In the light of such a nationally significant fact, it is easy to read the progress of the Morkan family as representative of the rise, in the wake of Catholic emancipation (the climax of what began in Back Lane), of an aspirant Irish Catholic middle class determined to make good the losses that had ensued on Protestant King Billy's conquest in 1690. And it was around King Billy's equestrian statue at College Green, in Gabriel's patronising anecdote, that Grandfather Morkan's horse had foolishly circled, when his master had decided 'to drive out with the quality to a military review in the park'.

Yet the Morkans's progress has been interrupted, or at least we must infer that his mother considered that it had been, when Gabriel had married a 'country cute' young woman from Galway by the name of Gretta. Galway, however, is the site of remembered passion in the story, which is summoned to Gretta Conroy's mind not by any Italian aria or melody from 'mellifluous Moore',[2] but by a ballad in the old tonality with its atavistic burden of betrayal, loss and pain. The strains of 'The Lass of Aughrim' stir in Gretta memories of a more compelling ardour than anything her bourgeois life with Gabriel can offer. The music rises indeed as if out of some more primal, elemental, passionate Ireland than the lower middle class, respectable decencies of Usher's Island or the suburban, attenuated cultural provincialism of Monkstown. 'The Dead' therefore sets in apposition the music with which an Irish Catholic lower middle class at the turn of the century could feel comfortable and a music which speaks from a more vital, dangerous territory of the national consciousness.

It is wholly appropriate that the *Irish Melodies* of Thomas Moore should be associated by Joyce with the former term in this socially and culturally salient apposition. For Moore had been among some of the earliest to avail himself of the opportunities opened to Catholics by the Relief Act of 1793. The son of a grocer in Aungier Street in the capital, he graduated from Trinity College, Dublin, in 1800 with a keen ambition to make his way in the world of letters. *The Irish Melodies* were his route to both fame and fortune. Yet in the wake of the rebellion of 1798 and Emmet's futile, romantic attempt of 1803 to defy the Act of Union (1800), to make Ireland a literary and musical subject involved attendant difficulties, not to say risks. For the music of a primitive people could all too easily be associated with political instability by English audiences. It could call to mind all that made the wild Irish a suspect people. Had they not risen with violent and terrible consequences in 1798 and might they not do so again? Moore was at pains therefore as his career progressed in the first decade of the nineteenth century to reassure his readers and auditors that they had little to fear from him, however Irish the subject matter of the verses which he set to Irish airs. He outlined his intentions with a careful eye on the English audiences he had charmed in Regency drawing rooms.

Moore of course was all too conscious of what kind of feelings could be vested in at least some of the Irish melodies to which he chose to set words. So he was circumspect as he began his defence of his own exploitation of these materials. He recognised the dilemma he faced:

It has often been remarked, [he wrote] and oftener felt, that our music is the truest of all comments upon our history. The tone of defiance, succeeded by the languor of despondency – a burst of turbulence dying away into softness – the sorrows of the moment lost in the levity of the next – and all that romantic mixture of mirth and sadness, which is naturally produced by the efforts of a lively temperament to shake off or forget the wrongs which lie upon it. Such are the features of our history and character, which we find strongly and faithfully reflected in our music; and there are many airs which, I think, it is difficult to listen to without recalling some event to which their expression seems peculiarly applicable.[3]

Moore tried in this subtle piece of self-justification to discharge the dangerous energies of such a national inheritance in two ways. Firstly, he sought to argue that despite the widespread belief that Irish music is very ancient, 'it is certain that our finest and most popular airs are modern'.[4] As modern creations, 'the origin of most of those wild and melancholy strains which were at once the offspring and solace of grief' can be attributed not to Irish history as a whole but to 'the last disgraceful century'.[5] This speculative musicology permits Moore, in a new century, when the Penal Laws of the eighteenth century no longer bear so heavily, to begin a process in which music can be released from immediate, perhaps subversive, political exigencies and be made the basis of an essentially unthreatening form of national sentiment. It also permits him to develop the second stage of an apologia.

The recent provenance of what is reckoned to be Irish music, for Moore accounts for one of its most characteristic and exploitable aspects: its sweetness. Moore's is a curious enough argument, but its conclusions were important both for himself and for the course of music in nineteenth-century Ireland. He posits of archaic Irish music that 'the irregular scale of the early Irish … must have furnished wild and refractory subjects to the harmonist'.[6] It was only in comparatively modern times when strings were added to harp music in Ireland that Irish 'melodies took the sweet character'[7] that interests him as a vastly popular poet. He continues: 'In profiting, however, from the improvements of the moderns, our style still kept its originality sacred from their refinements.'[8] In other words it did not become artificially ornate, allowing it to please by its unsophisticated charm in a period of decorative Regency elaboration of style in music and architecture. So it had been possible for a contemporary collector of Irish music like Edward Bunting and the arranger Sir John Stevenson 'to restore the regularity of its form, and the chaste simplicity of its character'.[9] As a result of all this, Irish music will appeal, Moore believes, to the kind of people who can be depended upon not to be inflamed by political fervour of a dangerous kind. To those who might still fear the impact of Moore's *Irish Melodies*, their author reassuringly writes:

I beg of these respected persons to believe that there is no one who deprecates more sincerely than I do any appeal to the passions of an ignorant and angry multitude; but that it is not through that gross and inflammable region of society a work of this nature could ever have been intended to circulate. It looks much higher for its audience and readers – it is found upon the pianofortes of the rich and educated – of those who can afford to have their national zeal a little stimulated without exciting much dread of the excesses into which it may hurry them; and of many whose nerves may be now and then alarmed with advantage, as much more is to be gained by their fears than could ever could be expected from their justice.[10]

So a sweet, simple chaste music could accompany poems of national sentiment. The songs would not unduly unsettle Irish public opinion, being restricted in performance to the comfortable middle classes, while in England they could remind, to useful effect, for all their charm, of the monster that someone else might awaken if England did not supply good government for Ireland in the new century. Moore's own analysis of his work supplies a complicated context which makes William Hazlitt's famous quip that Moore 'took the wild harp of Erin and made of it a musical snuff-box'[11] not the comprehensively damning indictment it is usually reckoned to be. For, as Seamus Deane has argued,[12] Moore had modernised Irish music in performance for an emergent Irish middle class who wished to escape the nightmare of history and to settle for a comfortable, eventually constitutional, nationalism. His concern for artistic elegance was the cultural expression of that aspiration. And by contrast the elemental passion which rises from the past in 'The Lass of Aughrim', in 'The Dead' is therefore the return of the repressed (of 'the dead') as a vital and demanding ghost. For the music and words of the song amid the gentility of a Dublin soirée seem possessed of energies that disturb the fragile complacency of an Edwardian Dublin social occasion.

Moore in the first decades of the nineteenth century sought to make music the agent of a sanitised modernity. By the mid-nineteenth century, as famine threatened to silence the 'land of song' completely, a new concern to salvage the music of pre-modern Ireland had quickly developed. It was as if it had become imperative to rescue all Moore had sought to exorcise from the Irish musical tradition, before it went finally into the dark. In 1851 the Society for the Preservation and Publication of the Melodies of Ireland was founded with George Petrie as its president. Petrie himself, in his introduction to his *Complete Collection of Irish Music*, wrote of how the nineteenth century had 'almost entirely denationalised its higher classes'[13] and of how the Famine had decimated the countryside. The ancient music of Ireland, redolent of national feeling, which Gaelic-speaking Ireland had preserved, was on the point of extinction. It must be revived, Petrie implies, if national feeling is to survive at all. And as Joep Leerssen has recently argued,[14] the impulse to regard Ireland as possessed in the past of a rich popular musical tradition, in the second part of the nineteenth century involved the idea of song playing a crucial part in the whole necessary project of national revival. Works such as M. J. Barry's *The Songs of Ireland* (published in three editions in 1845, 1846 and 1869) had their high cultural echo in such a work as Samuel Ferguson's *Lays of the Western Gael* (1865) and in the classic, seminal act of retrieval and translation, Douglas Hyde's *Love Songs of Connacht* (1893). Even the highly esoteric universe of Yeats's incorporation of the idea of the Celt into the enactments of ritual magic allowed, perforce in such a cultural context, for 'The Song of Wandering Aengus' and the nativist exuberance of 'The Fiddler of Dooney'. In 'To Ireland in the Coming Times', he identified his own poetic with 'A Druid land, a Druid tune' (Yeats was, strange to say, completely tone deaf and could scarcely tell one melody from another, which may have helped him to imagine for himself what such a tune, unknown to musicology, may have been like).

Paradoxically, the literary and cultural revival of the late nineteenth and early twentieth centuries, which so valorised the concept of song under threat in its idea of the nation, lacked a composer who could be associated with the movement in the way the poet and playwright Yeats so centrally was. The reason for this is not hard to seek. Orchestral music by the turn of the century had little purchase on the country's social and political life beyond the cities of Dublin, Cork and Belfast, and even there it tended to be identified with the worlds of Ascendancy pretension and anglicised social activity. As a result, such composers of orchestral music as Sir Charles Villiers Stanford, who '"worked the mines" of his native folk music as bequeathed to him by Bunting, Joyce, Petrie and Moore',[15] never became truly national figures, crucially identified, in the way Yeats was and continues to be, with the creation of a modern Irish identity. What this means is that Ireland in the high period of national fervour in Europe lacked its Grieg or Smetana and never even came close to producing a Bela Bartok or a Richard Wagner.

Curiously, it was a writer of the Irish Literary Revival who gave an idea of what such a music might have been like, had chance, circumstance and genius brought it into existence. In his account of his sojourn on the Aran islands, in that 'West' to which Gabriel Conroy is drawn in 'The Dead' and from which in that story Michael Furey hailed, the dramatist John Millington Synge describes an extraordinary dream that overtook him one night during a visit there. It is a dream of music, as if the islands themselves found absolute expression in an orchestral score as yet unwritten. The music of the dream, which begins with a faint rhythm 'far away on some stringed instrument' seems intimate with 'some moment of terrible agony'. As the dreamer listened, 'the music increased continually, sounding like the strings of harps, tuned to a forgotten scale, and having a resonance as searching as the strings of a 'cello'. Then a passage that evokes an Irish music of the romantic agony, modulating into a rite of pagan celebration (in 1907, when Synge published *The Aran Islands,* Stravinsky's *Rite of Spring* still lay six years in the future). The writer confesses: 'the luring excitement became more powerful than my will, and my limbs moved in spite of me'. He continues:

In a moment I was swept away in a whirlwind of notes. My breath and my thought and every impulse of my body became a form of the dance, till I could not distinguish between the instruments and the rhythm and my own person or consciousness.

For a while it seemed an excitement that was filled with joy, then it grew into an ecstasy where all existence was lost in a vortex of movement. I could not think that there had ever been a life beyond the whirling of the dance.

Then with a shock the ecstasy turned to an agony and rage. I struggled to free myself, but seemed only to increase the passion of the steps I moved to. When I shrieked I could only echo the notes of the rhythm.[16]

This remarkable passage in the text seems like an orchestral consummation of the sounds and musical tones the writer has heard on the islands. For the very seagulls on the islands are constituents of its romantic music: 'Their language is easier than Gaelic, and I seem to understand the greater part of their cries, though I am not able to answer. There is one plaintive note which they take up in the middle of their usual babble with extraordinary effect, and pass on from one to another along the cliff with the sort of inarticulate wail, as if they remembered for an instant the horror of the mist.'[17] Irish spoken, for all its difficulty, is an authentic music too. Synge acknowledges: 'it is only in the intonation of a few sentences or some old fragment of melody that I catch the real spirit of the island'.[18] He hears it furthermore in the most ancient form of musical performance

Ireland can afford the modern ear, the cries of the keen, which surely resonated in his dream of an island orchestral music ('some moment of terrible agony'):

While the grave was being opened the women sat down among the flat tomb-stones, bordered with a pale fringe of early bracken, and began the wild keen, or crying for the dead. Each old woman, as she took her turn in the leading recita-tive, seemed possessed for the moment with a profound ecstasy of grief, swaying to and fro, and bending her forehead to the stone before her, while she called out to the dead with a perpetually recurring chant of sobs.

All round the graveyard other wrinkled women, looking out from under the deep red petticoats that cloaked them, rocked themselves with the same rhythm, and intoned the inarticulate chant that is sustained by all as an accompaniment.[19]

Synge summons to our imagination in the early twentieth century in *The Aran Islands* the possibility of an Irish music with its sources in pre-modernity, where Moore upwards of a hundred years before had sought to make Irish music acceptable in the modern world. Tellingly, Synge ends his account of his Aran dream with silence: 'there was no sound anywhere on the island'.[20] If we may read that silence metaphorically, we might also suggest that it was not until the 1950s, and the beginnings of Seán Ó Ríada's sadly brief career as a composer, that we had the chance in Ireland to hear that silence broken by an orchestral music with its sources in the pre-modern Irish world, a music of the kind Synge heard in imaginary form on Aran, during his visits there.

NOTES

1   J. V. Kelleher, 'Irish History and Mythology in James Joyce's "The Dead"', *The Review of Politics*, 27, 3 (July 1965), 414–33.
2   The phrase is John Betjeman's.
3   T. Moore, 'Prefatory Letter on Music', in *The Poetical Works of Thomas Moore* (Edinburgh: W.P. Nimmo, Hay and Mitchell, 1891), p. 430.
4   *Ibid.*
5   *Ibid.*
6   *Ibid.*, pp. 431–2.
7   *Ibid.*, p. 432.
8   *Ibid.*
9   *Ibid.*, p. 433.
10 *Ibid.*, pp. 433–4.
11 Cited in N. Vance, *Irish Literature: A Social History* (Oxford: Basil Blackwell, 1990), p. 102.
12 S. Deane, 'Thomas Moore', *The Field Day Anthology of Irish Writing*, Vol. I (Derry: Field Day Publications, 1991), p. 1055.

13 G. Petrie, 'Preface' in *The Complete Collection of Irish Music as Noted by George Petrie, Edited from the Original Manuscripts by Charles Villiers Stanford* (Cork University Press, 1996), p. viii.

14 See J. Leerssen, *Remembrance and Imagination: Patterns in Historical Literary Representation of Ireland in the Nineteenth Century* (Cork University Press, 1996), pp. 173–7. Leerssen also argues persuasively in this volume that Moore's *Irish Melodies* in the early decades of the nineteenth century did in fact contain a sufficiently powerful nationalist charge to make his disavowal of subversive intent necessary.

15 C. Pearce, 'Contemporary Irish Music', in B. Boydell (ed.), *Four Centuries of Music in Ireland* (London: British Broadcasting Corporation, 1979), p. 50.

16 Alan Price (ed.), *J. M. Synge: Collected Works*, Vol. II: *Prose* (London: Oxford University Press, 1966), p. 100.

17 *Ibid.*, pp. 73–4.

18 *Ibid.*, p. 74.

19 *Ibid.*

20 *Ibid.*, p. 100.

CHAPTER 4

Modernism and revolution: rereading Yeats's 'Easter 1916'

It is a commonplace of literary history to observe that what came to be known as the literary Modernism of the second two decades of the twentieth century was a reactive response to the disturbed, war-torn and revolutionary conditions of modernity itself. A familiar text can be cited to indicate how this association between a troubled period and radical aesthetic experiment was established even as the texts of high Modernism were appearing and receiving their earliest assessments. In T. S. Eliot's famous 1923 *Dial* review of Joyce's *Ulysses*, which had appeared in 1922, the same year that Eliot himself had published *The Waste Land*, the poet/critic argued that Joyce had employed a mythical method in his epic novel 'as a way of controlling, of ordering, of giving a shape and a significance to the immense panorama of futility and anarchy which is contemporary civilization'.[1] He had assumed, wrongly to my mind, that Joyce was reacting to the same conditions of post-war, post-revolutionary ennui and angst that he himself had so hauntingly evoked in *The Waste Land* in such sections as 'The Burial of the Dead', with its montage of *déraciné* central Europeans in the *Hofgarten,* or going south in the winter, its desolating love affair conducted to the strains of Wagnerian commentary and its underlying mythic allusiveness. Interestingly, for my purposes in this essay, Eliot in that review also suggests that this mythic method had been first employed by W. B. Yeats, thereby drawing the Irish poet for his own critical purposes (the justification of his own work) within the circle of literary experimentalists who were presumably reacting to the general crisis. Denis Donoghue, in noting this reference to Yeats,[2] has suggested that as he included Yeats in what we might now call the Modernist team, Eliot may well have been thinking of Yeats's poem 'No Second Troy'. And indeed that poem's elision of millennia to make twentieth-century Dublin an unworthy backdrop for an anachronistic Helen with 'beauty like a tightened bow' can bear comparison with Eliot's London evoked as Dantesque phantasmagoria or an Old Testament vision of a valley of dry bones.

Yeats composed 'No Second Troy' in December 1908, which, if we follow Donoghue's suggestion about Eliot's thinking, would make the poem an early entry in any anthology of the Modernist literary canon. The poem was written, one reflects, a year or so before the point in which history so definitively changed, as Virginia Woolf later asserted,[3] as to demand quite new forms of literary production. Poems more usually associated with literary Modernism in Yeats's oeuvre are those works of troubled times, underpinned by the mythic structures of *A Vision,* which appear in *Michael Robartes and the Dancer* (1921) and among the opening sequences of *The Tower* (1928). They are such poems as 'The Second Coming', with its source in the poet's response to events in war-torn Russia, 'Meditations in Time of Civil War' and 'Nineteen Hundred and Nineteen' (first published as 'Thoughts Upon the Present State of the World'), which make Irish violence symptomatic of epochal transition symbolised in the centrally placed poem in *The Tower,* 'Leda and the Swan', with its panoramic, mythic perspectives.

The critic who wishes to include poems by Yeats in a putative anthology of modern literary experimentalism (as Eliot it seems was inclined to do) certainly has good grounds to number these great poems in the volume. He or she might baulk, however, *pace* Donoghue on Eliot, at 'No Second Troy', deeming it too coherent, dramatically univocal a performance credibly to find a place in such a collection.[4] Casting about for earlier poems by Yeats which could work their passage along with Eliot's 'The Love Song of J. Alfred Prufrock' and Ezra Pound's 'Hugh Selwyn Mauberley' in such an anthology, the critic might make a case for 'In Memory of Major Robert Gregory', pointing out that the figure ostensibly elegised in that poem was a victim of modern mechanised warfare (an air pilot, no less) and that the poem makes much of different orders of time (the domestic quotidian, the naturally vital and the apocalyptic) while announcing its own unfinished state. Indeed the poem breaks off before the elegy proper gets into its stride as a thought 'of that late death' takes all the poet's heart for speech, and we are left, in a period of Modernist fragmentation of poetic form, with a fragment of an implied complete poem. This poem cannot be written because the poet has been overcome with emotion. Poetic silence becomes the most profound tribute to the dead.

Yeats's 'Easter 1916', I will argue in this essay, is a poem which bears rereading in the light of Eliot's assumption in his review of *Ulysses* that Yeats could be included among those who were responding to the challenges of the contemporary moment in aesthetically experimental ways.

To this end, I will concentrate on the poem's literary aspects. I believe this is necessary because the poem, dealing as it does with so crucial an historical event in its Irish context, has had to carry so great a burden of historical analysis that its poetic mode of being can be occluded. That mode of being can, I think, be made vitally alive to us once again if we consider it as displaying certain key Modernist characteristics.

However, before we turn to the poem to attempt a detailed analysis of it as poetry, it is well to consider what kind of event it was to which Yeats reacted in this remarkable work.[5] The Rising of 1916, like Yeats's poem indeed, has also had to carry its weight of nationalist and revisionist historical analysis so that the reality of that grim week in a city's springtime has been neglected. What in fact occurred, though the death toll was minimal in comparison to the charnel house that would open that summer on the Somme, was the infliction of modern warfare for the first time on a city of the United Kingdom, in which civilian casualties probably exceeded those among armed participants. And the city experienced both street fighting with its snipers and bombardment of defensive positions by artillery and fire from a small gunship that left its handsome central streets in ruins.

Yeats, who was in England during the fateful week in which the Rising took place, visited the city in early June. He saw with shock the devastation it had left in its wake in a city still under emergency policing. As Roy Foster tells us, he 'needed a pass from the Dublin Metropolitan Police to travel even as near as Greystones'[6] to visit his brother, the artist Jack Yeats. The brief sojourn in Dublin seems to have confirmed the poet in the conviction that we can see forming in his famous letter about the Rising written to Lady Gregory on May 11, that the event was bound to have profound consequences both for his country and for his own life. In that letter he had reflected, 'I had no idea that any public event could so deeply move me and I am very despondent about the future. At the moment I feel all the work of years has been overturned, all the freeing of Irish literature and criticism from polities.'[7] Intriguingly, in this same missive, Yeats tells Gregory that Maud Gonne, with whom he had been in correspondence, had reminded him that in the first few days of the world war then raging she had had a vision of 'the ruined houses about O'Connell Street, and the wounded and lying about the streets'.[8] Yeats had thought that vision could have only symbolic import. Now the Western Front of the Great War had become the Home Front, as it would do most powerfully in Sean O'Casey's play of Easter Week, *The Plough and the Stars*. There was no immunity in Dublin from the

condition of modernity that had unleashed industrial slaughter on the
European continent. All was indeed changed.

On 23 May, accordingly to Foster, Yeats informed John Quinn that
he was 'planning a group of poems on the Dublin Rising'[9] and shortly
thereafter, still during the poet's Dublin visit, his sister Lily told the same
John Quinn that her brother was 'writing a series of poems on things
here'.[10] In the event Yeats did not write a 'series' of poems about the
Rising that summer, but the single poem 'Easter 1916', the typescript of
which bears the completion date 25 September 1916. However, the poem,
it can be argued, is itself suggestive of a series of poems that give a hint
in embryonic form of the kinds of sequences in which Yeats was to react
to public events in his great later poems in *The Tower* and *The Winding
Stair*. It must be acknowledged, of course, that the poem does effect a
degree of narrative progression in its four stanzas (or sections, as I will
term them; Helen Vendler describes them as 'four carefully delineated
parts'[11]), moving as it does from hesitancy about the Rising's martyrs to
incorporation of them in the pantheon of the nationalist dead. But what
is striking about the work in Yeats's oeuvre is that, apart from the series
of poems composed over several years for Mabel Beardsley and published
in 1917 as 'Upon A Dying Lady', Yeats had written no single poem before
'Easter 1916' with quite its sense of a whole in the process of creation,
which, without the centripetal refrain and controlling trimeters, could
have seemed a fissiparous set of observations in several sections (Maud
Gonne in fact complained when Yeats sent her the poem that it was 'not
a great WHOLE … which would have avenged our material failure by
its spiritual beauty'[12]). Without those, the transitions from the opening streetscape at evening, to the characterisation of a set of unnamed
individuals to an imagistic landscape of stream and stone, concluding
with political commentary and specific honorific could have seemed to
involve the kind of unsettling juxtapositions that mark some of Yeats's
later works and that are characteristic of Modernist poetry in general (in
which the sequence poem helps to define the movement). In 1913 Yeats
himself had noted how 'an absorption in fragmentary sensuous beauty
or detachable ideas' had deprived contemporary poets 'of the power to
mould vast material into a single image', and he had questioned 'What
long modern poem equals the old poems in architectural unity, in symbolic importance?'[13] It was as if he was anticipating the development of
the twentieth-century sequence poem in which, when poets sought to
deal with material of major significance, they could have recourse to a
poetic mode that eschewed obvious 'architectural unity', the quest for

a 'single image'. Yeats's poem 'Easter 1916' can be read as proleptically signalling that Modernist stratagem.[14]

As we noted, 'In Memory of Major Robert Gregory' is a self-referential poem, which indicates as it breaks off that it is in fact an introduction to the poem that cannot be written; and it is that which in part allows us to consider it in the context of early twentieth-century Modernism with its markedly self-consciously textual productions. 'Easter 1916' is also a poem which in the writing highlights that it is a poem in the process of being composed.

There were probably specific biographical/historical reasons for this, which account for the complex rhetorical procedures of the work. The poet who may indeed as a young man have sworn the Irish Republican Brotherhood's oath,[15] when he was under the influence of the old Fenian leader John O'Leary, by 1916 was remote both from the feelings that had made him a political activist in the months leading up to commemoration of the United Irish Rebellion in 1898 and from the cabals of republican plotters with whom he once consorted. Furthermore some of his prose writings ('Poetry and Tradition', for example) and most notoriously his poem 'September 1913' had served provocative notice, the latter in the Unionist *Irish Times* newspaper, no less, of his conviction that the era of heroic sacrifice in Ireland's cause had well and truly passed. 'Romantic Ireland' was 'dead and gone' he intoned; it was 'with O'Leary in the grave'.[16] So the poet who had long thought of himself as occupying a national role with national poetic duties had a difficulty if he was to respond convincingly, as he knew he must, to the epochal events that had unfolded in Ireland in the spring and early summer of 1916. How, given such opinions, could he be taken seriously as the poet of 1916? His recourse was first to title his poem 'Easter 1916', as if christening this new date of birth and resurrection in answer to the threnody for 'romantic Ireland' he had himself chaunted over the grave of John O'Leary, just over two years earlier in 'September 1913'. Then it was to gain the credit due to the magnanimous by suggesting that he now knew he had been in error about the period in which he was living. He had got it wrong. The poem accordingly calls to mind the earlier writing and draws attention to itself as an act of literary revisionism.

A further way in which the poem draws attention to itself as poem is through the altering status in the work of the first person pronoun. In the first section of 'Easter 1916', 'I' as in 'I have met them at close of day', or 'I have passed with a nod of the head' (p. 228) is the everyday, social self addressing the reader or auditor. It is contrasted with the others adverted to in these lines, 'they and I' of line 13. The opening section employs the personal pronoun four times in sixteen lines. The second section avoids its usage for fourteen lines, until lines fifteen and sixteen when the poet avers, 'This other man I had dreamed / A drunken vainglorious lout' (p. 229), associating the pronoun not with everyday social exchange but with poetic vision (throughout Yeats's oeuvre 'dream' is a positive force, a mode of truth telling, 'In dreams begins responsibility'). The poet is donning his bardic robes, so that he can say even of that dubious character, 'Yet I number him in the song' (p. 229). By section four of the poem, 'I' is subsumed in a collective 'our' in the reflection 'our part to murmur name upon name', which means that when at the last he himself proclaims the martyrs' names in a poetic epitaph for them and states, 'I write it out in a verse' (p. 230), he is speaking as the poet among the people. I/They is now a national unity. The grammar has allowed us to see that transformation from social being to visionary bard fulfilling a public role in a way that parallels what has happened to the executed men themselves. And the statements 'I number him in the song' and 'I write out in a verse' highlight how the poem is about a poem in process of becoming both performance and textual artifact.

Such a trajectory involves striking modulations in tone, from the conversational, to the dismissive, the analytic, to the tender, the rhapsodic to the bewildered, the declarative to the chiliastic. So that the poem becomes a poem of many voices, more multivocal, I think, than any single poem by Yeats to that date. And this alerts us indeed to how involved the poem is with issues of tone and voice. It is as if the poet is signalling to his readers and auditors (for the poem surely demands public performance) that he is wrestling as poet with the matter of tone and register as he seeks to respond to an overwhelming event. Section one speaks of 'polite meaningless words' (p. 228) and the mocking tones of clubmen. Section two regrets the woman's voice that 'grew shrill' in argument when it had once been 'sweet', as 'sweet' as another's 'thought'. In section three 'hens to moor-cocks call' (p. 229), giving an aural charge to Nature's visual dynamism in that section. In section four it is the 'murmur' of a mother naming her child that offers a possible register for intimate commemoration before the stark reality of death enforces a more troubled tone. 'All that is done *and said*' (p. 239, emphasis mine) in the same final section suggests the cruelty of deed and *word* amid the uncertainties of history. The tonal range of the work, I am arguing, is how we discern the presence of many voices in the poem, a presence which in the Modernist fashion denies the work a dominant register. Even the chaunt-like refrain that all readers remember from the poem is set in striking contrast with the matter of sections one and two and is absent in section three before it becomes a summation in section four.

Such tonal fluctuation can be read too as the correlative of the work's indeterminate generic status. If we are unsure about the work's controlling 'voice', we are also in doubt about what 'kind' of a poem it is. This problem has stimulated significant critical debate. For example, Helen Vendler reckons 'Easter 1916' an elegy if not one of his greatest,[17] but at the Yeats International Summer School in 2007, the director Patrick Crotty challenged that designation, arguing that although the poem has a 'threnodic dimension', it is is 'explicitly – less concerned with death than with birth'.[18] Such disagreements derive I think from the poem's own uncertainty about itself. Yeats as poet in the poem is aware indeed that his commemorative performance is a speech act among speech and communicative acts of various kinds (including 'a nod of the head') and that his poem must establish its authority as an utterance of a special but oddly undefined kind. The poem adverts to the 'tale', the 'gibe', 'argument', 'song', 'verse'; and the famously memorable refrain suggests a ballad tradition in Ireland in which every event of note (and many of little note) is recorded and given textual and oral publicity. The charged political ballad, of the sort Yeats had emulated in 'September 1913', is one generic model that Yeats clearly had in his mind as he offered a compelling refrain in this poem to trump that in the earlier one. And as he concludes his new poem, he alludes unmistakably to one of the most famous of all Irish political ballads, that poem of the grim aftermath of the United Irish Rebellion of 1798, 'The Wearing of the Green'. Yeats declares that the martyrs of 1916 have been 'changed utterly', 'Wherever green is worn' (p. 230). The particular ballad and the ballad genre as a whole are therefore present subtextually in Yeats's poem, complicating our sense of its poetic mode of being. Indeed 'The Wearing of the Green' had been made hugely famous in Irish America by its use in Dion Boucicault's play *Arrah-na Pogue*; so one of the places green was unquestionably worn in 1916 and in 1920 (when Yeats's poem was published) was Fenian Irish-America.[19] This gave Yeats's poem an undeniable political edge which ran counter to the poem's otherwise ambivalent attitude to the political significance of what had transpired ('England may keep faith', p. 230).

Other allusive aspects of the work add to the strange, haunted air of poetic indeterminacy that is one of the works most powerful effects, giving it a curiously ghostly quality (it is after all a poem of spirits who will live forever in the national pantheon). I am thinking of the Blakean note struck in the poem (Yeats of course was a profound student of Blake) when in its final section the anguished question about the 'stone of the heart', 'O when may it suffice?', draws from the poet the response 'That is Heaven's part' (p. 229). The imagined setting of the following five lines recalls to mind Blake's song of innocence 'The Echoing Green', with its spring-time children called from their play as night comes on (Yeats's term 'nightfall' here, in 'What is it but nightfall' (p. 230), is an altogether more innocent, benignly evocative term than the drab, terminal 'close of day' with which his poem began). 'Easter 1916' becomes accordingly a song of bitter experience, in which poetic imagining ('their dream') meets brute fact ('No, no, not night but death') (p. 230). A set of contraries is thereby set in motion that allows progression to the Blakean positive, 'excess of love' (the road to Palace of Wisdom for the Blake of 'The Marriage of Heaven and Hell' is by the way of excess) which brought about the deaths by which bewildered men were ultimately apotheosised. In a Blakean paradox, bewilderment is transformed into a kind of wisdom, reminding us that in 'September 1913' Yeats had celebrated 'all that delirium of the brave'. So a poem that summons a ballad's immediacy of poetic impact to mind also engages with matters of Blakean psychological and spiritual import that the political ballad could not easily encompass. The term 'song' in Yeats's poem accordingly faces in two directions at once, towards the ballad sung in direct defiance of imperial authority and towards the poetry of complex spiritual process epitomised in the Blakean antithesis of *Songs of Innocence* and *Songs of Experience*.

This generic indeterminancy in Yeats's poem and the allusive texture it achieves (alluding both to his own past work and to other texts[20]), which makes it an intertextual performance among the other kinds of performance it refers to ('gibe', 'tale', etc.), adds to our deepening sense that this is a transitional poem in Yeats's oeuvre, one that anticipates later works of his that have more readily been associated with multivocal, intertextual Modernist experiment. The way the poem is shadowed by another art form reinforces that impression.

Much Modernist literature, as is well known, aspires to the condition of music. Literary Modernism has among its masterpieces *The Waste Land*, with its use of Wagnerian leitmotif, *Ulysses* with its 'Sirens' episode predicated upon fugal form and 'Anna Livia Plurabelle', where language becomes 'the music of what happens' (in Seamus Heaney's memorable phrase). 'Easter 1916' has its own mesmeric, dissonant music to be sure (not the drum taps Helen Vendler claimed to Patrick Crotty that she hears in its trimeters, defending it as elegy, but repeated notes expressive of a stunned sense that nothing will be the same again),[21] but it is the drama to which it can be seen to aspire as the art form most appropriate to what has occurred on the streets of Dublin.

There was a certain historical appositeness about this. Though the Rising was a serious business, in its first few days, before the big guns began to pound, it all had an unsettling unreality for the citizens of Dublin, as if it were an event being staged with the city as *mise-en-scène,* rather than a political revolution being attempted. In 1938, as Yeats awaited the death he knew could not be long postponed, he in fact remembered the theatricality of that momentous week and the way history and stage had seemed imbricated with the life of his nation. For not only did he guiltily wonder whether his play *Cathleen ni Houlihan* had sent out 'Certain men the English shot' (p. 392) ('Man and the Echo'), but in 'Come gather round me players all' he invited his audience of fellow Irish men and women to attend to his warning about future acts in the national drama ('And no one knows what's yet to come', p. 378). The poem, the third of the set entitled 'Three Songs to the One Burden', recalls to mind how it was indeed a well-known actor who was the first of the insurgents to die in the fighting, as if by his death to synthesise theatre and reality in a symbolic moment which made of reality, theatre and of theatre, reality. Both are played out before a 'painted scene' at the behest of a historical process that is, as the refrain suggests, a fiercesome agent of conflict:

> Who was the first man shot that day?
> The player Connolly,
> Close to City Hall he died;
> Carriage and voice had he;
> He lacked those years that go with skill
> But late might have been
> A famous brilliant figure
> Before the painted scene.

From mountain to mountain ride the fierce horsemen. (p. 378)

And as if to show the whimsical ironies indulged in by history as stage director, the play advertised to open at the Abbey Theatre on the Tuesday immediately following that fateful Easter Monday was *The Spancel of Death* by one T. H. Nally. It was never produced, falling victim to the violence.

A transition from the comedic to the tragic is the central trope of Yeats's 'Easter 1916' as a whole, and this governs its fundamental logic. For section one reckons the present age a clownish one 'where motley' (p. 228) is worn and section two has the 'drunken, vainglorious lout' among its dramatis personae 'resign his part / In the casual comedy' (p. 229). By contrast the phrase 'a terrible beauty' suggests a Yeatsian reformulation (perhaps by way of the Burke of *The Sublime and the Beautiful*) of the Aristotelian categories pity and terror, productive of catharsis in tragedy. The refrain announces change as the poem's preoccupation, but it is change in dramatic mode that so overwhelms the poet. Characters he had thought fit only for comedy have become tragic figures in a compelling drama.

Yeats in the spring of 1916 had we know been pondering the nature of comedy and tragedy, for since 1908 he had been at work on a lengthy stage play (that is lengthy for Yeats) that would bear the name *The Player Queen* when he completed it in 1917. In 1908 he had envisaged that the play would be a tragedy to be played by that great tragedian Mrs Patrick Campbell. She, however, had lost interest in the project and Yeats had had trouble with the text. Then in the summer of 1914, he conceived the idea of casting the play not in a tragic mode, but a comic one. He wrote to his father: 'I shall have almost finished my new play, to be called perhaps *The Woman Born to Be Queen.* It is a wild comedy, almost a farce, with a tragic background – a study of a fantastic woman.'[22] In May 1916, in that letter to Lady Gregory which I have already quoted, where he writes of 'the Dublin tragedy', which 'has been a great sorrow and anxiety' and where he advises Gregory 'terrible beauty has been born again', Yeats refers to *The Player Queen*, concluding, 'I have been able to do little work lately and that chiefly on *Player Queen* which always needs new touches in its one bad place – first half of second act.'[23] In the early summer of 1916, reworking his play, which had been conceived as a tragedy and reborn as a wild comedy, must have reinforced the poet's awareness of comedy and tragedy as radically different modes, a contrast which was to be the basis of the great poem he would complete by September of that year (with some slight emendations when it was published in October 1920). That contrast had been borne in upon the poet indeed from the point of the play's conception. For in the year in which Yeats began what would prove to be the protracted task of writing *The Player Queen*, he had been reading *The Mask*, a theatre journal which Gordon Craig (the stage designer who so influenced Yeats's own theatrical practice) was publishing from the Arena Goldini in Florence. In the journal's first number, Craig had reproduced Sebastiano Serlio's woodcuts, taken from the second book of his treatise *Five Books of Architecture* (1545), of the Comic Scene and the Tragic Scene.

We know these terms (and presumably the images they referred to) stuck in Yeats's mind, for as late as 1938, in his poem 'Lapis Lazuli', the poet has his mountain sages of the poem's concluding lines stare 'on all the tragic scene'. Liam Miller in his book *The Noble Theatre of W. B. Yeats* has even suggested that Serlio's description of the comic scene, part of which was given in translation in the first edition of *The Mask*, may have influenced Yeats's stage directions to the first act of *The Player Queen*: 'The comic scene shall represent the exterior of the dwellings of private persons such as citizens, lawyers, merchants, parasites and other like men.' It is 'An open place at the meeting of three streets. And at some little distance it turns, showing a bare piece of wall lighted by a hanging lamp.' The opening section of 'Easter 1916' has, I would suggest, something of Serlio's comic scene about it, with its citizens, offices (as synecdoche present in 'counter or desk'), its 'grey eighteenth-century houses' and its club, while the final lines of the poem suggest the monumentality of Serlio's 'tragic scene', with its public space dominated by the statues of noble men, the legend of their deeds inscribed (like the names McDonagh and MacBride, Connolly and Pearse) beneath them. Arguably the controlling logic of Yeats's poem had some of its imaginative inspiration in the contrasting scenes from Serlio that must have been in his mind when, as he was pondering the events of Easter 1916, he was also working on *The Player Queen*.

Yeatsian dramaturgy is relevant as well as how his theatrical aesthetic bore on the occasion of this poem. The poet had a less than high view of comedy. He was willing to admit to the stage of the Abbey Theatre 'the art of extravagant comedy', or 'exuberant and vivid comedy',[24] the kind Synge had mastered in *The Playboy of the Western World* (and no doubt what he was attempting to provide for the same stage in *The Player Queen*), but what passed for comedy on the contemporary commercial stage he associated with the superficiality of modern, urban life, with its materialism and merely social concerns. In 1907, the year in which John O'Leary died, he had reflected on how the death of romantic Ireland was also the death of tragedy. 'I do not think', he wrote, referring to his fellow poet Lionel Johnson,

either of us saw that, as belief in the possibility of armed insurrection withered, the old romantic Nationalism would wither too, and that the young would become less ready to find pleasure in whatever they believed to be literature. Poetical tragedy, and indeed all the more intense forms of literature, had lost their hold on the general mass of men in other countries as life grew safe, and the sense of comedy which is the social bond in time of peace as tragic feeling is in times of war, had become the inspiration of popular art. I always knew this, but believed that the memory of danger, and the reality of it seemed near enough sometimes, would last long enough to give Ireland her imaginative opportunity. I could not foresee that a new class, which had begun to rise into power under the shadow of Parnell, would change the nature of the Irish movement, which needed no longer great sacrifices, nor bringing any great risk to individuals, could do without exceptional men, and those activities of the mind that are founded on the exceptional moment.[25]

And in 1910 Yeats recorded how he had discovered 'an antagonism between all the old art and our new art of comedy', recognising how he was carrying on in his own mind a 'quarrel between a tragedian and a comedian'[26] with, it is clear, the tragedian having the better of it. Now in 1916, tragedy had been enacted on the stage of Irish history, with the poet as awe-struck chorus. The sense of awe, indeed, is powerfully registered in the poem, reminding us that for Yeats tragic art had a supernatural dimension. In ''The Tragic Theatre', he had written of how 'in the supreme moment of tragic art there comes upon one that strange sensation as though the hair of one's head stood up'.[27] And he concludes the essay with an evocation of how such art, which he contrasts with modern art, 'which is under command of our common moments', affects its audiences, inducing in them a heightened state of consciousness: 'Tragic art, passionate art, the drowner of dykes, the confounder of understanding, moves us by setting us to reverie, by alluring us almost to the intensity of trance. The persons upon the stage, let us say, greaten till they are humanity itself. We feel our minds expand convulsively or spread out slowly like some moon-brightened image-crowded sea.'[28]

'Easter 1916', it can be argued, approaches the condition of tragic drama. It does so as, through its several sections, normal, quotidian time, the repeated 'minute by minute' of section three, that mode of time which in the terms of Yeats's essay 'is under command of our common moments', is sheered away to enter the poem and its auditors in a sacred order of time: 'Now and in time to be / Wherever green is worn'. In this sacral time, whenever the poem is read or declaimed, it is always eschatologically 'Now' and the people will be hearing the names of the transfigured dead for ever, 'in time to be'. The effect is uncanny, 'as though the hair of one's head stood up'.

So 'Easter 1916' as a Modernist text is shadowed by the drama and achieves some of the effects of tragic art as Yeats himself understood them. Furthermore this sense that the poem seeks to induce an altered state of consciousness that Yeats associated with tragedy adds to the impression that the poem can be read as an entry in the Modernist canon. For a poem that responds to the executions of individuals who had risen in

armed insurrection, with modern, if inadequate, weapons and with political hopes of German support, amid the slaughter of industrial war, has
a distinct air of the pre-modern about it. This, of course, accords with
Yeats's own belief that comedy was the characteristic art of the present
age, while tragedy was that of the ages, 'all the old art and our new art of
comedy'. This air of ancient things, I think, is especially marked in the
third section of the poem, which offers archetypical images of stream,
stone, road, horse and rider, cloud, birds that range and which also introduces to the psychic economy of the poem the near-occult concept of
enchantment: 'Hearts with one purpose alone / Through summer and
winter seem / Enchanted to a stone' (p. 229). Which is to say that the
poem seems not only to set in apposition drably comical modernity 'where
motley is worn', with numinous tragedy, but everyday forms of awareness
with their 'polite meaningless words' in apposition with a mythic consciousness that can be expressed only in imagistic terms. For the third
section of the poem implies that the Rising and its transfigurations have
been the consequence of perennial spiritual truths about the human heart
made available in the mythic image of stone troubling the living stream.
Perhaps Yeats in invoking this dynamic was remembering what he had
read in Ernest Renan's lecture *La poésie des races celtiques* (which we
know Yeats read in translation, for he quotes from it in his own essay
of 1898, 'The Celtic Element in Literature'). There Renan wrote: 'The
worship of forest, and fountain, and stone, is to be explained by ... primitive naturalism which all the Councils of the Church in Brittany united
to proscribe. The stone, in truth, seems the natural symbol of the Celtic
races. It is the immutable witness that has no death. The animal, the
plant, above all the human figure, only express the divine life under a
determinate form; the stone on the contrary, adapted to receive all forms,
has been the fetish of peoples in their childhood.'[29]

The key third section of the poem, therefore, performs the task of
'nudging history towards the condition of myth', to quote a recent essay
by Peter Nicholls on similar processes at work in the poetry of Pound
and Eliot, in which, as in Yeats's 'Easter 1916', 'myth is valued at once
for its antiquity and for its alteriety'.[30] Yeats's great poem accordingly
joins the classic Modernist texts which seek to 'discover' as Joe Cleary
has it in another recent study, 'some aboriginal sense of totality in the
form of universal archetypes or collective myths (which would explain
the Modernist fascination with classical anthropology, the primitive, the
occult, and religious and/or aristocratic ritual'.[31] In his later great poetry,
that has more and more been reckoned by the critics to set Yeats firmly in

the context of the twentieth century's literary Modernism, the interpretative powers of myth are more extensively invoked than in 'Easter 1916', no more resonantly than in that late, troublingly obscure poem of bronze and marble monuments, 'The Statues', where Yeats wrote:

> When Pearse summoned Cuchulain to his side,
> What stalked through the Post Office? What intellect,
> What calculation, number, measurement, replied?
> We Irish, born into that ancient sect
> But thrown upon this filthy modern tide
> And by its formless, spawning fury wrecked,
> Climb to our proper dark, that we may trace
> The lineaments of a plummet-measured face. (pp. 384–5)

It is in 'Easter 1916', however, as I have been arguing, that Yeats most probably began that Modernist ascent to a mythic 'proper dark', from which height the 'filthy modern tide' could be magisterially dismissed, as the ancient Irish sect found a 'terrible beauty' in the visage of a strange avatar.

NOTES

1 T. S. Eliot, '*Ulysses,* Order and Myth', *The Dial*, 75, 5 (November, 1923), 483.
2 Donoghue made this point in a lecture broadacst on the BBC third programme.
3 Virginia Woolf identified this watershed in her famous Hogarth Press pamphlet of 1924, *Mr Bennett and Mrs Brown*.
4 In fact, in Laurence Rainey's *Modernism: An Anthology* (Oxford: Blackwell Publishing, 2005), Yeats is well represented, though he does not include 'No Second Troy'. The earliest poem by Yeats that Rainey includes is 'A Coat', written in 1912 and first published in 1914. He also includes 'In Memory of Major Robert Gregory' and 'Easter 1916'.
5 C. Townshend's *Easter 1916: The Irish Rebellion* (London: Allen Lane, 2005) is a detailed account of the events of that momentous week and its aftermath.
6 R. Foster, *W. B. Yeats: A Life*, Vol. II: *The Arch-Poet 1915–1939* (Oxford University Press, 2003), p. 54.
7 A. Wade (ed.), *The Letters of W. B. Yeats* (London: Rupert Hart-Davis, 1954), p. 613.
8 *Ibid.*
9 Foster, *W. B. Yeats: A Life*, Vol. II, p. 53.
10 *Ibid.*, p. 54.
11 H. Vendler, 'Four Elegies', in A. N. Jeffares (ed.), *Yeats, Sligo and Ireland* (Gerrards Cross, Colin Smythe Ltd, 1980), p. 216.
12 A. N. Jeffares and A. MacBride White (eds.), *The Gonne–Yeats Letters 1893–1938: Always Your Friend* (London: Hutchinson, 1992), p. 385.

13 W. B. Yeats, *Essays and Introductions* (London and Basingstoke: Macmillan, 1961), p. 354.

14 See Anne Fogarty's excellent essay 'Yeats, Ireland and Modernism', in A. Davis and L. Jenkins (eds.), *The Cambridge Companion to Modernist Poetry* (Cambridge University Press, 2007), pp. 126–46, where she not only argues that 'Yeats's poetry and aesthetics are of pressing relevance to the history of modernism because of their exacting self-reflexivity' but sees 'his espousal of a modernist aesthetic' (p. 128), made fully apparent as early as the publication of his volume *Responsibilities: Poems and a Play* in 1914, with its 'formal variety and miscellaneous moods' suggesting that 'Ireland is now splintered into numerous conflicting zones' (p. 135).

15 See R. Foster, *W. B. Yeats: A Life*, Vol. I: *The Apprentice Mage* (Oxford and New York: Oxford University Press, 1997), pp. 112–13, where he reckons that it was 'not unlikely' that Yeats did in fact take the oath as a young man, despite mature denials that he had done so.

16 D. Albright (ed.), *W. B. Yeats: The Poems* (London: Everyman's Library, 1991), p. 159. Subsequent page references in the text to Yeats's poems are to this edition.

17 Vendler, 'Four Elegies', 216–20.

18 I am grateful to Professor Crotty for making the text of his lecture available to me.

19 In her doctoral thesis 'Dion Boucicault's Irish Melodramas; National Identity, Politics and the Press' (Trinity College, Dublin, 2007), Deirdre McFeely has shown how Boucicault's use of a version of this ballad in his play *Arrah-na Pogue* gave it both long-lasting popularity and political potency in republican and nationalist Irish-America. I am indebted to her study.

20 Helen Vendler, in *Our Secret Discipline: Yeats and Lyric Form* (Cambridge, MA: Belknap Press of Harvard University Press, 2007), hears another Blakean echo in this poem. She associates the phrase 'terrible beauty' with the 'fearful symmetry' of Blake's 'fiery tiger' (p. 20.). She also senses its allusive quality, not only hearing allusions to Blake and to 'The Wearing of the Green' in its lines but to Shakespeare's *Hamlet*, in 'That is heaven's part', a version of old Hamlet's injunction about Gertrude, 'Leave her to heaven.'

21 In *Our Secret Discipline* (p. 17) Vendler states, 'Yeats chooses, for his elegy, a quick trimeter march rhythm suitable both to military enterprise and to the second subject of the poem, the rapidity of natural change.' My sense of the poem is that the trimeters at moments give a note of urgency to the poem's pained, sometimes poignant reflections, but that the cadences of many of the lines are neither those of march rhythm nor of rapid change. If we are to hear martial drumbeats here, I would suggest that they are muffled by complex emotional ambivalence.

22 Cited L. Miller, *The Noble Drama of W. B. Yeats* (Dublin: The Dolmen Press; North America: Humanities Press Inc. 1977), p. 183. I am indebted to this work's account of the gestation of *The Player Queen*.

23 Wade (ed.), *The* Letters *of W. B. Yeats.* p. 614.

24 These phrases occur in a lecture Yeats wrote in 1910 entitled 'The Theatre'. The lectures were published in R. O'Driscoll, 'Yeats On Personality: Three Unpublished Lectures', *Yeats and the Theatre* (London and Basingstoke: Macmillan, 1975). See p. 23 of this volume.

25 Yeats, *Essays and Introductions*, p. 259.

26 *Ibid.*, pp. 241–2.

27 *Ibid.*, p. 243.

28 *Ibid.*, p. 245.

29 E. Renan, *The Poetry of the Celtic Races, Translated, With Introduction and Notes, By William G. Hutchison* (Port Washington, NY and London: Kennikat Press, 1896), p. 23. This is a scholarly reprint (published in 1996) of Hutchison's translation. Yeats undoubtedly used the translation to prepare his essay of 1898, 'The Celtic Element in Literature', in which he quotes Renan in Hutchison's English (with some emendations).

30 P. Nicholls, 'The Poetics of Modernism', in Davis and Jenkins (eds.), *Modernist Poetry*, p. 59.

31 J. Cleary, *Outrageous Fortune: Capital and Culture in Modern Ireland* (Dublin: Field Day Publications, 2007), p. 123.

CHAPTER 5

Shakespeare and the Irish self

> Our Irish servant has piqued me this morning by saying that her
> Father in Ireland was very like my Shakespeare only he had more
> colour than the Engraving.
>
> John Keats, 'Letter to Georgina Keats'

Jorge Luis Borges in his remarkable meditation on Shakespeare's career
entitled 'Everything and Nothing' strikingly begins: 'There was no one in
him.' For the South American fabulist, Shakespeare was a man who from
boyhood sensed an 'emptiness' that made his life a quest for a cure from
the 'ill' of non-identity which so terribly afflicted him. For Borges, the
bard's career as actor and playwright was a long demonstration 'of simu-
lating that he was someone'. Borges eloquently contends:

No one has ever been so many men as this man who like the Egyptian Proteus
could exhaust all the guises of reality. At times he would leave a confession hidden away in some corner of his work certain that it would not be deciphered;
Richard affirms that in his person he plays the part of many and Iago claims
with curious words 'I am not what I am'. The fundamental identity of existing,
dreaming and acting inspired many famous passages of his.[1]

Borges has Shakespeare retire from the theatre to play a final role as
a litigious, wealthy Stratford burgher, until, at the last, he stands before
God. Shakespeare asks his creator, as one who has been so many men, to
be allowed to be himself.

The voice of the Lord answered him from a whirlwind, 'Neither am I anyone;
I dreamt the world as you dreamt your work, my Shakespeare, and among the
forms in my dream are you, who, like myself, are many and no one.'[2]

Borges's Shakespeare is a god of 'negative capability' whose nature
imagined in these protean terms reminds us of John Keats's famous letter to Richard Woodhouse of 27 October 1818, where he brooded on the
'poetical Character':

it is not itself – it has no self – it is everything and nothing – It has no character – it enjoys light and shade; it lives in gusto, be it foul or fair, high or low,

61

rich or poor, mean or elevated – It has as much delight in conceiving an Iago as an Imogen.[3]

For Keats, Shakespeare is exemplary in his exuberant indifference as poet to the moral virtue or otherwise of his creations: 'What shocks the virtuous philosopher, delights the chameleon poet.[4] Accordingly, for Keats the selflessness of the great dramatist is a relished opportunity for the gusto of creativity, whereas for Borges it is a burden and an affliction – though interestingly they share a sense of Shakepeare as a man and artist who was no one.

To turn from Borges and Keats to the Shakespeare of Victorian English criticism is to leave the nothingness of non-identity for the secure certainties of what was then comprehended as character. A Shakespeare of anonymous emptiness who could assume any shape becomes an artist whose works bespeak a certainty that the world is to be understood in terms of individual character in action. Character is, famously, destiny in Bradley's *Shakespearian Tragedy*. In his chapter 'Shakespeare as Artist', he identifies the 'chief difficulty in interpreting his works' as follows:

Where his power or art is fully exerted it really does resemble that of nature. It organises and vitalises its products from the centre outward to the minutest markings of the surface, so that when you turn upon it the most searching light you can command, when you dissect it and apply it to the test of a microscope, still you find in it nothing formless, general or vague, but everywhere structure, character, individuality.[5]

This passage makes Shakespeare a kind of scientist of human character. There is a faith here in the integrity of the human subject, a faith that the self possesses the givenness of a natural phenomenon, something which Shakespeare's 'power or art' can anatomise from core to periphery, discovering at every level 'structure, character, individuality'.

In this essay I will argue that Shakespeare in Ireland has been recurrently associated with the concept of the self, of the human subject, as fictively open to dramatic representation in various guises, rather than with any kind of Victorian notion of 'character' as a given in which destiny is implicit. The Irish Shakespeare in his person and his works is a Keatsian or Borgesian phenomenon, who at crucial moments in the country's twentieth-century experience has been imagined by Irish writers in terms that align his drama with crises of identity, with the exploration of multiple roles in which subjectivity finds expression and with the radical indeterminacy of the self.

Though Joyce's *Ulysses* might at first seem the most apposite text, it is Yeats who furnishes my example. In April 1901 the poet, at a point in his life when he was uncertain whether England or Ireland would be the location for the dramatic movement he sought to develop, attended a cycle of the history plays at Stratford (*King John, Richard II*, the second part of *Henry IV, Henry V*, the second part of *Henry VI*, and *Richard III*), which was being produced by Francis Robert Benson. Yeats had a particular interest in this event for he was anxious that Benson would soon produce his own *Diarmuid and Grania*. He wrote of his experience to Lady Gregory that he felt he was 'getting deeper into Shakespeare's mystery than ever before'.[6] A compelling passage in the essay this visit provoked, dated May 1901, suggests how very deep was the mystery Yeats was seeking to penetrate that week in Stratford. It can be set revealingly against Bradley's confident summation of the dramatist's 'power and art'. Yeats writes in 'At Stratford-on-Avon':

> the theatre has moved me as it has never done before. That strange procession of kings and queens, of warring nobles, of insurgent crowds, of courtiers, and of people of the gutter, has been to me almost too audible, too visible, too full of unearthly energy. I have felt as I have sometimes felt on grey days on the Galway shore, when a faint mist has hung over the grey sea and the grey stones, as if the world might suddenly vanish and leave nothing behind, not even a little dust under one's feet. The people my mind's eye has seen have too much of the extravagance of dreams.[7]

In the body of Yeats's writings this essay is, it must be said, one of the very few moments in which he responds with any enthusiasm to an English setting. England (away from London, 'bitter hatred' for which is 'becoming a mark of those that love the arts'[8]) for once can offer an idyllic world: 'One passes through quiet streets, where gabled and red-tiled houses remember the Middle Ages, to a theatre that has been made not to make money, but for the pleasure of making it, like the market-houses that set the traveller chuckling.'[9]

So Stratford is attractive, but it is indisputably substantial with its red tiles and market-houses. The magic of the drama by contrast transposes Yeats to the insubstantial dream-world of a Galway shore, which may vanish of a sudden and leave not a wrack behind. That imaginary landscape with its grey colouration, its mists, on the point of vanishing into nothingness, seems the antithesis of the ancient settled town in England with its 'old farm-houses … and old churches among great trees', its 'inn parlour, under oak beams blackened by time, showing the mark of the adze that shaped them'.[10] The contrast between the two locations in the essay – the one a permanent, substantial product of actual physical labour and proficient craft pride, the other a landscape of dream – does of course reflect some of the self-division Yeats must have been experiencing at this stage of his life and career, when he was undecided about his future. Would it be in materialistic England, which might supply the wherewithal to establish a theatre of beauty? Or would it be in the Ireland (with its western landscapes and sea) that he identified with the life of the imagination, but also with extraordinary practical difficulties? Yeats may have found, as he tells us, nothing to dislike in Stratford 'but certain new houses' and the theatre itself. It is telling, nevertheless, that he associates the power of the drama to suggest what he calls 'high dream' not with the palpable English town in which he had seen the plays, but with a western Irish liminal state, bordering, at a sea shore, on immateriality. For in the complex divisions of his nature, Ireland held *very* powerful sway.

The locational contrast also bears significantly on the central point of Yeats's essay – its comparison between Richard II and Bolingbroke as images of human possibility. In the essay, as is well known, Richard, *contra* Yeats's father's friend Edward Dowden, author of *Shakespere [sic]: A Critical Study of His Mind and Art*, is a poetically exquisite failure but preferable as such to Henry V, the hero of utilitarians and admirers of schoolboy heroics. As William Murphy has demonstrated in his biography of the poet's father, brilliantly entitled *Prodigal Father,* Yeats probably derived the substance of the argument of his essay from J. B. Yeats; for in 1874 Dowden had written to his friend John Butler Yeats to tell him of his forthcoming lecture on Richard II:

In K. Richard II Shakespeare represents the man with an artistic feeling for life, who isn't an artist of life. The artist of life is efficient and shapes the world and his destiny with strong creative hands. Richard likes graceful combinations, a clever speech instead of an efficient one, a melodious passion instead of one which achieves the deed … If things can be arranged so as to appeal gracefully or touchingly to his esthetic sensibility he doesn't concern himself much more about them. And so all his life becomes unreal to him through this dilettantism with life.[11]

J. B. took, as Murphy describes it, what was a more-or-less personal affront. Since Dowden had accepted his Chair of English literature at Trinity in 1867, he had represented for the apprentice painter the terrible danger to the artistic temperament that a need for bourgeois security occasioned. As a man who had abandoned a career in the law which family contacts might have made financially rewarding, he was not pleased to have his college friend, now in secure employment, appear to read him a lecture on dilettantism. For J. B. Yeats, 'In the rules of goodness, of bravery and chivalry and comradeship and true love, Richard is admirably proficient.'[12]

The poet shared his father's preference for Richard and scorn for Bolingbroke but, crucially, attributed Dowden's views not as J. B. would have done, to the self-justificatory instincts of a man who had destroyed the poetry in himself for domestic and professional security, but to his Irish residence. 'He lived in Ireland', Yeats somewhat pompously announces, 'where everything has failed, and he meditated frequently upon the perfection of character, which had, he thought, made England successful ...'[13] As Yeats sees it, Dowden, as a Unionist in Ireland, was necessarily obsessed by 'character' and how success was dependent upon it.

In Yeats's essay the concept of 'character' as moral fibre and 'character' as figure in a drama begin to seem interchangeable. Dowden is interested in Richard as a *theatrical* character in apposition to Bolingbroke because he has an Irish Victorian Unionist obsession with *personal* character as a guarantee of worldly success. Yeats, in opposition to Dowden, is not interested in Shakespeare as a creator of 'characters' who might serve as models of right action of any kind. (J. B. Yeats, the Victorian despite himself, admired Richard because he seemed to endorse his own indolent character and aesthetic mode of life.) Rather, Yeats is in awe of the dramatist as a powerful dreamer, whose six plays presented in sequence have 'something extravagant and superhuman, something almost mythological'[14] about them. And Shakespeare's nature, as Yeats imagines it in this essay, is not itself that of any kind of stable 'character' who was a creator of characters in plays which could supply role models for his audiences. For the Shakespearian nature, like his own, is fascinated by antithesis and the extravagant drama it generates. He writes:

The Greeks, a certain scholar has told me, considered that myths are the activities of the Daimons, and that the Daimons shape our characters and our lives. I have often had the fancy that there is some one myth for every man, which, if we but knew it, would make us understand all he did and thought. Shakespeare's myth, it may be, describes a wise man who was blind from very wisdom, and an empty man who thrust him from his place, and saw all that could be seen from very emptiness.[15]

Shakespeare's is thus a nature in the grip of a dialectic, his character in the control of a Daimon-shaped myth of antithesis between blind wisdom and empty but effective power that imposes its will on all it sees. This dualistic sense of life finds expression, Yeats believes, in all the plays. They do, as Yeats admits, 'pose character against character', but not because the dramatist is interested in character as such, in the Victorian way, but because he relishes the spectacle antithesis arranges for a detached eye. For Yeats, Shakespeare, although he must have looked on 'his Richard II with … sympathetic eyes', nevertheless also 'watched Henry V not indeed as he watched the greater souls in the visionary procession but cheerfully, as one watches some handsome spirited horse, and he spoke his tale, as he spoke all tales, with tragic irony'.[16]

Shakespeare indeed contained within him a Keatsian gusto and a Borgesian tragic irony. He created as his myth impelled him. He was able in different moods to create and contemplate a Richard and a Henry, a Hamlet and a Fortinbras. The play of antithesis was the thing. His own identity, the 'mind' Dowden had sought to explore and define in his famous book, was realised beyond simplistic definition in his protean art, with its 'blind ambitions, untoward accidents, and capricious passions',[17] its strange processions of men and women as in a dream.

It is difficult to trace the immediate impact of Yeats's exposure to the history plays at Stratford in 1901 to the poetry and drama. It has been argued (by Liam Miller) that the season 'prompted him to think of the epic nature of the six plays played in sequence, perhaps forming the germ of the idea behind his later attempt to create a cycle of dramas based on the old Irish epic the *Táin*'.[18] And his play, *On Baile's Strand*, begun in January 1902, does have a Shakespearian verse form. Declan Kiberd has pointed out that Patrick Pearse 'heard echoes of Hamlet on the lips of the Cuchulain'[19] of the play and has argued interestingly that the conflict between Richard and Bolingbroke in Shakespeare's cycle of plays 'emboldened' Yeats to write his own cycle, with its conflict between Cuchulain and Conchobar. Yeats paid a second visit to Stratford in March of that year to see a further cycle of the plays.

What I think can be affirmed is that Yeats saw his Shakespeare in performance (if we except his youthful and very compelling exposure to Henry Irving's *Hamlet*) at a time when he was beginning to develop his theory of the mask, in which the self finds an escape from vitiating incoherence and self-division in performative acts of verse and drama. He had in fact, from his boyhood onwards, for all the Victorian quality of his response to Irving, associated the figure of Hamlet with self-division. For in *Reveries Over Childhood and Youth*, he recalls how he saw in Irving's Hamlet, as a boy still expecting models of behaviour in the theatre in the Victorian way, 'an image of heroic self-possession for the poses of youth and childhood to copy, a combatant of the battle within myself'.[20] In the first decade of the twentieth century, Yeats pondered how that battle within the self, through the mask, could be made the basis both of a dramatically charged poetic and of a dramaturgy.

By 1911, with his theory of the mask well advanced, Yeats naturally took great interest in Gordon Craig's design for the Moscow Art Theatre's production of *Hamlet*, paying special attention to the famous woodcut 'Hamlet and the Daimon', with its haunting image of a proud, strong man, in contemplative anguish, shadowed by a sternly upright other at his back – head directly lowered, bent in serious sorrow to contrast with the more fraught angles of Hamlet's posture. Yeats included this image in an exhibition of Craig's stage designs which was mounted in Dublin, under the poet's direction, in 1913. Even in 1901, the problem of the self and its public representation had not been far from his mind as he brooded on what he had seen in the Stratford theatre. There he had recalled a Balzac novel, *La peau de chagrin,* that explores the conflict between a 'true self' and 'the momentary self which acts and lives in the world, and is subject to the judgement of the world'.[21] By the end of the decade he had become less attached to the notion of a 'true self' as more and more he sought to express what he called 'the personality as a whole'.[22] In a key passage in *Discoveries,* the series of prose reflections he published in 1906, Yeats recalls how this change in his sense of the self occurred. He is remembering how in his early poetry he had sought to put his 'very self into poetry'. Yeats continues:

I thought of myself as something unmoving and silent living in the middle of my own mind and body, a grain of sand in Bloomsbury or in Connacht that Satan's watch-fiends cannot find. Then one day I understood quite suddenly, as the way is, that I was seeking something unchanging and unmixed and always outside myself, a Stone or an Elixir that was always out of reach, and that I myself was the fleeting thing that held out its hand.[23]

It may have been at Stratford that some of the seeds of this recognition were sown: that the struggle to put the 'very self' into art was futile. For there he had seen a cycle of plays by a dramatist whose vision was of a procession of kings, queens and other personages, in a drama which delighted with Keatsian gusto in the antithesis of human personality but told its tales with tragic irony. The Shakespearian history plays may indeed have helped Yeats to his mature sense of the self as an arena of creative tension released in acts of dramatic representation through the adoption of a mask. We note too how, in the passage from *Discoveries* already quoted, where the poet considers the integrity of a putative essential self, and the stresses of actual social existence, it is in terms of the same geographic opposition that had emerged in the essay on Stratford.

In the one, Galway had been in apposition to the English town, to reflect a key aspect of his current self-division; in the other, Bloomsbury is in apposition to Connacht. In both, geography is implicated in the problematic of selfhood, while topography is a sign of subjectivity conscious of its own conflicts.

In 'At Stratford-on-Avon', Yeats averred that 'Shakespeare cared little for the State', yet he 'did indeed think it wrong to overturn a king, and thereby to swamp peace in civil war'.[24] When Ireland was swamped by civil war in 1922, Yeats's artistic response was to compose what became that great sequence poem 'Meditations in Time of Civil War'. The first poem of the sequence, 'Ancestral Houses', had been begun at a country house in England before the fratricidal violence actually broke out, but the further six poems of the sequence were written in Ireland in 1922, mainly at Thoor Ballylee, where they are set. 'Meditations in Time of Civil War', with its controlling metaphors of buildings, wind and symbolic tower, is concerned at fundamental levels with the poet's role in the world; with the problematic of his artistic and human identity in a period of tubulence. The poet of the sequence ponders with intensifying uncertainty how it may be possible to perform what Borges dubbed 'the trick of making believe he was somebody', as the waves of violent destruction threaten even his 'loosening masonry'. The acts of linguistic conjuration in the sequence become increasingly desperate, until the poet at last acknowledges that the various masks he has donned over the years as man and artist have left him a misunderstood survivor at best, making do with a selfhood that transcends time and its depredations only in its obsession with occult knowledge.

> I turn away and shut the door, and on the stair
> Wonder how many times I could have proved my worth
> In something all others understand or share;
> But O! ambitious heart, had such a proof drawn forth
> A company of friends, a conscience set at ease,
> It had but made us pine the more. The abstract joy,
> The half-read wisdom of daemonic images,
> Suffice the aging man as once the growing boy.[25]

'Meditations in Time of Civil War' imagines the poet and man in a variety of public and semi-public guises, each found to be inadequate in face of the knowledge of a nation racked by civil war. In 'Ancestral Houses', the elegant world of 'a rich man's flowering lawns' where 'slippered Contemplation finds his ease' is dependent on a foundation of expropriatory violence and bitterness. Civilisation is originated and sustained by barbarism. His poem has the poet as troubled interrogative presence, assailed by historical ambiguity, amid 'buildings that a haughtier age designed', buildings that would be at risk in the violence of a new era. 'My House' is no more assured. The image of the poet as philosophic guide for a people, whose 'midnight candle glimmering' could be a point of reference for 'Benighted travelers / From markets and from fairs' is set against the recollection of the military disturbances a 'tumultuous spot' has known. Aspirations to the role of instructive sage seem the wistful sentiments of peacetime in this poem, which promises the poet's bodily heirs only 'befitting emblems of adversity'. Poem III, 'My Table', by contrast, reckons with the poet as ethical aesthete rather than Platonist, as it engages a Keatsian dialectic of changeless works of art and of the 'aching heart'. Yet the accompaniment to this almost Keatsian vision of the poet as refined moralist of 'soul's beauty' and 'the soul's unchanging look' is no nightingale or 'unheard' melody, but the scream of 'Juno's peacock'. Poem IV, 'My Descendants' contemplates selfhood in terms of dynastic duties and is haunted by fears of familial disintegration which threaten such achievements as the poet can claim as his own. The images of ruination and eugenic catastrophe in this poem make the poet's investment of intact selfhood (highlighted syntactically and structurally) in bricks and mortar, seem a desperate ploy indeed:

> The Primum Mobile that fashioned us
> Has made the very owls in circles move;
> And I, that count myself most prosperous
> Seeing that love and friendship are enough
> For an old neighbour's friendship chose this house
> And decked and altered it for a girl's love,
> And know whatever flourish and decline
> These stones remain their monument and mine.[26]

Poem V, 'The Road at My Door', highlights how 'Meditations' contemplates the roles a poet might play on the stage of national life in a time of crisis, for it introduces a bold dramatic metaphor:

> An affable Irregular,
> A heavily-built Falstaffian man,
> Comes cracking jokes of civil war
> As though to die by gunshot were
> The finest play under the sun.[27]

We know from *Discoveries* that Yeats considered Falstaff, whom he termed there 'an episode in a chronicle play', the one Shakespearian creation, even including Hamlet and Lear, 'who will follow us out of the theatre as Don Quixote follows us out of the book'.[28] Such extra-textual existence undoubtedly made Sir John readily available for allusive recruitment by the poet in this poem. Yet, there is evidence in the sequence that Yeats is remembering, as a focus of his meditation, the context of the chronicle plays in which Falstaff found his first life on stage.

In 'Ancestral Houses', Yeats imagined the superb indifference to others that wealth endows to be an 'abounding glittering jet'. The image is a reiterated one in Yeats's oeuvre: we find it in 'The Gift of Harun Al-Raschid', in *The Tower* and in 'Blood and the Moon'. In *Discoveries* the poet offers a definition: 'Art bids us touch and taste and hear and see the world and shrinks from what Blake calls mathematical form, from every abstract thing, from all that is of the brain only, from all that is not a fountain jetting from the entire hopes, memories and sensations of the body.'[29]

In 'At Stratford-on-Avon', Richard II is crucially deemed to possess a lyricism which rose out of his 'mind like the jet of a fountain to fall again where it had risen', apt accompaniment of a 'fantasy too enfolded in its own sincerity to make any thought the hour had need of'.[30]

In 'Meditations', Yeats certainly seeks to make a thought the hour has need of, but he does so in the knowledge of the thoughtless 'inherited glory of the rich' and of the lyricism and physical beauty of 'the abounding glittering jet' of life lived without such burdensome necessity. So wearying indeed is the exercise of thought and meditation that the poet in 'The Road at My Door' envies the soldiers, including the Falstaffian irregular, who come to his door, as if he might solve the problems of his identity and role in unthinking action, in the 'finest play under the sun'. But action is denied him, for he is 'caught / In the cold snows of a dream'. Where the extravagant spectacle of a history of civil war and eventually restoration of order on a Stratford stage had provoked the poet to imagine the world vanishing away in faint mists hanging over grey sea and stones, now the drama of Irish civil war enacted before him is the occasion of a chill dream in his chamber in Thoor Ballylee. Poem VII of the sequence overwhelms us with the contents of such a dream. Its ghastly intensity makes nugatory the prayerful incantation of poem VI, 'The Stare's Nest By My Window' (for this is a meditation that concludes in nightmare, not prayer). And it is a dream that re-enacts in symbolic terms the Shakespearian transition from Richard II, all lyricism and sincerity, to Henry V who, as Yeats describes him in 'At Stratford-on-Avon', is 'remorseless and undistinguished as some natural force'.[31]

In Yeats's poem we see in procession, as on some phantasmagoric stage, a history play in which, as one era gives way to another, 'Magical unicorns bear ladies on their backs'. These creatures and their riders inhabit a zone of being that transcends even 'life's own self-delight': 'Their minds are but a pool / Where even longing drowns under its own excess'. But they are completely vulnerable, despite an aristocratic superiority of demeanour and bodily frame. In the 'visionary procession' of this drama they 'give place', as Richard did to Bolingbroke and eventually to Henry V, to the remorselessness of what seems both a natural force and an abstract mechanical horror, an 'indifferent multitude' figured as 'brazen hawks':

> Nor self-delighting reverie,
> Nor hate of what's to come, nor pity for what's gone,
> Nothing but grip of claw, and the eye's complacency,
> The innumerable clanging wings that have put out the moon.[32]

In 'Meditations', I have been arguing, as Yeats tests various roles for the self in time of civil war and finds them all inadequate, he offers us a dramatisation of a Shakespearean antithesis, similar to that which had fascinated him at Stratford-on-Avon over two decades earlier. Then he had been uncertain about the stage upon which he was to play his main roles as man and artist, but had begun to see how self-division could be the basis of a performative, dramatic art. In 'Meditations', in which he explores his sense of selfhood and of the roles it might play in radical crisis, that dramatic art can be seen in one of its most Shakespearean moments – as Yeats would have understood the term 'Shakespearean'. For the Yeatsian Shakespeare is to be comprehended in a myth whereby a blind wise man gives way to an empty one. On the symbolic level, the second movement of the final poem of 'Meditations', which I have just quoted, follows an historical trajectory governed by the same order of antithesis, as indeed the title of the poem indicates: 'I see Phantoms of Hatred and the Heart's Fullness and the Coming Emptiness.'

It would be possible, I believe, to establish a history of the Irish Literary Revival that reads some of its principal texts as Irish revisions of the Victorian Shakespeare – both Philip Edwards, in his paper 'Shakespeare and the Politics of the Irish Revival' and Declan Kiberd in *Inventing Ireland* in his chapter entitled 'Writing Ireland, Reading England' have inaugurated such a project. I also believe that in this context we would be required to explore in detail an Irish interrogation of the idea of the self. In this the Keatsian and Borgesean version of a Shakespeare who contained multitudes, who was everyone and no one, who created a world of dramatic antitheses, would, I think, be found critically enabling.

This essay has sought to show how it might be so enabling in relation to two occasions on which Yeats engaged imaginatively with the Shakespeare of the history plays. In a more extended reflection, the presence of Shakespeare's *Hamlet* in the texts of the period would require extended analysis, especially Hamlet as rendered in Joyce's *Ulysses*. That curious moment in 'Circe', the episode in which the very basis of individual identity is fundamentally undermined in a collective hallucination, springs instantly to mind as especially apposite. There, we remember, both Bloom and Stephen see the face of Shakespeare when they look together into the mirror in a Dublin brothel – the cracked looking-glass of Irish art? Such a history, were it to be culturally situated, would also have to engage with the question as to whether the Irish recruitment of Shakespeare to a version of selfhood that emphasised the dialectical and performative quality of personal identity did not bear on the problematics of social and national identity, when these things were in crisis and flux in the early years of this century. It might be instructive too to assess how the presence of Shakespeare in the Irish literary imagination has diminished since that heady period when national independence has been consolidated and to note that the Keatsian and Borgesean Shakespeares (with very few textual exceptions) in the later twentieth century found their dangerous home in literature north of the Irish border, where the issue of national identity was still so fraught.

I am thinking in respect of this point not only of Seamus Heaney's identification in some of his poems of anguished introspection with the gloomy Dane, but also of a poem such as Michael Longley's 'Fleance', collected in the mid-1970s in *Man Lying on a Wall,* at the height of the violence in the northern province. Fleance in this poem presents himself as a creation of mere words and shadowy theatricality, a bit part indeed, a product of illusion whose very identity is in doubt in a world where the self faces the immediate danger of violent extinction:

> But as any illusionist might
> Unfasten the big sack of darkness,
> The ropes and handcuffs, and emerge
> Smoking a nonchalant cigarette,
> I escaped – only to lose myself.
> It took me a lifetime to explore
> The dusty warren beneath the stage
> With its trapdoor opening on to
> All that had happened above my head
> Like noises-off or distant weather.
> In the empty auditorium I bowed

To one preoccupied caretaker
And, without removing my make-up,
Hurried back to the digs where Banquo
Sat up late with a hole in his head.[33]

And such a history might conclude with a detailed analysis of Ciaran Carson's complex, haunting poem in *Belfast Confetti* (1989) entitled 'Hamlet'. This eerie monologue concludes a volume in which human identity, the self, has been dispersed in a violent city of protean, indeterminate origins and contemporary plurality of contingent consciousness (MacNeice's famous poem 'Snow' with its 'incorrigible plurality' is tellingly rewritten early in the book) in the midst of ongoing urban destruction and political crisis. The ghost in this poem is the rattle of a tin can in a street in which the spirit of a soldier killed in 1922 reminds that the Irish word *fál*, meaning a hedge (from which the Falls Road in West Belfast takes its name) is 'also *frontier, boundary* as in *the undiscovered frontier / From whose bourne no traveller returns,* the illegible, thorny hedge of time itself'. Carson makes complicated, subtle play in this work with a fast clock in a bar, with memories of the Armada lost (stimulated by an image of a salvaged vessel on a beer-stained banknote) that evokes that Elizabethan disaster set in motion at the beginning of the imperial age and that is now running down in the Belfast of the 1990s. In this poem, the city, suffering demolition by bomb and bulldozer, is a place of necessary restoration of self and society in a recognisably human order of things, in a living community of conversation:

Like some son looking for his father, or the father for his son,
We try to piece together the exploded fragments. Let these
    broken spars
Stand for the armada and its proud full sails, for even if
The clock is put to rights, everyone will still believe it's fast:
The Barman's shouts of time will be ignored in any case, since
    time
Is conversation; it is the hedge that flits incessantly into the
    present,
As words blossom from the speakers' mouths, and the flotilla
    returns to harbour
Long after hours.[34]

NOTES

1 J. L. Borges, 'Everything and Nothing', in *Labyrinths* (London: Penguin Books, 1970), p. 285.

2 *Ibid.*

3 J. Keats, 'Letter to Richard Woodhouse', 27 October 1818, in Douglas Bush (ed.), *Selected Poems and Letters of John Keats* (Boston: Houghton Mifflin Company, 1959), p. 279.

4 Keats, 'Letter to Woodhouse', p. 279.

5 A. C. Bradley, *Shakespearean Tragedy* (London: Macmillan, 1932), p. 77.

6 W. B. Yeats, 'To Lady Augusta Gregory', in J. Kelly and R. Schuchard (eds.), *The Collected Letters of W. B. Yeats*, Vol. III (Oxford: Clarendon Press, 1994), p. 62.

7 W. B. Yeats, *Essays and Introductions* (London: Macmillan, 1961), p. 97.

8 *Ibid.*, p. 98.

9 *Ibid.*

10 *Ibid.*

11 Cited in William M. Murphy, *Prodigal Father: The Life of John Butler Yeats* (Ithaca: Cornell University Press, 1978), p. 97.

12 *Ibid.*, p. 99.

13 Yeats, *Essays and Introductions*, p. 104.

14 *Ibid.*, p. 109.

15 *Ibid.*, p. 107.

16 *Ibid.*, p. 109.

17 *Ibid.*, pp. 106–7.

18 L. Miller, *The Noble Drama of W. B. Yeats* (Dublin: Dolmen Press, 1977), p. 53.

19 D. Kiberd, *Inventing Ireland* (London: Jonathan Cape, 1995), p. 162.

20 W. B. Yeats, *Autobiographies* (London: Macmillan, 1955), p. 47.

21 Yeats, *Essays and Introductions*, p. 102.

22 *Ibid.*, p. 272.

23 *Ibid.*, p. 271.

24 *Ibid.*, p. 106.

25 W. B. Yeats, 'Meditations in Time of Civil War', in D. Albright (ed.), *W. B. Yeats: The Poems* (London: Everyman's Library, 1992), p. 252.

26 Albright (ed.), *Yeats: The Poems*, p. 249.

27 *Ibid.*, p. 250.

28 Yeats, *Essays and Introductions*, p. 273.

29 *Ibid.*, pp. 292–3.

30 *Ibid.*, p. 108.

31 *Ibid.*

32 Albright (ed.), *Yeats: The Poems*, p. 252.

33 M. Longley, 'Fleance', in *Poems 1963–1983* (Edinburgh: The Salamander Press; Dublin: The Gallery Press, 1985), p. 136.

34 C. Carson, 'Hamlet', *Belfast Confetti* (Oldcastle: Gallery Press, 1989), p. 108.

CHAPTER 6

Irish literature and the Great War

In 1979, ten years after the modern Irish 'troubles' broke out, Seamus Heaney included in his volume *Field Work* a poem entitled 'In Memoriam Francis Ledwidge'. In so doing he was invoking an iconic figure, almost the only Irish poet who might be included among the soldier poets who died in the First World War and who made that conflict seem in cultural memory, a poet's war. In his poem Heaney ponders how it can seem an enigma in the late twentieth century, in the midst of a conflict between loyalism and Irish republicanism, that a nationalist Irishman should have been among the British soldiery who perished in the Great War, among whom, we remember, were such renowned war poets as Julian Grenfell, Isaac Rosenberg and Wilfred Owen. Heaney designates Ledwidge 'our dead enigma'[1] and recalls his County Meath origins, the tender Georgian pastoralism of his verses, and quotes from a letter written by Ledwidge shortly before his death in action in France at the Battle of Passchendale, on 31 July 1917. In that letter the poet, serving in the King's uniform in the Royal Inniskilling Fusiliers, had regretted that 'party politics should ever divide our tents' and hoped for a time when a new Ireland would 'arise from her ashes in the ruins of Dublin, like the Phoenix, with one purpose, one aim and one ambition. I tell you this in order that you may know what it is to me to be called a British soldier while my own country has no place amongst the nations but the place of Cinderella.'[2] In so writing, Ledwidge was responding to the events of April and May 1916 when the Easter Rising had been crushed by other soldiers wearing the King's uniform, an outcome that had affected him profoundly. Indeed the figure of the soldier poet that shadows Ledwidge's wartime verses was no victim of the Dardanelles or the Western Front. Rather it is the martyrs for Ireland who had paid the ultimate sacrifice when cut down by the executioners' bullets in Dublin, Thomas McDonagh, Patrick Pearse and Joseph Plunkett, who preoccupy him. It is they who are honoured in his poem 'The Blackbirds', written in July 1916, with its nationalist iconography and tones of lament:

> I heard the Poor Old Woman say:
> 'At break of day the fowler came,
> And took my blackbirds from their songs
> Who loved me well thro' shame and blame.
> …
> And when the first surprise of flight
> Sweet songs excite, from that far dawn
> Shall there come blackbirds loud with love,
> Sweet echoes of the singers gone.
> But in the lonely hush of ever
> Weeping I grieve the silent bills.'
> I heard the Poor Old Woman say
> In Derry of the little hills.[3]

And perhaps Ledwidge's best-known poem is 'Thomas McDonagh' with its plangent, sorrowing cadences:

> He shall not hear the bittern cry
> In the wild sky, where he is lain,
> Nor voices of the sweeter birds
> Above the wailing of the rain.[4]

The actual experience of war is not directly represented in Ledwidge's poetry (he makes graphic reference to it in some of the letters he sent back from the war zone), but the intensifying homesickness it registers may be taken as a symptom of the increasing alienation he felt both as an Irishman in British uniform after 1916 and as a 'unit in the Great War, doing and suffering' while facing the prospect of likely violent death. That homesickness expressed itself in poems like 'In France' where 'Wherever way I turn… / The hills of home are in my mind / And there I wander where I will.'[5] In poem after poem, rural County Meath is evoked in idyllic terms, as a pastoral place of fairy lore and sweet birdsong. One senses that Ledwidge as poet, in so concentrating on the pastoral antithesis to his life as a soldier, was in fact unwittingly aligning his work with other war poets who did admit the conditions of industrial warfare to their work (where Ledwidge does refer to the war itself, it is in rather conventionally poetic terms, without the realism that was to mark some of the most compelling of Great War poetry). For a good deal of the poetry of the Great War did in fact highlight the gulf between the pastoral landscapes close to the front and the horrors of trench life and the desolate, shell-ruined zone of no-man's-land. One thinks of Rosenberg's 'Returning, We hear the Larks', with its 'heights of night ringing with unseen larks, / Music showering on our upturned list'ning faces' of soldiers returning to camp and 'a little safe sleep'.[6] It is as if Ledwidge, sick with longing for his native place, fixed his being on the pastoral mode that fellow poets of the Great War in their poems set in apposition to the realities of trench warfare and the ruined towns amid the poppy fields in Picardy and Flanders.

In Heaney's Ledwidge poem, the pastoral quality of the Meathman's verse is sensitively acknowledged in its invocation of 'the leafy road from Slane / Where you belonged';[7] but it is the enigma of Ledwidge that most engages the Derry poet who is stimulated to his reflections by a war memorial in the northern seaside resort of Portstewart, with its 'loyal fallen names on the embossed plaque',[8] that he remembers first encountering as an uncomprehending child. Not that adulthood has brought much greater understanding, For the poem concludes by reckoning that Ledwidge followed 'a sure confusing drum', and that he was not 'keyed or pitched like these true-blue ones',[9] commemorated in Portstewart, who perhaps knew what they were dying for. It is as if the varying motives that took men to their deaths earlier in the century epitomise for Heaney an island still riven by divided loyalties – party politics still divide the tents. The only certainty in the muffled pain of this memorial is 'all of you consort now underground'.[10]

Heaney's invocation of an 'underground' at the conclusion of this poem mysteriously enters it as a Great War poem in more than its subject matter. It reminds, of course, of Wilfred Owen's great poem 'Strange Meeting', in which mortal enemies encounter one another after death in a 'sullen hall' that is accessed 'down some profound dull tunnel, long since scooped / Through granites which titanic wars had groined'.[11] In that poem the soldier's experience of the trenches, in which life became a matter of beneath ground-level survival is made the basis of a mythic perspective. And the imagery of mining that Owen's lines encapsulate also reminds us that much of the war was fought underground by the sappers who sought to undermine the enemy's front-line defences. Sebastian Faulk's well-known novel of 1993, *Birdsong*, was powerfully alert to this aspect of Great War strategy and the mole-like burrowing 'underground' it involved. He was accurately reflecting the fact that as the historian Eric J. Leed has observed, the Great War was 'in general … a war of engineers' and was, as Paul Fussell has termed it, 'a troglodyte war'.[12] Leed comments: 'the silence, darkness, disorientation, and almost unbelievable tension suffered by the mining solders was an intensification of the experience of trench warfare'.[13] So powerful indeed was the sense of the war as a conflict being fought beneath the surface of the earth that, as Leed argues, the concept of 'underground' achieved a near-mythic explanatory force in the minds of many soldiers, who felt themselves trapped in a terrible cave (in Owen's poem the only escape from the trenches is through death and the ultimate sleep with which that poem concludes).

A couple of prose works by the Irish writer Patrick MacGill (known as 'the navvy poet'), who served with the London Irish and was injured in France, powerfully evoke the subterranean world of the common soldier. *The Red Horizon* (1916) describes, for example, a shell bombardment in the following terms:

> The suspense wore us down; we breathed the suffocating fumes of one explosion and waited, our senses tensely strung for the coming of the next shell. The sang-froid which carried us through many a tight corner with credit utterly deserted us, we were washed-out things; with our noses to the cold earth, like rats in a trap, we waited for the next moment which might land us in eternity. The excitement of a bayonet charge, the mad tussle with death of the blood-stained field, which for some reason is called the field of honour, was denied; we had to wait and lie in the trench, which looked so like a grave, and sink slowly into the depths of depression.[14]

One notes here the suggestion of entrapment and underground death-in-life. In *The Great Push: An Episode of the Great War* (an account of the battle of Loos, also published in 1916), MacGill also captured the periods of awful anxiety involved in such warfare, in which the earth itself is no protection: "The shells were loosened again; there was no escape from their frightful vitality; they crushed, burrowed, exterminated, obstacles were broken down, and men's lives were flicked out like flies off a window-pane. A dug-out flew skywards, and the roof-beams fell in the trench at our feet. We crouched under the bomb-shelter, mute, pale, hesitating.'[15]

There was a more general sense in which the experience of fighting men in the Great War was open to metaphoric representation as an underground world. It was underground in the sense that many on the Home Front did not wish to be told of its true nature. There is accordingly a powerful sense of taboos being broken in the English war poetry of the period, of the suppressed being provocatively exhumed. One thinks of Owen's 'Dulce et Decorum Est' with its graphic images of intolerable suffering, that give the lie to conventional patriotic pieties and of his admonitory preface to his poems, which restricts the poet to the role of one who must issue warning, eschewing poetry. If an Owen felt driven to such aesthetic asceticism, the Irishmen who might have wished to register in literature experience of the Great War's front lines would have laboured under a double disadvantage. For not only were those at home disinclined to have their noses rubbed in the mud and blood of Flanders or elsewhere, but after 1916 and the events that led to partition and the establishment of the Irish Free State, there were obvious ideological and political reasons that made literary treatment of the Great War highly problematic. A poem by the nationalist intellectual and university teacher Thomas Kettle, who had enlisted in the British Army in passionate support of 'gallant little Belgium' and who would lose his life in September 1916 at the Somme, anticipated how one such as he could be disavowed 'in time to come' (that phrase is from Yeats's poem 'Easter 1916, completed in its first form in the same month as Kettle met his death). In 'The Gift of God', Kettle addresses a daughter whom he imagines asking 'in wiser' days why he abandoned her for the dangers of the soldier's calling ('to dice with death'). His answer movingly, if unconvincingly, makes his action seem an anti-imperialist Christian solidarity with the wretched of the earth, as if he knows his sacrifice will be misunderstood:

> So here, while the mad guns curse overhead,
> And tired men sigh, with mud for couch and floor,
> Know that we fools, now with the foolish dead,
> Died not for Flag, nor King, nor Emperor,
> But for a dream, born in a herdsman's shed,
> And for the Secret Scripture of the poor.[16]

The attitude of the poet W. B. Yeats to the Great War was that it should be buried and stay buried as a poetic and artistic subject, especially in the case of non-combatants. In February 1916 he composed a poem which on its first publication was titled 'A Reason for Keeping Silent', and subsequently 'On Being Asked for a War Poem'. In this he wrote:

> I think it better that in times like these
> A poet's mouth be silent, for in truth
> We have no gift to set a statesman right;
> He has had enough of meddling who can please
> A young girl in the indolence of her youth,
> Or an old man upon a winter's night.[17]

It might have been observed when this poem first appeared in 1916 that Yeats had not hitherto felt inhibited about commenting on political matters, as the first edition of his volume *Reponsibilities* strenuously indicated. Published in 1914, that volume had made no bones about his elitist disdain for Irish political mediocrity. And those familiar with the Yeats circle might have been tempted to read in the poem's invocations of an indolent young girl and an old man some hint of the amatory confusions that were in fact assailing Yeats in 1916. For upon the execution of John MacBride following the Easter Rising, he would feel obliged once again to propose marriage to MacBride's estranged widow, his own great love of youthful years, Maud Gonne, and when she one more refused him, he would turn his attention to her daughter, the fitful and often indolent Iseult Gonne. Yeats would have known of Iseult's moody laziness from concerned letters he had been receiving from Maud during the war, which also told him how terrible were the battles unfolding in France. In this context, Yeats in his poem can be seen as repressing this knowledge in preference for the cultivation as poetic subject of amatory feeling within a circle of intimates. Gonne's letters, however, would have alerted him to the personal costs of the war. For she had reported the deaths-in-action of a nephew and of her first lover's son, mourned the death of Hugh Lane, Lady Gregory's nephew, in the sinking of the Lusitania and worried for Lady Gregory, when her son Robert chose to enlist in the British forces. And she wrote passionately of the suffering of the French army, whose wounded she and Iseult helped to nurse:

I am nursing the wounded from 6 in the morning till 8 at night & trying in my material work to drown the sorrow & disappointment of it all – & my heart is growing up in wild hatred of the war machine which is grinding the life out of these great natures & reducing their population to helpless slavery & ruin, among all the wounded I have nursed only one man who spoke with real enthusiasm of returning to the front.[18]

Gonne's experience as a nurse brought her, as she wrote, 'in contact with awful suffering & heroic courage & a great deal of the waste & squalor of war'.[19] One death amid all that waste Yeats could not suppress or disregard for it involved his own immediate circle in the most brutal way. On 23 January 1918, Major Robert Gregory was killed on the Italian Front when, returning from a mission, his plane was brought down by 'friendly fire' in a dreadful accident. So Yeats's patron, close friend and collaborator lost her only son, father of her three grandchildren, the man upon whom her hopes for the future of a family, house and estate at Coole, County Galway rested. It was a most terrible blow that Yeats as poet could not ignore. Silence was not an option. Yeats wrote four poems in Gregory's memory all of which involved complex negotiations of a central unpalatable fact about the Major: he was an unabashed imperialist who had enlisted as Roy Foster has it 'with alacrity early in the war'.[20] The best-known of the four poems Yeats composed in his memory, 'An Irish Airman Foresees His Death', exhibits the poet engaged in the avoidance, if not quite suppression, of this uncomfortable facet of Gregory's character, which was at odds with his mother's and Yeats's Irish Nationalism.

Yeats's ploy in the poem is to disregard Gregory's known patriotism and to attribute his participation in the conflict to parochial loyalties and affections ('My country is Kiltartan Cross / My countrymen Kiltartan's poor') and to a 'A lonely impulse of delight' which 'drove' him to a 'tumult in the clouds'.[21] In other words, the Irish airman risked the death of which he had prescience, in loyalty to the home ground and in an act of radical self-definition. And in so doing, it was as if he had not died in the war at all, but in some private, chivalric wager of his own, bred of regard for a native place and of high adventure. Yet in writing in this way, as Foster has commented, Yeats had composed the 'war poem' which he had earlier claimed he would not provide.

'An Irish Airman Foresees His Death' is a 'war poem' in two special senses, beyond the fact that it immediately addresses the death of a combatant. Firstly, in imagining Gregory at a great height 'Somewhere among the clouds above',[22] Yeats was, whether he knew it or not, giving expression in his war poem to a general mode of consciousness that had emerged in the terrible conditions of trench warfare. To quote Leed once more:

The aerial perspective – assumed to belong to the flyer – was one of the most significant myths of the war. The necessity for this myth lay precisely in those constrictions that so fragmented the perceptions and purpose of the frontsoldier. The myth of the flyer, of adventure in the air as the last home of chivalric endeavor, is clearly a compensatory notion. It serves to keep open the realm of purpose and meaning with which many entered the war.[23]

So Yeats's airman was able to assess and welcome his own version of fate far above the random slaughter of earth-bound engagements. And in imaging this zone of near metaphysical elevation, Yeats was occupying as poet the same almost mythic dimension as is envisaged in what are indisputably war poems by an Irish survivor of the Great War, Thomas MacGreevy. In his 'Nocturne', dedicated to a soldier who 'died of wounds', MacGreevy sets earth and starry universe in absolute apposition: 'I labour in a barren place /Alone, self-conscious, frightened, blundering; / Far away stars wheeling in space'.[24] In 'De Civitate Hominum', an 'airman' 'high over' the battlefield is shot down, 'a stroke of orange in the morning's dress' to the awestruck horror of an observer: 'My sergeant says, very low, "Holy God! / 'Tis a fearful death".'[25]

Secondly, the final lines of Yeats's poem, in their carefully managed rhythmic equilibrium, suggest, as an historian of Irish aviation observed to me, the actual experience of piloted flight in a small plane, its controlled exhilaration:

> I balanced all, brought all to mind,
> The years to come seemed waste of breath,
> A waste of breath the years behind
> In balance with this life, this death.[26]

The poem floats on its fixed, phrasal wings in one of the very few moments in Yeats's poetic oeuvre when the technology of modernity impacts on the poet's imagination.

The Great War was, of course, a conflict marked by the deployment of innovative technology in an imbroglio that saw the triumph of the machine at the expense of the human. This was something the dramatist Sean O'Casey fully understood as is evidenced not only by his Great War play *The Silver Tassie* (1928) but by his drama of the 1916 Rising, *The Plough and the Stars* (1926). The latter had made significant reference in its dialogue to the Great War context in which the Easter Rising took place, but as theatrical spectacle one of its most striking effects is to dramatise how the Irish Volunteers and Citizen Army with their showy uniforms and flags are overcome and decimated by the overwhelming force of modern munitions. And there is, too, an awareness of how in the twentieth century war had become 'total', with civilians being caught up and even targeted in generalised assaults on towns and cities. The final image of British Tommies brewing tea and singing 'Keep the Home Fires Burning' (a popular song at Great War fronts) in a Dublin tenement amid the flames of destruction is a powerful symbol of the domestic invaded by the overwhelming violence of modern warfare.

The insight shown by O'Casey into Great War realities in *The Plough and the Stars*, a play Yeats admired, makes Yeats's notorious decision to reject *The Silver Tassie* when the dramatist sought to have it produced on the Abbey Theatre's stage, all the more troubling. And in light of *The Plough and the Star*'s sense of how the Easter Rising like the Great War saw romantic chivalry pitted against ruthless dehumanising force, Yeats's assertion, in a letter to the dramatist, that O'Casey was 'not interested in the great war' because he had 'never stood on its battlefields or walked its hospitals'[27] seems uncharacteristically obtuse.

The Silver Tassie takes Dublin football hero Harry Heegan from sporting success by way of the collective slaughter of the Western Front, to injury and a convalescence that does nothing for his permanent disablement. The horror of industrial warfare is powerfully represented in its experimental, expressionist second act. In central position on stage is howitzer gun, which points directly at the audience as if to threaten them with the fate that awaits the cannon fodder in the cast. As Nuala Johnson has remarked of this *coup de théâtre*, 'this piece of military hardware is one of the most enduring symbols of the machinery of the war',[28] and in the play it demands that audiences become fully aware of the terrible attrition wrought by mechanized carnage and of the suffering it left in its wake, knowledge, the play insists, that must not be suppressed or kept 'underground'.

O'Casey's *The Silver Tassie* had found some of its inspiration in a poem by Wilfred Owen entitled 'Disabled' (and echoes Robert Burns's tender lyric 'My Bonnie Mary'). The play's final images of a former athlete in a wheelchair as the dance of heterosexuality is joined without him clearly derives from Owen's lines (also about a cruelly wounded former football star and soldier): 'To-night he noticed how the women's eyes / Passed from him to the strong men that were whole'.[29] *The Silver Tassie* caught, indeed, some of the poem's bitterness about the Home Front as a world of women who would offer pity to the war's surviving sacrificial victims, but little more, as the vital possibilities of peace beckoned. Perhaps Yeats in damning O'Casey's play in 1928 detected something in it of the slightly maudlin atmospherics of its source. Certainly in the letter in which he gave his views on the play, he seemed to regret that O'Casey had not struck the appropriate tragic note, in a play governed by 'opinions' worthy only of a newspaper. Be that as it may, by 1936 when his own view of the necessity for tragedy in art had hardened into the near-doctrine encompassed in his phrase 'tragic joy', it would be Owen himself who would bear the brunt of Yeats's denigration. In what seemed to many an act of wilful suppression, Yeats excluded Owen from the *Oxford Book of Modern Verse*, edited by him and published that year. In the Introduction to this volume, he justified his decision by stating that 'passive suffering' was not a proper theme for poetry, and he extolled the masculinity of John Synge's verse, as if in exemplary contrast. In a letter he was unabashedly dismissive of Owen: 'When I excluded Wilfred Owen, whom I consider unworthy of the poet's corner of a country newspaper, I did not know I was excluding a revered sandwich-board man of the revolution ... He is all blood, dirt and sucked sugar-stick ... There is every excuse for him, but none for those who like him.'[30]

By that act of exclusion, Yeats appeared to compound the impression given in 1928 that somehow the Great War should be off-limits as an artistic subject for most writers, and especially for the Irish writer (though

The Silver Tassie did get an Abbey production in 1935). For the Oxford book not only dispatched Owen to oblivion and excluded other English war poets but included swathes of verse by Irish poets who did not advert to the Great War at all. It was as if that catastrophe had only tangentially registered in the aesthetic sphere, while it had completely passed the Irish poetic imagination by (apart from Yeats's own poem "An Irish Airman' and a cursory reference to 'bombs and mud and gas' in a poem by Louis MacNeice). In this way, Yeats could be seen as giving a kind of imprimatur to what the historian Keith Jeffery has identified as the 'amnesiac tendency of southern Ireland to the war'.[31] And indeed there has been a sense in those works by Irish writers who have directly broached the subject of the war in their works of the breaking of the Yeatsian interdiction and of a cognate infringement of cultural and social conventions involved in the unearthing of Great War experience. In Jennifer Johnston's novel of 1974, *How Many Miles to Babylon*, for example, a sense of recovering buried experience makes the Great War front a site of complex sexual and class alliances that cement mysterious male solidarities. Frank McGuinness's play *Observe the Sons of Ulster Marching Towards the Somme* (1985) takes up as it were, where O'Casey left off in *The Silver Tassie* in exploring the homoerotic implications of military comradeship, which had been explicit in O'Casey's poetic source and hinted at at moments in his play. Sebastian Barry's novel *A Long Long Way* (2005) combines a gruesome realism of blood and mud with a sensuous lyricism as if to endorse and extend Wilfred Owen's aesthetic that Yeats had so excoriated, even as it revives the subject of conflicting loyalties of the kind Ledwidge had suffered in relation to the events of 1916 in Dublin. And the poet Michael Longley, who has made the Great War and the image of the 'war poet' a central poetic preoccupation, in his poem 'In Memoriam' (composed for a father who survived Great War service) introduced this theme in tones that suggested he was deliberately resurrecting familial memories that must be given their full due if his poetry is to avoid mere poeticism:

> My father, let no similes eclipse
> Where crosses like some forest simplified
> Sink into my mind, the slow sands
> Of your history delay till through your eyes
> I read you like a book.[32]

The irony of all this vis-à-vis Yeats, it must be said, was that despite his words and actions, his own poetry was certainly affected by the Great War. Notably, after 1918 his work takes on a marked internationalist aspect. Where formerly Yeats's verse had its eye fixed on the personal life of the poet, on Ireland and on eternity, after the Great War it is the current condition of the world that begins to alarm him. In his protracted spiritualist experiments with his wife George that began in the autumn of 1917, history and the meaning of the historical moment in the scheme of things become a dominant concern of that strange activity. So much so that when Yeats reacted in verse to Black-and-Tan atrocities in Lady Gregory's district (the events took place in 1920), he did so in a poem that on its first publication bore the title 'Thoughts Upon The Present State of the World'. And that poem, with its historical perspectives on how a long Victorian and Edwardian peace had given way to 'dragon-ridden' days, can be read as a Yeatsian commentary on the break-up of empire that the Great War set in motion. Epochal historical changes in this poem come home to roost in the local world with a particular viciousness, revealing 'the weasel's twist, the weasel's tooth'.

Furthermore, a poem that was to acquire some of its imagery from George's automatic writing seems to have had its inception in the poet's alarm in the summer of 1918 at events in distant Russia. For Jon Stallworthy has shown how an early draft of Yeats's famous poem of world historical crisis and apocalypse, 'The Second Coming' (begun in the late summer of 1918), contains the phrase 'the Germans are ( ) now to Russia come', and he argues that the poem went through a process of composition whereby what were probably allusions to revolutionary events in Russia and to German territorial acquisitions became buried in a panoramic vision of violent transformation. Stallworthy can assert accordingly that this poem stems 'from a mood of depression brought on by the First World War'.[33]

The internationalism of mind that found expression in Yeats's great post-war poetry was of course something he shared with his fellow-writer James Joyce, who had spent some of the war years at work on his experimental, encyclopedic novel *Ulysses* (published in 1922). Set in Dublin in 1904, it could of course make no direct reference to the events of 1914–18 that had compelled Joyce to take refuge in neutral Switzerland. Arguably, however, in its various references to battles ancient and modern and in its profound sense of history as a nightmare from which it is necessary to awake, it too can be read as a work upon which the Great War had significant literary impact. The fact, therefore, that its ultimate response to the spectacle of human history, which so appalled even as it excited Yeats in 'The Second Coming', can perhaps be discerned in Leopold Bloom's pacifism, makes that text, finally, a salutary point at which to conclude this survey: 'But it's no use, says he. Force, hatred, history, all that. That's not a life for men and women, insult and hatred.'[34]

NOTES

1   S. Heaney, *Field Work* (Faber and Faber, 1979), p. 60.
2   This letter is quoted in H. Dunn, *Francis, Ledwidge and the Literature of His Time* (Ireland [*sic*]; Booklink, 2006), p. 254. I am indebted to this work and to A. Curtayne's *Francis Ledwidge: A Life of the Poet* (London: Martin Brian & O'Keefe, 1972).
3   Quotations from Ledwidge's poetry are taken from *The Complete Poems of Francis Ledwidge* (New York: Bretano's, 1919), pp. 209–10.
4   *Ibid.*, p. 206.
5   *Ibid.*, p. 265.
6   I. M. Parsons (ed.), *Men Who March Away: Poems of the First World War* (London: Chatto and Windus, 1965), p. 53.
7   Heaney, *Field Work*, p. 59.
8   *Ibid.*
9   *Ibid.*, p. 60.
10 *Ibid.*
11 Parsons (ed.), *Men Who March Away*, p. 169.
12 E. J. Leed, *No Man's Land: Combat and Identity in World War I* (Cambridge University Press, 1979), p. 138; Paul Fussell, *The Great War and Modern Memory* (Oxford University Press), pp. 36–74.
13 Leed, *No Man's Land*, p. 138.
14 P. MacGill, *The Red Horizon* (Dingle: Brandon, 1984) p. 196.
15 P. MacGill, *The Great Push* (Edinburgh: Birlinn, 2000), p. 13.
16 Gerald Dawe, *Earth Voices Whispering: An Anthology of Irish War Poetry, 1914–1945* (Belfast: Blackstaff Press, 2008), p. 55.
17 D. Albright (ed.), *W. B. Yeats: The Poems* (London: Everyman's Library, 1992), p. 205.
18 A. MacBride White and A. N. Jeffares (eds.), *The Gonne–Yeats Letters, 1893–1938* (London: Hutchinson), p. 151.
19 *Ibid.*, p. 158.
20 R. Foster, *W. B. Yeats: A Life*, Vol. II: *The Arch-Poet 1915–1939* (Oxford University Press, 2003), p. 118.
21 Albright (ed.), *W. B. Yeats: The Poems*, p. 184.
22 *Ibid.*
23 Leed, *No Man's Land*, p. 134.
24 T. Dillon Redshaw (ed.), *Collected Poems of Thomas MacGreevy* (Dublin: New Writers' Press, 1971), p. 15. MacGreevy, born Tarbert, County Kerry, was twice wounded in the war. He became Director of the National Gallery of Ireland in 1950.
25 *Ibid.*, p. 17.
26 Albright (ed.), *W. B. Yeats: The Poems*, pp. 184–5.

27 Allan Wade (ed.), *The Letters of W. B. Yeats* (London: Rupert Hart-Davis, 1954), p. 741.

28 Cited N. C. Johnson, *Ireland, The Great War and the Geography of Remembrance* (Cambridge University Press, 2003), p. 133.

29 Parsons, *Men Who March Away*, p. 143.

30 Wade (ed.), *The Letters of W. B. Yeats*, p. 874. Saros Cowasjee first linked O'Casey's play with Owen when he suggested the latter's poem 'Disabled' as a source for *The Silver Tassie*. See S. Cowasjee, *Sean O'Casey: The Man Behind the Plays* (Edinburgh and London: Oliver and Boyd, 1965), pp. 114–15.

31 Keith Jeffery, *Ireland and the Great War* (Cambridge University Press, 2000), p. 57.

32 M. Longley, *Collected Poems* (London: Cape Poetry, 2006), p. 30.

33 Jon Stallworthy, *Between the Lines: Yeats's Poetry in the Making* (Oxford: Clarendon Press, 1963), p. 24.

34 J. Joyce, *Ulysses* (World's Classics, Oxford University Press, 1993), p. 319. James Fairhill, in his *James Joyce and the Question of History* (Cambridge University Press, 1993), considers *Ulysses* as a Great War text.

CHAPTER 7

Ireland, Modernism and the 1930s

The *annus mirabilis* of literary Modernism was 1922, when *Ulysses* and *The Waste Land* were first published in two metropolitan centres, Paris and London. In Ireland, the year 1922 saw the founding of the Free State, a coincidence of chronology that ought to have stimulated more reflection than it has. For that moment when a national revolution achieved even a partial success represented an experiment in social and cultural expression just as the publication of those two works represented experiment in the artistic sphere. Each event, the founding of a post-imperial state, the publication of a novel which set in question the adequacy of realist fiction to the present moment and the issuing of the poem which sought to exploit a 'mythical method' the better to comprehend the 'immense panorama of futility and anarchy' of 'contemporary history' were symptomatic occasions, signs of the times, manifestions of, and reactions to, the general crisis of post-war Europe.

Ulysses and *The Waste Land* are of course customarily entered in the roll-call of Modernist masterpieces even by those who suspect that Modernism is so capacious a term, so 'completely lacking in positive content', that it is 'the emptiest of all cultural categories'.[1] The Irish revolution and the foundation of the Free State have not, by contrast, been considered in the context of the international Modernism of the period, however accommodatingly conceived. And this despite the fact that the Irish society which in 1922 embarked on its own national experiment was the same society which gave to the world the Oscar Wilde whose *fin de siècle* art and criticism were a precursor of Modernist aesthetics, two major Modernist writers in Yeats and Joyce and would in Beckett produce a writer whose preoccupations would be significantly defined by Modernist characteristics while anticipating post-modern effects.

The reasons are not far to seek. Modernism, in as much as it can as a term provide descriptive insights on widely variegated phenomena, is radically internationalist in scope and vision, cosmopolitan in its dramatis personae. Its characterising conditions are literary and artistic exile, *déraciné,* cosmopolitan and metropolitan rather than national foci, a highly self-conscious eclecticism and near-universality of cultural forms. A nationalist revolution values none of these things and the state it inaugurates may be reckoned to contribute to a movement like Modernism only through provoking that exile which so evidently marks the sociology of the twentieth-century European avant-garde.

Artistic and cultural expression in the Irish Free State in the 1920s, and especially in the 1930s, would certainly give the cultural historian apparently sufficient grounds for concluding that Modernism and post-imperial nationalism (another capacious and acccommodating term) are antithetical in their particular manifestations. The predominant literary form of the period was the short story which for the first time in Ireland employed a sustained realism to assess the condition of the country in its new-found and less than inspiring freedom. Its principal practitioners were antagonistic to literary experimentalism. Both Frank O'Connor and Seán O'Faoláin entered objections, for example, to Joyce's *Work in Progress.* In painting, a fascination with landscape, which in the early work of an original painter like Paul Henry had involved avant-garde interest in Post-Impressionism, by the 1930s had hardened into convention and stereotype which were readily exploited by less able painters. Indeed, Henry recalled of the 1920s in Dublin that there was a deep-rooted 'ignorance and prejudice ... against any form of art which savoured, even remotely, of modernism'.[2] By 1937 John Dowling, in *Ireland To-day,* could hail Sean Keating, who was aggressively opposed to Modernism in painting, as the chief glory of the Irish school. Sculpture was entirely academic and architecture almost unaffected by the experimentalism of the Bauhaus (though a few houses in Dublin's suburbs built in the 1930s suggest that Modernist ideas were not completely unknown). Furthermore in 1920s and 1930s Ireland, symphonic music was scarcely established and no real audience existed for it. Aloys Fleischmann, the country's leading musicologist, in 1936 declared *'this* is the land without music, a land that is literally music starved ... The intelligentsia does not give music a thought' (emphasis in original).[3] In 1937 Eamonn Ó Gallchobhair concurred. He declared 'musically speaking Dublin is a city of barbarians'.[4] So while composers like Fleischmann himself were aware of developments in twentieth-century European art music and sought to make them known in Ireland, there were few opportunities, beyond those afforded by occasional broadcasts and gramophone records, for interested individuals to hear such large-scale works as Stravinsky's *The Rite of Spring,* which had announced itself as the harbinger of Modernist iconoclasm in music as early as 1913. Nor was there much chance that Irish audiences could get to see the great Modernist experiments in cinema, where such radical techniques as montage had defined for Modernism as a whole its quintessential structural method (though the Irish-made *Guests of the Nation* does show the influence of Eisenstein).[5] Liam Ó Laoghaire, that notable and in the 1930s almost unique Irish cinéaste, wrote in 1932 that 'the quality of creative film work shown in Ireland, particularly in recent years, has been as drops in an ocean of commercialised vulgarity'.[6] In 1937 he reported that only the 'cheapest and most inferior products of modern film production' were screened in Dublin.[7]

A very telling indicator of the Irish cultural condition in the 1930s is the achievement and reception of the Gate Theatre company in the Dublin of the period. Founded by Micheál Mac Liammóir and Hilton Edwards in 1928 to explore the international repertoire that the Abbey felt unable on account of its brief to stage, the Gate endured constant disapproval. Writing in 1932 in *Motley*, the theatre's journal which ran for a couple of years during what Mac Liammóir called 'these early drab days of the present drab decade',[8] a contributor commented of the Gate's repertoire:

Since this theatre was founded we have presented comparatively few realistic plays, and have already avoided realism in production. We consider that realism has been badly overdone, and if the drama has a future that that future will not be found to lie in a realistic direction.[9]

Perhaps this unfashionable espousal of non-realistic modes, when the Abbey was effectively patenting Peasant Quality in its realist plays as the indigenous dramaturgy, accounted for the state of affairs the journal had reported on earlier in the same year:

From the very first moment of its inception in this city, the Gate Theatre has suffered more carping criticism from friend and foe than any other Little Theatre in these Islands. Perhaps it is the modern progressive element in us.[10]

Not that even the Gate was in any very real sense dedicated to Modernist experimentalism. In its journal the idea of an avant-garde is certainly bruited, and the word 'modern' is employed quite frequently in positive contexts. There is no evidence, however, that the critics and writers ready to associate with the Gate venture were the dedicated vanguard of a movement which took seriously the radical engagement with the disorientating aesthetics that Modernism, through movements like vorticism, cubism, futurism, surrealism, had sponsored. Certainly, as Richard Pine has argued, the influences which had complicated Mac Liammóir's *fin de siècle* aestheticism as a stage designer had included an 'affinity with Gordon Craig'[11] and a fascination with the colour effects of Leon Bakst whose work with the Russian Ballet, where he saw the dancing of Nijinsky, he so admired, and where he heard the music of Stravinsky and Ravel under the inspired management of Diaghilev. Yet reading through the files of *Motley* and considering the repertoire of the early seasons when the theatre was striving to distinguish itself from its competitor in Abbey Street, one is struck by the odd mixture of classics, experiments, international successes and pot-boilers that graced the boards and the lack of a ruling engagement with ideas. What this suggests is a theatre whose ethos was style for style's sake rather than a theatre that shared the Modernist movement's intense desire to be present at the birth of the 'Savage God'. Nor indeed does one gain a sense that the theatre was directed by individuals truly aware of Modernism's crusading aspirations. For all its brilliance, its bravura cosmopolitanism, one detects in the Gate Theatre of the 1930s the subversive energies of both the Decadence and the modern becoming somehow unthreatening in the provincial Irish air.

In fact what now strikes the reader of such literary periodicals as there were in the period is an absence of that urge to make it new which so informed the manifestos, treatises and prophesies which in Europe had stimulated Modernist experiment. A curious atmosphere, for example, pervades the pages of *The Dublin Magazine* (the only well-established literary periodical in the period) in the 1930s. Work by experimental poets such as Lyle Donaghy appears in its pages; Samuel Beckett's early remarkable poem 'Alba' was published there in October 1931. But the overall impression is not of an editorial engagement with the way modern letters since the era of the French symbolists had sought to represent strikingly original modes of human consciousness in new poetic forms, but of literary and artistic connoisseurship. The shock of the new is absorbed in the general atmosphere of cultivation and informed, self-consciously urbane taste.

A tendency to absorb and discharge the energies of the most original Modernist texts and techniques may in the Irish context be the most persuasive evidence that Ireland and Modernism were an antithetical congeries of feeling and sensibility in the 1930s. An intriguing case in point is a work by Thomas MacGreevy. A poet who in the 1930s composed a small body of rhythmically exquisite verse indebted to the experimentalism of Pound and Eliot (which stimulated an admiring celebratory essay from the young Samuel Beckett and the respect of Wallace Stevens), MacGreevy's volume of 1931, *T. S. Eliot: A Study*, is a very odd performance indeed.

MacGreevy's essay is an early attempt (eight years in advance of Cleanth Brooks's classic, more subtle, Christian account in *Modern Poetry and the Tradition*) to read *The Waste Land* in positively Catholic terms. 'The subject' MacGreevy announces 'that overtook him was nothing less than death and resurrection. What he made of it is *The Waste Land,* a poem which, in its own more nervous way, has influenced us all almost as much as Mr Joyce's *Ulysses*.'[12] It is not, however, the poem's nervousness that MacGreevy emphasises in his literal-minded account but the worthy Christian conclusions the poem can be read as attaining. En route to this happy terminus, MacGreevy opines of the famous prophetic passage in 'The Burial of the Dead': 'For my own purposes I take the broken images to be the weakened churches of to-day, the dead tree to be dead faith, and the cricket to represent the inadequacy of mere natural companionship (or perhaps sermonless, message-less natural science).'[13] But what is even more surprising is the critic's determination to read Eliot as formally nothing very new – certainly nothing to get excited about. It is as if the orthodox believer in him, who as poet learned from Eliot how modern free verse can be written, must make his precursor a questing man of the spirit and deny to him any really disturbing originality of form, inappropriate to one who is to be recruited by the critic to the secure, unshakeable traditions of Catholic faith and art. Apropos of Eliot's 'associative way of writing', MacGreevy is at pains to insist 'the method is not really very new'. He continued:

In France it is at least as old as Arthur Rimbaud. Mr Pound got it in France, and it is possible that it is amongst the things for which Mr Eliot acknowledges his indebtedness to Mr Pound in the introduction he wrote to his selected poems. Mr Joyce uses it also. It forms an inherent element in the 'interior monologue' for which he acknowledges his indebtedness to the French novelist, M. Édouard Dujardin. But it is not, in reality, very important … For what it sets out to be, it seems to me, therefore, that *The Waste Land* is practically beyond mere literary criticism, and to criticise the religious and moral attitude expressed in it would be to criticise the strictest Christianity.[14]

So there is, according to MacGreevy, nothing new under the literary sun and Eliot's poem simply employs an existing method to produce 'this Old, almost Jacobean, if not Elizabethan, English (and above all, London) shorthand masterpiece',[15] in which the devout reader may find nothing at variance with the 'strictest Christianity'. To read MacGreevy's *T. S. Eliot* is to be reminded of how perspicacious was Wallace Stevens when he wrote to MacGreevy, 'You were … a young man eager to be at the heart of his time' but that he had also been affected by '"the nostalgie du divin" (which is obviously endemic in Dublin)'.[16] In that endemic Dublin state of feeling, the dangerous implications for the Christian world-view of the major Modernist texts can be rendered anodyne in an oddly Olympian conception of tradition which may in fact be the symptom of a certain self-protective provincialism of mind before the arresting challenge of true and threatening originality. It was possibly the unruffled conservatism of Irish intellectual and cultural life in the 1930s, rather than more obvious indignities such as the Censorship of Publications Act of 1929 (which had begun to work its absurd will in the country in the banning of books by Irish and international authors alike) and regular episcopal fulmin-ations against the cinema and the dangers of jazz, which gave their special tone to the two indisputably Modernist manifestos issued by Irish artists in that decade. These were Mainie Jellett's 'Modern Art and the Dual Ideal of Form Through The Ages', published in *Motley* in 1931 and Samuel Beckett's 'Recent Irish Poetry', published in *The Bookman* in 1934. Jellett, the disciple of and fellow-worker with Albert Gleizes, who had begun to show her cubist works in Dublin in the 1920s and who would achieve only limited recognition in the 1930s, writes in 1932 with the painstaking caution of one who expects to be misunderstood:

A picture or work of art evolved with the mobile non-materialistic ideal of form is, first and foremost, a complete formal organism in itself; and secondly, if the forms are derived from nature, descriptive. If the work of art is a painting, it is considered two dimensionally as a flat surface to be filled and made alive by forms born of its own shape and obeying the natural laws of the surface and the shape of the surface they are filling. If the work of art is sculpture, then the third dimension is recognised, it being the material property of the sculptor's material. His ideal would be, first and foremost to make his block of stone or marble live as an harmonious mass of form and secondly to introduce description.[17]

She continues, somewhat wearied in tone, as if having to explain what should be well known by 1931, even in Dublin:

In Western art since the Renaissance, the tendency has been more and more towards realism and materialism, but with the opening of the twentieth century came the first sign of reaction. The reaction started with Cézanne in France, and the Italian Futurist group, and has continued with the Cubist movement and Expressionist movement ... When a work of art which is striving towards a dif-ferent ideal of formal expression than that which is commonly accepted at the moment, is being judged, it should be approached with the same ideal of form as that with which it is conceived.[18]

By contrast the young Samuel Beckett, knowing that the gulf between subject and object, so necessary to all forms of realism, has broken down in modern epistemologies, inveighs against those mired in artistic anachronism with the intemperance of the prophet who knows he will be without honour in his own country. Addressing a 'rupture in the lines of communication' he advises, in what J. C. C. Mays has precisely identified as 'an exacerbated analysis':[19]

The artist who is aware of this [rupture] may state the space that intervenes between him and the world of objects; he may state it as no-man's-land, Hellespont or vacuum, according as he happens to be feeling resentful, nostalgic, or merely depressed. A picture by Mr Jack Yeats, Mr Eliot's 'Waste Land', are notable statements of this kind. Or he may celebrate the cold comforts of apperception. He may even record his findings, if he is a man of great personal courage. Those who are not aware of the rupture, or in whom the velleity of becoming so was suppressed as a nuisance at its inception, will continue to purvey those articles, which in Ireland at least, had ceased to be valid even before the literary advisers to J. M. Synge found themselves prematurely obliged to look elsewhere for a creative hack. These are the antiquarians, delivering with the altitudinous complacency of the Victorian Gael the Ossianic goods.[20]

Modernism requires definition; we must identify its salient features the more convincingly to assess the justice of our view that 1930s Ireland was largely bereft of its artifacts and the prevailing culture apparently unmoved by its concerns. Eugene Lunn lists four primary characteristics of Modernist art forms: (1) aesthetic self-consciousness or self-reflexiveness; (2) simultaneity, juxaposition or 'montage'; (3) paradox, ambiguity and uncertainty; (4) dehumanisation.[21] Michael Bell also suggests that Modernism as well as manifesting 'aesthetic self-consiousness' involves issues pertaining to 'the transcendence of realism' (a variant of Lunn's second and third set of terms); 'the presentation of identity' (related to Lunn's fourth definition) and 'the treatment of time'.[22] Simply to list these, reflecting as one does how they bear on works as diverse as *Ulysses*, *The Tower*, *The Cantos*, *À la recherche du temps perdu*, *To the Lighthouse*, without even considering developments in music, painting and film, is initially to be confirmed in the judgement arrived at above that Ireland in the 1930s was not significantly attentive to Modernism. Yet in the 1930s Yeats was still at work, Joyce was to complete *Work in Progress* as *Finnegans Wake* and Samuel Beckett was at the start of his career, as if to rebuke any too summary assumption that the matter is simple and can without further thought be put down to the invincible provincialism of Irish cultural reality. For to list these several characteristics of works which find themselves enumerated under the general rubric of Modernism is to realise how the Literary Revival in Ireland in its symbiosis with Irish

Nationalism (which was in part responsible for the foundation of the Irish Free State in which Modernism apparently foundered) shared many of the attributes more generally associated with the presumably internationalist artistic movement.

It is commonplace to account for both the Irish Literary Revival and Irish Nationalism, when they are set in other than a local context, as late versions of European Romanticism. The obsession with the past, the veneration of the primitive and the rural, the cults of the hero and of blood sacrifice, give both a genuinely Romantic inflection.[23] What is less frequently addressed is the degree to which Nationalism and the Literary Revival, itself so imbricated with that Nationalism, allow parallels to be drawn with Modernism. This is not, I hasten to add, to state that the Revival in its Irish Nationalist context is a version of Modernism, but rather to observe that the relationship between that movement and the Modernist movement is complex, since both share the figure of W. B. Yeats, and in an even more complex way, that of James Joyce.

In nationalism the nineteenth century's sense of time is challenged. No longer a secular, sequential process in which progress unfolds, time becomes an element in which the sacred national saga of ancient glory and recurrent defeat can be played out in iterative and, it is hoped, climactic fashion. The past intrudes on the present to offer typologies and prophetic instances. Vast stretches of mere chronological time can be elided. Past and present instances are significantly juxtaposed like images in some symbolist text. Historical time and mythological timelessness are woven together in a seamless garment of national imagining. Time is not only the individual's possession but the shared reality of the collective. Literary production conducted in the context of nationalist feeling accordingly revives and translates texts from the dim past not for antiquarian reasons but to allow them to exist again in the timeless spirituality of the nation's continuous being. This, as we saw earlier in this volume, involved a kind of occult communing with the dead, in which literature ceased to be a matter of personal expression, but a matter of collective imagining, embodied in translated, reconstructed texts. The ubiquitous ambition of writers in the period to provide the nation with a sacred, magical book of the people (which would exist in its own ideal time) involved revisions and reworkings, fabrications in, for example, Yeats's volumes *The Wind Among the Reeds* or *The Secret Rose*. But such ambition was simultaneously an idealisation of the movement's elevation of literature's national provenance over its personal significance. Such works as made things, which sought to function as powerful illusions that the dead past had indeed been resurrected in textual form, inevitably drew attention to the fact that a literary artifact is not simply to be reckoned an apparent reflection of a contemporary or historical social world in the manner of a realist literary work. Rather, they advertised how writing obeys its own internal laws of narrative structure, employing as it does juxtaposition, temporal and contextual elisions, reiterated motifs and conventional descriptions of locale and *personae*. As such, it broke the canons of classical realism as well as undermining the Romantic notion that a text is an expressive phenomenon rooted in the unitary, organic self of an originating creator. That the Revival depended for its sources as a revived national literature on the ancient Celtic sagas, on folk tale and on the self-conscious interlacing narratives of the storyteller's oral art, as well as on the revelatory capacities of myth, assuredly meant that the defining characteristics of its key texts would have little in common with the prevailing literary norms of Victorian literature where the realist novel, the discursive essay and the subjective lyric met the expectations of a bourgeois audience.

Through what initially seems an historic accident therefore, the Revival's distinguishing literary forms in its nationalist context were those which in several respects anticipated and paralleled what commentators have isolated as the nexus of features which allow the term Modernism such critical valency as it possesses. Nationalist consciousness cut across conventional awareness of time, and Revival texts in effect were entered in a temporal zone akin to that which classical Modernist texts like Pound's *Cathay* and Eliot's *The Waste Land* would so compellingly occupy. They revealed themselves as literary constructions (even sometimes admitting their fragmentary nature) which must obey their own laws of narration, presentation and a self-reflexive trajectory. Their sources in various modes of discourse and textuality were made plain to the reader. As works which aspired to the condition of myth, they represented meaning as ambiguous and uncertain, only available in the irrational structures of primitive imagining and in the depths of communal consciousness. They denied to the literary artifact the authority of an originating creative mind, situating it in the dimension of the collective, thereby setting in question the significance of individual identity and the coherence of the self. Realism was rarely admitted as a governing possiblity.

Sociolgists of Modernism tend to adopt the internationalism of the phenomenon they investigate. Notable among them is Perry Anderson, who set the agenda for some important theorising. For Anderson, Modernism emerges in the context of a crisis in European capitalist society. What he calls 'a *conjectural* explanation' (emphasis mine) has Modernism as 'a cultural force-field "triangulated" by three decisive coordinates'.[24] These are, in summary, formalised academicism in the arts complicit with the *ancien régime*, modern technologies of communication and the expect-ation of revolution. In a pan-European context, Modernism emerges as a non-national, internationalist art movement exhibiting the characteris-tics we have noted above. What is not explained in such accounts is why such circumstances result in such aesthetic effects. Though by associating Modernism with the city, in which new technologies in communications and visual representation of experience were taking place in cinema and advertising, such explanations suggest that high art was readily adapting to the novel means of communication rapidly becoming available in the capitals of the continent as a whole.

What such a thesis ignores is what W. J. Mc Cormack has identified as the 'issue of national, regional or local provenance' in Modernism.[25] Alex Callinicos, in a sympathetic critique of Anderson, does indicate how such matters of 'local provenance' can be of import when we consider why Modernism as an international event of the period 1890 to 1930 is not uniformly thick on the ground in the various parts of Europe. For Callinicos, England made a very limited contribution to the movement because 'Britain by the late nineteenth century did not offer the sharp contrast between old and new provided by the comparatively sudden onset of industrial capitalism in genuinely *ancien régime* orders such as Prussia, Russia, and Austria-Hungary.'[26]

A task exists then to establish the socio-cultural construction of Modernism which takes account of the varying levels of European modernisation and identifies how elements deriving from different local contexts coalesce (or were coalesced in critique and propaganda) into the more general movement. From such a perspective, it may be possible to isolate two things as particularly salient: the adoption of techniques based on the new means of communication, film, wireless, advertising – with montage as a unifying preoccupation – and the employment of tech-niques deriving in part from cultural developments of a less general kind, of which the Irish Literary Revival is one telling example. Indeed, for all Joyce's and Beckett's documented antagonism to the cultural limitations of the Revival, their sense, as often impatient readers of its products, of what might constitute a literary text was obviously more akin to that of the Revival itself than to, for example, that sponsored in the tradition of the nineteenth-century realist novel. Nor did they merely exploit pro-cedures becoming available as the pace of technological change quick-ened, though both were highly attentive to these. Joyce, indeed, in the

'Cyclops' episode in *Ulysses*, may satirise the textual forms of the Revival, but he registers in doing so the highly textual nature of the phenomenon he is himself satirising in a work which announces its own undeniable, labyrinthine, even scholastic sense of ubiquitous textuality on every page. Beckett uses in the first trilogy the self-reflexive, interlacing procedures of Irish anecdote and tale to deconstruct the very basis of narrative itself. And both writers shared with Yeats an awareness that time, as history in Ireland would have had them know, is a matter of repetitions, an endless present tense, comic, tragic, a matter of pathos by turns. Riverrun. What stalked through the Post Office? Another happy day.

What I have been arguing is that the Irish Literary Revival in its nationalist context was contiguous with Modernism rather than merely concurrent. Context and text formed a culture in which the kinds of technical devices and the sense of reality Modernism and its accompanying critique would internationalise were contemporaneously aspects of the Revival project and probably influenced, consciously and unconsciously, the Irish contribution to the general movement. As John Wilson Foster has reminded us in his pioneering essay 'Irish Modernism', it was to that quintessential Revival writer James Stephens (possibly the closest in practice of all Revivalists to the fabular, folkloric indigenous tradition) that Joyce turned to invite him 'to complete *Finnegans Wake* ... in the event of his own death'.[27] By such a proposal Joyce, however eccentric it seemed to his biographer,[28] gave notice that the experimental qualities of his own art were not so very far removed from what the local tradition had generated in the work of Stephens. He could hope in the man (who shared with him a Christian name and day of birth) for comprehension of his most radical experiment in fiction and a sufficiently sympathetic sensibility in a writer who might on superficial examination appear to lack appropriate Modernist credentials. It was on reading Stephens's *Deirdre,* it should be noted, that Joyce conceived this idea.

In sum, the Revival and Modernism can be seen as exhibiting parallels of outlook and method. At moments in the work of the Irish Modernists, the literary historian is conscious of overlappings, points of contact as well as parallels and similarities. And the Revival context can be seen as one likely to produce writers who, formally at the very least, can be reckoned as contributors to the international phenomenon of Modernism.

Most post-Treaty Irish writers reacted against the Romantic idealism of the Literary Revival, which seemed too intimate with the political wave that had broken on the rocks of civil war and republican failure. Seán O'Faoláin (a highly representative figure, as ex-IRA man, language-enthusiast and caustic post-revolutionary social critic), in his biography *Vive Moi!*, recalls how in the 1930s he attended four Irish Academy of Letters dinners. He calls them to mind the better to 're-evoke the sense I gradually got of a tide receding about me'.[29] Yeats, the presiding genius of those occasions, as he was the doyen of the Revival itself, struck O'Faoláin as one whose nature required him as man and poet 'to live a foot off the ground, a foot or two or more, away from common life'.[30] O'Faoláin was determined to be true to that common life and to employ realism as the instrument of his integrity. In rejecting the idealism of Yeats and his confederates, O'Faoláin and others who shared his post-revolutionary disillusionment also by the same token rejected the forms in which that idealism had apparently most readily expressed itself – saga, heroic narrative, translated antique text, folklore and myth. Character returned with a vengeance to Irish fiction. Self-obsessed young men would come of age again and again in a depressed Irish environment that demonstrably allowed for none of the mythic and structural fictional complexity of Joyce's classic Irish *Kunstlerroman, A Portrait of the Artist as a Young Man*. It was as if the challenge to realism effected by both the Revival writers and the Modernist movement had not taken place. A debilitating air of anachronism hangs over the whole of what gets called in the literary histories 'the Irish short story'. It reads as if Joyce had not already in *Dubliners* and in that short story writ large, *Ulysses*, taken the form to its limits. And in poetry Austin Clarke, who wished to establish himself as a post-Revival writer, after his youthful infatuation with its achievement, opposing the unstable heteroglossia and fertile invention of the preceding period, turned to the tradition of Irish-language religious poetry – 'another imaginative world which remains entirely neglected'.[31] He found there 'a world of art in which emotion is pure, choice and disciplined'.[32] Anything but Romantic, and certainly not Modernist. Indeed Clarke, identifying the learned tradition he wished to emulate, spoke of a desire to express 'our own casuistic mentality as deeply as we can'.[33]

So disillusioned, post-revolutionary literary Ireland seems to have thrown out the Modernist baby with the Romantic bathwater of the Literary Revival, leaving the 1930s to produce only a few writers, like genetic sports, who wrote in varying degrees of awareness of the Revival's formal originality or of Modernism's revolution of the word. At the very least, until Flann O'Brien in 1939 published *At Swim-Two-Birds*, there did not occur that curious coincidence of literary taxonomies in which a work rooted in aspects of Revival poetics (I am thinking of the parodic Revival epic descriptions and the version of *Buile Suibhne* which it contains) is also an entry in the Modernist (and even the post-modern) canon.

Irish Nationalism and literary Modernism in the 1930s do, however, share some parallel concerns, even if their aesthetics appear markedly antithetical. Both responded to a perceived international crisis and sought in history explanations for, and solutions to, the challenge of the present moment. Accordingly, it may be that the paucity of an explicit, developed interest in Modernism in Ireland in its post-independence phase also has to do with the fact that nationalism itself as a structure of feeling allowed for the expression of what elsewhere became identified with the reactionary cultural politics of the general movement. Irish writers and ideologues could dispense with the formal originality of the Revival's poetics, with its links to, and parallels with, Modernist experiment, but could nevertheless indulge themselves, in the midst of general crisis, in conservative ideological accounts of past and present which were elsewhere the basis of Modernist sociological and historical expatiation. A crucial figure in this respect is Daniel Corkery, the principal ideologue of independent Ireland in the 1930s.

It would be instructive to attempt a comparative analysis of the social and historical thought of Corkery and Yeats in the 1930s, that decade in which Yeats became increasingly obsessed by European history and the role Ireland must play in it. It would, I believe, be evident in such a study that what in Yeats is a characteristically Modernist set of reactionary political and social theses (culminating in the second version of *A Vision* in 1937, and *On the Boiler* in 1938) in Corkery is paralleled by Irish nationalist convictions and preoccupations. The fact, however, that Yeats frequently expresses his essentially Modernist world-view through meditations and polemics on Irish reality, and shares a basic Irish Nationalist outlook with Corkery would make such a comparison seem less interesting than a comparison with that other Modernist ideologue at work in the 1930s and 1940s, T. S. Eliot, on whom Irish Nationalism had no impact whatsoever (to ignore an Irish nurse in a St Louis childhood).

Corkery published his *Hidden Ireland* in 1924, a study of Gaelic poetry in eighteenth-century Munster. It is prefaced by a general reflection on the nature of a national literature which must, if it is to express the national life, eschew the false cosmopolitan values of the European Renaissance. For Corkery, the Renaissance represented a 'fall' from the pre-lapsarian world of national culture which could be restored in modern writing where 'everything is creeping back to the national hearth'.[34] It might be thought that it would be difficult to find a more anti-Modernist set of observations (and indeed Corkery seems to oppose T. S. Eliot's elevation of Dante over Shakespeare in the course of his argument) than the critic offers in this introduction to his subject. Yet Corkery and Eliot share an assumption that the European rot set in with the Renaissance. Then, for the American Modernist, a 'dissociation of sensibility' occurred which thereafter sundered fact and value, mind, emotion and body. For the Irish Nationalist, the Renaissance introduced a 'common strain into the art-consciousness of all European countries' that was certainly brilliant, shapely, worldly-wise, strong, if not indeed gigantic, overbounding in energy, in life! Yet all the time there was a latent weakness in it, a strain, a sham strength, an uneasy energy, a death in life'.[35] In Corkery's bizarre reading of things, Shakespeare as an Englishman was free of the malign influence of the Renaissance: 'what did Shakespeare's native wood-notes wild know of the Unities. Happy England! – so naively ignorant of the Renaissance at the close of the sixteenth century'.[36] It is a theme he returns to in his second book *Synge and Anglo-Irish Literature,* published in 1931. There he deems England a 'normal country' where writers are 'at one with what they write of'.[37] Ireland in this text is not such a happy place for its writers are almost all alien to the real experience of the people. In Corkery's thinking, Renaissance moulds were external things. Thus, in *The Hidden Ireland*, Romanticism is read as 'a protest against the external-ity of Renaissance moulds'.[38] In Ireland, *Synge and Anglo-Irish Literature* insists, the 'literary Irishman' knows of Anglo-Irish literature that 'what-ever moulds exist in this literature are not the inevitable result of long years of patient labour by Irish writers to express the life of their own people in a natural way'.[39] As a consequence, the Irish endure a condition remarkably akin to that identified by Eliot as a 'dissociation of sensibil-ity'. Corkery writes of the education of a typical Irish child: 'No sooner does he begin to use his intellect than what he learns begins to undermine his emotional nature … His surroundings begin to seem unvital.[40] What is most revealing is that Corkery, like Eliot, envisages culture both as a whole way of life and as a collective experience. For the Irish critic/prose writer, culture can, if literature expresses it, heal the nation's broken psy-che. For the American poet/critic, culture, expressing as it does the whole life of the people, can unify the fragmented self of the modern individual. Corkery in 1931 writes:

I recall being in Thurles at a hurling match for the championship of Ireland. There were 30,000 onlookers. They were as typical of this nation as any of the great crowds that assemble on Saturday afternoons in England to witness Association football matches are typical of the English nation. It was while I looked around on that great crowd I first became acutely conscious that as a nation we were without self-expression in literary form.[41]

And he goes on to imagine the defining constituents of the typical Irish culture which Irish writing has not yet expressed: 'the fair, the hurling match, the land grabbing, the *priesting*, the mission, the Mass'.[42] Eliot in 1948, in his *Notes Towards a Definition of Culture*, writes of culture as comprising all the characteristic activities and interests of a people: 'Derby day, Henley regatta, Cowes, the twelfth of August, a cup final, the dog races, the pin table, the dartboard, Wensleydale cheese, boiled cabbage cut into sections, beetroot in vinegar, nineteenth-century Gothic churches, and the music of Elgar'.[43]

The nationalist and the Modernist can it seems share, as well as convictions about a historic fall from some previously existing state of European grace, a nostalgic, evasive vision of an integrated way of life (neither admits industrialism or the city to his thumbnail sketch of the national culture). They thereby indicate, in this precise conjunction of preoccupations, how parallels could exist between the two movements which can seem entirely antithetical. For in Ireland, impulses which elsewhere could find expression in reactionary Modernist stances and polemics were channelled into nationalist feeling and the exposition of its sustaining ideology.

NOTES

1 P. Anderson, 'Modernity and Revolution', in C. Nelson and L. Grosberg (eds.), *Marxism and the Interpretation of Culture* (London: Macmillan, 1988), p. 332.
2 P. Henry, cited by S. B. Kennedy, *Irish Art and Modernism* (Belfast: The Institute of Irish Studies, Queen's University of Belfast, 1991), p. 20.
3 A. Fleischmann, 'Ars Nova: Irish Music in Shaping', *Ireland Today*, 1 (2 July 1936), 42.
4 E. Ó Gallchobhair, *Ireland Today*, 2, 9 (September 1937), 62.
5 See K. Rockett, '1930s Fiction', in K. Rockett, L. Gibbons and J. Hill (eds.), *Cinema and Ireland* (Syracuse, NY: Syracuse University Press, 1988), p. 61.
6 Liam Ó Laoghaire, *Motley*, 1 (5 October 1932), 3.
7 Liam Ó Laoghaire, 'Irish Cinema and the Cinemas', *Ireland Today*, 1 (January 1937), 74.
8 M. Mac Liammóir, 'The Hectic Twenties', *Motley*, 1 (7 December 1932), 11.
9 'Realism', *Motley*, 1 (7 December 1932), 3.
10 'An Open Letter to the *Leader*', *Motley* 1, 2 (April 1932), 12.
11 R. Pine, in Peter Luke (ed.), *Enter Certain Players* (Dublin: Dolmen Press, 1978), p. 74.
12 T. MacGreevy, *T. S. Eliot: A Study*, Dolphin Books, No. 4 (London: Chatto and Windus, 1931), p. 34.
13 *Ibid.*, p. 42.
14 *Ibid.*, p. 56.

15 *Ibid.*, p. 57.

16 Cited in S. Smith, 'From A Great Distance: Thomas MacGreevy's Frames of Reference', *The Lace Curtain*, 6 (Autumn 1978), 54.

17 M. Jellett, 'Modern Art and the Dual Ideal of Form Through the Ages', *Motley*, 1, 5 (October, 1932), 8.

18 Jellett, 'Modern Art', 9.

19 J. C. C. Mays (ed.), *The Collected Poems of Denis Devlin* (Dublin: Dedalus, 1989), p. 26.

20 S. Beckett, 'Recent Irish Poetry', in Ruby Cohn (ed.), *Disjecta: Miscellaneous Writings and a Dramatic Fragment* (London: John Calder, 1983), p. 70.

21 Cited in A. Callinicos, *Against Postmodernism: A Marxist Critique* (Cambridge: Polity Press, 1989), pp. 12–13.

22 M. Bell, 'Introduction: Modern Movements in Literature', in M. Bell (ed.), *The Contexts of English Literature 1900–1930* (London: Methuen, 1980), p. 3.

23 See G. Costigan, 'Romantic Nationalism: Ireland and Europe', *Irish University Review*, 3, 2 (Autumn 1973), 141–52.

24 Anderson, *Marxism and the Interpretation of Culture*, p. 324.

25 W. J. Mc Cormack, 'Austin Clarke: The Poet as Scapegoat of Modernism', in P. Coughlan and A. Davis (eds.), *Modernism and Ireland: The Poetry of the 1930s* (Cork University Press, 1995), p. 75.

26 Callinicos, *Against Postmodernism*, p. 44.

27 J. W. Foster, 'Irish Modernism', in *Colonial Consequences: Essays in Irish Literature and Culture* (Dublin: Lilliput Press, 1991), p. 48.

28 See R. Ellmann, *James Joyce* (Oxford University Press, 1959), p. 604, where he describes Joyce's proposal as 'one of the strangest in literary history'.

29 S. O'Faoláin, *Vive Moi!* (London: Rupert Hart-Davis, 1963), p. 270.

30 *Ibid.*, p. 277.

31 A. Clarke, 'Irish Poetry Today', *The Dublin Magazine* (10 January–March 1935), 31.

32 *Ibid.*

33 *Ibid.*, 32.

34 D. Corkery, *The Hidden Ireland* (Dublin: Gill and Macmillan, 1970), p. 15.

35 *Ibid.*, pp. 12–13.

36 *Ibid.*, p. 13.

37 D. Corkery, *Synge and Anglo-Irish Literature* (Cork University Press, 1966), p. 13.

38 Corkery, *Hidden Ireland*, pp. 13–14.

39 Corkery, *Synge*, p. 12.

40 *Ibid.*, p. 14.

41 *Ibid.*, p. 12.

42 *Ibid.*, p. 13.

43 T. S. Eliot, *Notes Towards the Definition of Culture* (London: Faber and Faber, 1948), p. 31.

CHAPTER 8

Post-modernists: Samuel Beckett
and Flann O'Brien

BECKETT AND STORY

The English writer E. M. Forster admitted of the novel as a form: 'Yes – oh dear yes – the novel tells a story.'[1] It is difficult to imagine many Irish novelists so regretting story as the basis of their craft. Indeed, the novelist and playwright Thomas Kilroy has perceptively observed that that chromosome of story, the anecdote, is in the DNA of the Irish fictional tradition from at least the end of the eighteenth century. He advises, with reference to Maria Edgeworth's *Castle Rackrent* (1800):

The distinctive characteristic of our 'first' novel, that which makes it what it is, is not so much its idea, revolutionary as that may be, as its imitation of the speaking voice engaged in the telling of a tale. The model will be exemplary for the reader who has read widely in Irish fiction: it is a voice heard over and over again, whatever its accent, a voice with a supreme confidence in its own histrionics, one that shares with its audience a shared ownership of the told tale and all that it implies: a taste for anecdote, an unshakeable belief in the value of human action, a belief that life may be adequately encapsulated into stories that require no reference, no qualifications beyond their own selves.[2]

This is certainly a voice the reader can hear loud and clear in the novels of Samuel Beckett (1906–89), though subjected there to the kind of satiric deconstruction that the weight of so settled a tradition might require. For the narrative energies of the anecdote and the told tale are pervasive in Irish fiction, in a way that can make the short story seem culturally indigenous where the novel has never quite appeared so. And the Irish novel in that context has certainly been dominated by a rich zest for story-shaped worlds. It may indeed be, as Kilroy hints, that storytelling has offered Ireland in modern times what in other cultures philosophy, theology and science have struggled to provide: a means of apprehending life's enigmatic truths and of accounting for what transpires in the world. For many Irish writers and their readers, 'life' can be 'adequately encapsulated into stories'.

This is not an idea which Beckett would have entertained. A brilliantly adept storyteller, he nonetheless lacked the kind of faith in the efficacy of narrative Kilroy suggests is 'exemplary' in the tradition. Nor was he bereft of interest in other modes of knowing such unthinking confidence implies. For Beckett employed narrative to explore problems explicitly posed by philosophic reflection, to a degree that can make him seem an anomalous figure in an Irish context. Yet it was his peculiar predilection for addressing issues of philosophic import in complex narratives which in part accounts for his remarkable achievement as a novelist.[3]

Murphy

Samuel Beckett's *Murphy* (1938) was the author's first published novel (he had published a collection of interlinked stories, *More Pricks than Kicks,* in 1934) and the first work about which he felt reasonably secure as a writer. Most of the pretentious attitudinising and passages of tedious intellectual display which had marred the earlier fictional venture (only the bleakly sardonic final page of 'Belacqua and the Lobster' in *More Pricks than Kicks* gave a full hint of future powers) had been slewed away in a text that made a succinct comedy out of philosophic matter. For in *Murphy,* Beckett, the Trinity-college scholar, explores by means of a bizarre yet strangely affecting comic narrative the implications of the Cartesian dualism his studies had encouraged him obsessively to ponder.

Murphy, in exile from Ireland and resident in London (we do not learn his given names), by his own reckoning a 'chronic emeritus',[4] is pathologically averse to work. His chief delight is to while away the hours on a rocking chair in mental separation from the world, intent as he is on loving himself. He has, however, against his will fallen in love with a London prostitute (also Irish by origin), who urges him to seek employment, lest she, Celia, will be forced back on the streets. A major part of the narrative concerns his desperate stratagems to avoid both work and Celia (despite the sexual rapture they enjoy together – 'serenade, nocturne, albada', p. 46) and his eventual employment in a lunatic asylum, the Magdalen Mental Mercyseat (the MMM). There he encounters a patient, a Mr Endon, whose near catatonic imperviousness to the world about him is symbolised in the game of chess Murphy and he play, in which Mr Endon refuses to react to any of Murphy's moves, to the point where Murphy must abandon the non-existent contest. Mr Endon seems to Murphy the ideal type, who has resolved the Cartesian conundrum of how the mind can be connected in acts of the will to the body and to the external world of other people and of objects by retreating to the will-lessness of his own mind. Unable to make any contact with Mr Endon, Murphy is forced back to his rocking chair, now set up in a garret in the asylum, where he meets his death in an apparently accidental gas explosion. He is cremated and his ashes strewn among the waste matter on the floor of a London pub. In an elaborate subplot, a gallery of Irish grotesques for complicated amatory reasons are set on discovering Murphy's London whereabouts, mounting indeed an increasingly futile philosophic quest for one whose intention it is to disappear into the serene stasis of his own mind.

Murphy, it must be stressed, is no merely clever, arid novel of ideas (though it has its moments of intellectual showmanship) in which a philosophic conundrum is presented in narrative form. Rather, its power as a work of fiction derives from the way in which the implications of an idea are tested in the crucible of human feeling. The story it tells in comic mode is also a poignant one. For in the text, Celia is sketched tenderly as a victim of her own needy heart and Murphy's death represents for her the end of her hopes. Furthermore, in anticipation of a central theme of Beckett's oeuvre as a whole, the novel is constantly alert to the dimensions and particulars of human suffering, mental and physical. In the course of a book that climaxes with Murphy's suspicious death, we hear of two suicides (that of 'the old boy', a grisly affair indeed) and bodily afflictions of one kind or another (Miss Dew has Duck's Disease, Cooper is unable to sit, while Celia's paternal grandfather, Mr Willoughby Kelly, can do little but sit, since he is confined to a wheelchair). In the MMM, we are afforded a glimpse of well-regulated mental and physical sadism, while the narrative voice of the book insists almost to the point of a ghastly relish that suffering is an ineluctable fact of the human condition. Of Neary's night panics, for example, the narrator grimly observes: 'he simply had this alarming conviction that every second was going to announce itself as the first of his last ten minutes or quarter of an hour on earth. The number of seconds in one dark night is a simple calculation that the curious reader will work out for himself (p. 125). A prevailing assumption in the book is that Murphy has good reason to seek sanctuary in his mind, which pictures itself 'as a large hollow sphere, hermetically closed to the universe without' (p. 63).

Murphy is in fact trapped in a reality that can only be truly escaped by death. Although the narrator assures us that Murphy is in some sense a free agent in the novel, when the other characters are merely the narrator's puppets, the text is dominated by chronology (complicated flashbacks keep the reader alert to days and dates), by an awareness of astrological seasons and Newtonian physics, and by a sense of city districts as grid-maps of streets. Geometry is a controlling metaphor; the events of the novel compose complex patterns of echo and repetition. The effect is to suggest the vanity of human wishes in a deterministic universe, where the narrator's moods vary from bitter revulsion at the antics of his puppets to comedic satisfaction at the dark absurdity of life that occasions pity. Like Murphy's, the narrator's is a bifurcated nature, split between an intel-lect that indulges an allusive, cerebral style, exaggeratedly recondite in its word choice, and a sensibility open to atmospheres, locales, the pull of emotion on the heart-strings (the novel ends in an affecting scene, with Mr Kelly sending his kite into the 'pale limitless blue', p. 157). It is the self-contradictory voice of the narrator that we remember from the novel when the complexities of its philosophic purport and its structural detail begin to fade.

As text, *Murphy* retains a purchase on a recognisable social world. The residual constraints of fictional realism anchor the book in time and place, with occasionally obtrusive references to the actual conditions of newly independent Ireland suggesting, furthermore, elements of the *roman-à-clef* (the portrayal of the pot-poet Austin Ticklepenny is a libel-lous lampoon on the poet Austin Clarke). A Modernist consciousness of textuality, however (Celia is introduced to us, for example, in a colum-nar list of characteristics and vital statistics), indicates an author at work in the wake of Joycean experiment. And Murphy as alienated outsider suffering a grotesque fate is the precursor of the indigents and tramps who people Beckett's subsequent, more radically experimental novels, in which we enter a universe of imagining that cuts loose from the social almost entirely, to reveal a blackly comic world, relentlessly apprehended in a mental and emotional space of its own. Of these, *Watt* (1953) and a trilogy of texts – *Molloy* (1951), *Malone Dies* (1951) and *The Unnamable* (1953), henceforth the Trilogy – constitute works that subject the very idea of the novel to such interrogation that the form itself can seem to undergo a terminal, post-modernist meltdown. In each of these, as in *Murphy,* philosophic issues are explored in a story-shaped world.

Watt

In one respect, *Watt* is even more than *Murphy* a work of realism, since it engages in an obsessively rational inspection of the physical world of things and data. But this is in the context of a fiction the manifest purpose of which is to display the outright lunacy of such rational ambition, which makes its passages of hyper-realism an intellectual inanity. Watt is a temporary inhabitant as servant in the house of one Mr Knott. Beginning his service on the ground floor, he graduates in time to the first, without any increase in his knowledge as to who his master really is, or of the true nature of his surroundings, which seem to be in a constant state of alteration. Lacking absolute knowledge, partial information leaves open an endless field of possibility and alternatives that bifurcate to the point of madness. Watt's ultimate fate is residence in an institution, possibly an asylum, where he narrates his tale of Mr Knott's perplexing house to a fellow inmate.

To seek to know in Mr Knott's house is to condemn oneself to manic consideration of all the possible permutations that reality can present. And to imagine that the conditions of rational order obtain among copious alternatives, scrupulously adumbrated, is to enter a zone of the ludicrous, where certainty can be achieved only at the expense of the rational or common sense as conventionally understood. An extended refrain in the novel imagines how Mr Knott manages to have a starving dog come every day at the appointed time to consume the food superfluous to Mr Knott's needs on that day. This involves the summoning into wonderful, absurd, textual existence of the bizarrely numerous and physically afflicted Lynch family, whose role it is to service Mr Knott's canine requirements.

Watt subjects reason as epistemological tool to unremitting scorn. Where reason enters, alternatives proliferate with an inventive persistence that is cognate with narration. For in this text, story and the findings of reason seem to share the same status, each of them only ways of seeking to make sense of an unknowable reality. Where the prose style attempts in its reiterated subjunctives and conditionals, its untiring qualifications, to establish at least something for certain, anecdote, tale and story push their way into the text with an unsettling air of inconsequence. Characters (the Galls, father and son piano-tuners, to cite but two) appear and disappear, while the tangential tale of a west of Ireland research trip by a Trinity student is tied to the main narrative in a whimsically tenuous fashion. Narrative is invention, the text implies, and is no more trustworthy than reason, for all its histrionic self-assurance.

And text itself is a contingent thing, *Watt* gives us to understand. For we are advised midway and also later on that the words we are reading are derived from the record Watt's companion Sam has made in a notebook, in their place of refuge, which in part accounts for lacunae in the text indicated by question marks and gaps. Though Sam can also seem like an omniscient narrator, Beckett himself (another Sam) enters this complicated narrative equation when in 'Addenda (1)' – there is no Addenda (2) – he advises in a footnote that 'The following precious and illuminating material should be carefully studied. Only fatigue and disgust prevented its incorporation.'[5] The novel could, this implies, have been other than it is, rendering what we have been given disturbingly arbitrary. A sense of that contingent quality as an attribute of fiction itself is forced on the reader, who experiences the text as a highly unpredictable set of variations between almost detachable sections (though patterns are established among the four parts). In some of these, a prose of cold rational distinctions is extended to a preposterous degree. In other lengthy passages, oral discourse is foregrounded. In a book where reason has sought to set feeling aside, these passages sometimes carry a burden of emotion (as in Arsene's 'short statement' of about twenty-eight pages, with its tale of housemaid Mary's peculiar eating habits and its poignant, bitterly lyrical evocation of the seasons' endless cycle).

That language which both reason and storytelling depend on is also arbitrary is a further revelation of this subversive, proleptically postmodern text. Part of Sam's problem in telling Watt's tale is that Watt has been afflicted by a curious mental state which causes him to invert what he says in highly complicated ways. Some of Sam's account of Watt's experience in Mr Knott's house is in fact therefore a translation from Watt-speak, which as Sam acknowledges at length was 'so much Irish' to him. He admits that of all he heard in Watt's private tongue, he understood 'fully one half of what won its way through [his] tympan' (p. 169).

Watt was written in English, in France, during the Second World War. The major works that were to follow in the period 1946–53, culminating in the play *Waiting for Godot* that established Beckett's international reputation, were all written in French by the Irish author who had made Paris his home. Beckett's near bilingualism has its analogue in his multigenre versatility. The works of this period include the three novels of the Trilogy, the first of which was translated into English by Patrick Bowles in collaboration with Beckett, the second and third by Beckett himself. This fact of compositional and publishing history means that novels which in ramifying narratives exhibit, as we shall see, the philosophic impotence of discourse themselves hover in a kind of linguistic no-man's-land, where acts of translation highlight how language is both contingent and an inescapable fate.

BECKETT AND FRENCH

Beckett's shift from English to French[6] in this wonderfully creative period of his writing life was accompanied by a revision of his aesthetic ambition as artist. In an oft-quoted interview of the 1950s, he spoke of how he sensed at this time that literature could no longer seek the encyclopaedic totality that had governed the Joycean enterprise in fiction: 'The more Joyce knew the more he could. He's tending towards omniscience and omnipotence as an artist.' By contrast, he confessed: 'I'm working with impotence, ignorance. I don't think impotence has been exploited in the past. There seems to be a kind of esthetic axiom that expression is achievement – must be achievement. My little exploration is that whole zone of being that has been set aside by artists as something unusable – as something by definition incompatible with art.'[7] In other words, Beckett was prepared to accept that the less he knew, the less he could – that in consequence of epistemological despair, writing must be intimate with failure. The better to explore this 'zone of being', he turned to French, which would he felt allow him to write 'without style'.[8] For such a project involved paring language down, relieving it of the weight of centuries of familiar English usage that gave the illusion of expression as knowledgeable achievement.

Existing as if between two languages (in French the Irish proper names in the Trilogy are curiously defamiliarising, while in the English version they seem merely generic in a landscape that eschews geographic specificity), in the condition of translation as it were, the prose of the Trilogy manages to suggest a language constantly discovering its own contingency. The Trilogy seems inexorably driven to restate itself in the face of a recurrent failure, even adequately to explore failure. A result of this is to make it a perverse triumph of the deconstructive impulse which so characterised the post-modern turn in late twentieth-century culture. For in this trio of novels, story becomes the means by which a despairing philosophy of knowledge is made markedly available as a textual experience; a paradoxical experience, to be sure, of what it is like to know and feel that 'there is nothing to express, nothing with which to express, nothing from which to express, no power to express, no desire to express, together with the obligation to express'.[9]

THE TRILOGY

In the first novel of the Trilogy, *Molloy,* the textual status of the 'story' is established from the start. Molloy, the narrator, is in his mother's room (he presumes his mother is dead). Each week, a man supplies him with paper and gives him money for the pages he has managed to cover with words, and returns earlier work marked up with signs he does not understand. It seems (though this is not stated) we are reading the product of this strange exchange. The tale Molloy unfolds is of a mysterious quest in which the narrator, a grotesque derelict, describes how he set out to visit his mother and failed. How eventually he arrived at her room, he does not know. His journey, first by bicycle and then on crutches, involves an encounter with the police, the accidental killing of a dog, a prolonged sojourn in a lady's house in an extended passage that evokes Ulysses' enchantment on Calypso's island in the *Odyssey*, culminating in an attack on a charcoal burner in the wood where Molloy loses his way and falls into a ditch.

Throughout his 'story', Molloy reminds the reader that he is an artist of sorts, spinning a tale (like Homer, it could be said). He speaks of 'the heat of composition'[10] yet admits 'all I know is what the words know' (p. 31). Later he confesses: 'I weary of these inventions and others beckon to me. But in order to blacken a few more pages may I say I spent some time at the seaside, without incident' (p. 68). He senses that in some odd fashion his stories are telling him, as if he is possessed by narrative voices that make him their conduit. His prose style emphasises this doubt as to authorial control of his own narration (at one point he exclaims: 'What a story, God send I don't make a balls of it', p. 77). Although the narrative is of an onward journey, sentences constantly backtrack on themselves in qualification and reservation, as though governed by uncertainty. Yet this also creates the sense of an author who aspires to punctilious word choice in a manner suggestive of post-modernist textuality, where words offer a refined exactitude that only their self-conscious pastiche of literary expression would appear to warrant.

That in *Molloy* we are in fact experiencing something akin to pastiche is revealed in part II of the novel. Here we are alerted to the fact that in part I we have been immersed in what, if normal chronology had been followed by Beckett, could be read as the increasingly mysterious second part of a spy or detective story (a 'mystery' in genre terms), with hints of the boys' adventure yarn thrown in (much is made in part II of accoutrements gathered together for the task undertaken). For in part II, we learn how Moran works for a boss named Youdi, who sends agents out on missions, such as the one that he embarks on to discover Molloy's whereabouts and report back. Part II, apparently, is Moran's report on his fruitless quest.

The textuality of *Malone Dies* is even more pronounced than that of *Molloy*. Malone, another afflicted monologuist (he shares Molloy's disablement and even some of his possessions), awaits his death. To pass the time, he will tell stories, writing them in pencil in an exercise book (he promises four stories but only manages one), commenting on what he has written as he goes. What he gives us is a pastiche *Bildungsroman* about a boy named Saposcat, who grows up to become a man called Macmann (son of man, no less). We are recurrently made aware both of the difficulties involved in producing this text (at one point the pencil seems to have slipped from Malone's fingers and is only recovered 'after forty-eight hours ... of intermittent efforts', p. 222) and of the arbitrary quality of the story itself (although Malone affects to struggle for historical accuracy about his hero). Death will be a relief from the compulsion to narrative, Malone hopes. He is also at pains to distinguish himself as author from his creation: 'Nothing is less like me than this patient, reasonable, child, struggling all alone for years to shed a little light upon himself, avid of the least gleam, a stranger to the joys of darkness' (p. 193).

However, the tale Malone tells of Saposcat and Macmann might well be his own, or that of what in Beckett's work has become, with the publication of *Malone Dies,* the typical Beckettian persona. For the child Saposcat becomes the Macmann whose career ends in a lunatic asylum, amid black comic grotesqueries of the kind that have been the stuff of Beckett's fiction since *Murphy.* Beckett himself intrudes in the text, indeed, when he has Malone long for fictional closure in death: 'Then it will all be over with the Murphys, Merciers, Molloys, Morans and Malones' (p. 236). At this juncture, the text implodes as artifice in its allusion to previous works by Beckett about which the invented Malone cannot be presumed to know. The very act of fiction is for the reader deconstructively set in question, therefore, in a way which can make the Trilogy a work subversive of literature's claims to represent reality in any way. In such an interpretation, what we have been reading, as we have followed our author's novelistic career, are narratives spun out of Beckett's head, ways of spending the time before death to be sure, but no more than that. Accordingly, it can seem entirely apt that as *Malone Dies* ends with Malone's presumed death, the narrator and his character Macmann begin to seem one and the same person. Beckett, as author, and his creations have begun to seem indistinguishable, both existing as arbitrary fabrications in a story-shaped world, in which the death of the author is implicit in the death of literature. Nor should it surprise that the final work in this trilogy of novels should bear the title that it does. For in *The Unnamable,* it is not at all certain who actually possesses the narrative voice to which we are invited to attend.

In *The Unnamable,* it is narrative itself which seems to generate the text. The text's implied author refers impatiently to his 'Murphys, Molloys and Malones' (p. 303), a gallery of literary personae who have wasted narrative time, instead of allowing what is now merely a narrative voice, without context or setting, to achieve a real goal: 'if I could speak and yet say nothing really nothing?' (p. 303). For that would be truth in face of the lies fiction perpetrates.

The Unnamable makes that attempt to coerce language to represent its own essential impotence as a means of expression and mode of knowledge. As it does, the prose becomes more and more the voice of entrapment, as the text becomes an urgent, oppressive tirade that cannot be arrested. It seems that the more the voice of narrative tries to escape from the grotesquely, blackly comic stories (about another Beckettian persona *in extremis*) that flower rampantly even from this stony ground, as it struggles to express nothing, the more it is immured in the prison house of language. *The Unnamable* seeks to speak from the abyss of deconstructed discourse where neither writer nor text can be granted ontological authority, as if to transcend language and its arbitrary significations in some new impotent and ignorant form of utterance; but the voice presses unrelentingly on, damned by its inauthenticity, doomed to speak pointlessly of its unquenchable lust for silence.

So the Trilogy can persuasively be read as a work of deconstruction, anticipatory of a cultural turn which has been identified with the postmodern moment of the later twentieth century. Philosophy and story both find themselves subverted in its radical raid on a desired inarticulateness on the edge of all linguistic occasions. Yet to restrict its significance to the deconstructive *mise en abyme* would be, it must be said, seriously to limit to a particular cultural moment what is one of the most multivalent of twentieth-century literary masterpieces; for many other readings have found eloquent advocates. Critics have not been slow to interpret its compulsively readable pages as offering genuine, achieved insights into the human condition. There have been those, for example, who have studied the Trilogy as an interrogation of the concept of an originary, integrated selfhood, subjecting the work to an existentialist critique, while others have read it as the expression of a Schopenhauerian pessimism or of a Swiftian satiric recoil from life, both made bearable by a fundamentally comic spirit in debt to Rabelais and Sterne. Some have accounted for its hold on readers by reading the work as a searching study of Man as a rational, self-conscious being in a godless, irrational world, where suffering is destiny. The bodily indignities that Beckett's personae are forced to endure would make belief in a benign Christian deity, frequently referred to by the narrators, seem simply absurd.[11]

Perhaps, however, the Trilogy's capacity to hold the attention of the reader is less to do with its possible meanings or with its post-modernist subversion of meaning than with its indisputable literary power. For the Trilogy as a whole is a work of wonderfully variegated moods, shifting from lunatic comedy (at its zenith in *The Unnamable*, when Mahood is imagined leading his legless and armless existence in a jar outside a restaurant near the shambles) to a weird poetry of improbable loves (as between Moll and Macmann in *Malone Dies*). It manages, too, mesmerically to inhabit a world close to the experience of dream, in which bizarre encounters with an imagined world and with its unlikely inhabitants are poised on the edge of mythic awareness of a revelation that never quite comes. The contents of the unconscious seem available to its bleak, haunting lyricism, in what become a species of poetry that touches the depths of desire, as the prose cadences of pathos and of nostalgia are challenged by the manic exercises of a deranged reason (at its most inventively florid in the extended sucking-stones passage in *Molloy*). A distinctively Beckettian tone establishes itself over the three volumes, compact of great syntactical and semantic command with exacting rhythmic control, that engages with terminal things in a manner that induces in the reader feelings of yearning and loss. For order set at naught seems the 'message' of the work as a whole. Alienation is its predominant register; displacement, dislocation, estrangement being the territories of feeling it is determined to occupy.

As the work of a sensibility imprisoned in self-exile, Beckett's Trilogy has also found a mode of interpretation in post-colonial theory. This is not just a matter of noting that the work often invokes a desolate landscape of the mind that incorporates details which suggest the constricted conditions of the putatively independent Irish Free State, nor of the way in which the experience of terminal states of feeling finds an appropriate setting in a phantom Dublin (a city beneath mountains, beside the sea, with its two canals), which haunts the text like the ghost of a lost poetics of place. It also involves reading the Trilogy – Beckett's oeuvre indeed – as so imbricated with dispossession and self-exile as to constitute an anatomy of the post-colonial condition itself. In David Lloyd's terms, the inauthenticity that he discerns in another of Beckett's works 'is … the perpetual condition of the colonized: dominated, interpreted, mediated by another'.[12] So for Lloyd, 'Beckett's … oeuvre stands as the most exhaustive dismantling we have of the logic of identity that at every level structures and maintains the post-colonial moment.'[13]

FLANN O'BRIEN: DISPOSSESSION AND DECONSTRUCTION

A sense of what can be characterised as post-colonial dispossession and inauthenticity also permeates the ostentatiously textual novels of Beckett's near contemporary, Brian O'Nolan (1911–66), who in 1939, as Flann O'Brien, published the first of his novels employing one of his several pseudonyms.[14] That book, *At Swim-Two-Birds* (1939), can seem so dependent as a ludic work of pastiche and parody on precursor texts as to lack any truly felt life of its own, as if meaning and authority are located elsewhere. *The Third Policeman* (completed 1940, posthumously published as a work by Flann O'Brien in 1967) offers in a curiously inert prose, accompanied by footnotes of preposterous academic decorum, the first-person narrative of a man who has in fact lost his life (the emptied-out language of dispossession indeed). *The Poor Mouth,* first published in Irish as *An Béal Bocht* in 1941 and published in English in a translation by Patrick C. Power in 1973, is a blackly comic report on the living death of Irish rural deprivation, which can only be mediated in parodic terms of a generic cliché popularised in newly independent Ireland – the western island and Gaeltacht pastoral. Furthermore, each of these works, his finest achievements in the novel form, can be read as a depressed commentary on the dismal conditions of life in 1930s Ireland, in the second decade of independence. The student narrator of *At Swim-Two-Birds* inhabits a cultural world of petit-bourgeois provincial inanity. *The Third Policeman* unfolds its grim tale of crime and punishment in a hell that is indistinguishable from the Irish midlands at their most stultifying, while *The Poor Mouth* makes misery and complaint in an exiguous setting an endogenous affliction of the Irish soul.

The English language cannot be taken for granted as a medium of communication in these texts. The narrator of *At Swim-Two-Birds* composes his narrative of seedy student life in an English that reads as if it had already achieved the condition of a dead language like Latin, oddly punctilious and formal.[15] From one of the book's interpolations that parody the weird 'translationese' through which Gaelic saga literature had been mediated since the nineteenth century and the Irish Literary Revival, we learn that its odd title is in fact a clumsy version of the Irish *Snámh dá-én,* as if to remind us that English is not native to the Irish ecosystem. That same landscape is evoked in *The Third Policeman* in a very 'queer' (a key word in the text) idiolect that suggests simultaneously familiarity and disorientation; and of course, *The Poor Mouth* owes its existence to *An Béal Bocht* and achieves its satiric effects through a parody of the Gaelic syntax and vocabulary deployed by nativist purveyors of Irish pastoral. All this suggests that language in Ireland is the site where the post-colonial condition of inauthenticity and dispossession finds an ambiguous, hybrid realisation.

It would be difficult, however, to contain these intriguingly experimental works within a single critical paradigm. Another seems immediately apposite. As with Beckett, their fascination with the textual makes O'Brien's key novels candidates for a post-modernist analysis, for readings in which they can be entered as a species of anti-novel. In this reading, anecdote, story, elaborate narrative (the staples of the Irish tradition and of O'Brien's entire oeuvre) and the genre of fiction itself can be seen as the objects of a fascinated inspection which, by revealing the techniques and protocols of fiction as they are enacted, robs them to a degree of expressive energy. When this post-modernist penchant for advertising what, in other forms of creativity, would be the taken-for-granted mechanics of an artifact is combined with a parasitic relish for parody and pastiche, then O'Brien's fiction can be seen to turn on itself in a sustained, deconstructive whimsy.

At Swim-Two-Birds

This is especially true of *At Swim-Two-Birds*. This zanily inventive text has as its presumed author a slothful University College Dublin undergraduate (there are obvious allusions to Stephen Dedalus's college milieu) who generates a manuscript about a novelist named Dermot Trellis. Trellis is at work on a novel which will display the deleterious effects of sin. The running gag of O'Brien's book is that Trellis's characters take on a life of their own when Trellis is asleep and eventually turn revengefully upon him. Levels of presumed reality and fictionality are elaborately intertwined. Trellis impregnates one of his characters, who bears him the son who begins to write a further novel in which he describes terrible violence done on his progenitor, employing the characters his literary father had invented. These include the Pooka ('a species of human Irish devil'[16]) and the Good Fairy – who together account for a good deal of the book's shape-changing brio, its magical realism – the giant Finn MacCool who, insistently and somewhat tediously (for characters and readers alike), chants from the saga legend of the mad king Sweeny, in extensive parodic interpolations into the text of high-falutin' translationese, and a cast of Dubliners, with their cliché-ridden demotic, who might have stepped in pastiche from Joyce's collection of that name to reveal a genius for inconsequential dialogue that is all their own. That is when they are not recalling cow-punching days in Ringsend in the style of cowboy pot-boilers. Throw in Jem Casey, the working man's Bard of Booterstown, with his banal verses, and a tasty Irish fictional stew is set to simmer.

As if this Chinese-box plot structure (narrative contained within narrative) is not enough to challenge the very status story might be assumed to enjoy in Ireland, O'Brien also out-Becketts Beckett in giving his book a vertiginous textuality. Chapter 1 begins with three separate openings (there is no chapter 2) and the book finishes in the logical absurdity of two conclusions (*antepenultimate* and *ultimate*). Throughout, sections are head-lined mock-sententiously – 'Biographical reminiscence, part the first', for example. Figures of speech are pedantically identified. Plot summaries of the action hitherto (some of them supplying new information) are provided and cross-referenced. Passages from the public press are cited as such, while the narrator has recourse at various points to a multi-volume *Conspectus of the Arts and Natural Sciences,* which surprisingly contains a biographical entry on Dermot Trellis, as well as the scarcely relevant matter the narrator chooses periodically to cite at confusing, if entertaining, length. The reader is constantly challenged as to the point of view at any given stage in this interlacing of story (the interlacing recalls a Celtic illuminated manuscript) with self-referring textuality. The novel as novel, as genre, scarcely survives the book's bravura display of subversive high spirits.

The Third Policeman

The Third Policeman also functions in certain respects as an anti-novel and post-modern text. A rum tale of envy, greed, murder and punishment, the book offers an unreliable narrator of a very special kind. He is in fact dead but does not know it. Nor as readers do we, until close to the final page of the novel. What our narrator takes for reality, therefore, we are given to understand by the book's conclusion, is the hell to which he has been consigned in punishment for his part in the vicious murder with which the narrative began. This strange conception turns the book inside out in a troubling way; for what we take as we read to be the real world, from which the narrator steps into a fantastical zone where Nature's laws of time and space no longer seem to apply, is in fact the reality he now occupies and what he and we have taken for normality is unreal, phantasmal.

This, oddly, makes *The Third Policeman* a book to reread, for a second reading will be different from the first to a greater degree than is customary in fiction, even of the *policier* and mystery kind. (The text shifts from a curiously deadpan prose appropriate to a hard-boiled crime novel to, in its final stages, the glooms of Gothic fiction.) On a second reading, we will notice all the indications that the narrator is dead but is unaware of this: frequent references to negative states, for example,[17] or the simple detail that he cannot remember his own name. As we read we will realise, too, that the repetition we are experiencing is also the narrator's fate, for he is condemned endlessly to re-live (re-die?) the novel's contents. We are made aware of this horrible truth by a lengthy textual repetition in which the narrator's approach to the police barracks, where so many extraordinary things transpire, is described. 'I had never seen a police station like it',[18] says the narrator on the final page, unknowingly repeating himself in apt punishment for a capital crime. He is namelessly condemned forever to that terrible first-person pronoun.

The Third Policeman, with its unreliable narrator, its disturbingly clever play on appearance and reality, its generic echoes and its key textual repetition, certainly draws attention to itself as artifice, in what we have come to recognise as the post-modern manner. The elaborate comedy of the footnotes adds to this. These concern the narrator's obsession with the lunatic theories of a savant named De Selby, among which is the belief, for which he argues with consummate logic, that the world is sausage-shaped. Perhaps, as Clissmann has argued, his theories pertain in thematic fashion to the hell the narrator inhabits where anything is possible,[19] but, as we read, their relevance is to exhibit how text itself is subject to bizarre exchanges in this world where time and space seem malleable. In the novel, much play is made of the atomic theory which allows O'Brien to fantasise how people become their bicycles and vice versa over the years, as atoms are exchanged in the riding. We see in this novel how the presumably! main text can be parasitically invaded by 'secondary' footnotes. Chapter 9 has a footnote that runs for six pages, splitting the print in two on each page, generating two narratives, where the priority of the 'main' story is set in question by a tale of academic in-fighting and skullduggery (in their way as reprehensible as the narrator's criminality). In this chapter, the footnote has become the narrative and the text a kind of footnote.

The Poor Mouth

The Poor Mouth also makes great play with literary artifice. Its narrative of outrageous Gaelic misery is presented as an edited version by Myles na gGopaleen (the pseudonym under which O'Nolan contributed a famous humorous column to *The Irish Times*) of a document written by an inhabitant of a stereotypical Gaeltacht. In the Irish version of the work, na gGopaleen represents himself as editor of a non-existent periodical, *The Day of Want.* By the time of the English translation, this had become *The Day of Doom.* Want and doom are indeed the fate of the Gael, in what is an obvious pastiche of such widely admired accounts of western Irish life as Tomás Ó Criomhthain's *An tOileánach* (1929; translated by Robin Flower and published as *The Islandman* in 1934).[20] *The Poor Mouth,* in its savage, wildly comic stories, its exaggerations of the kinds of set pieces and conventions these writings deploy, brings parody to a point where it preys as a negative energy on the precursor texts, swallowing them up, as it were, in a form of literary cannibalism. The anti-novel here becomes a predatory thing, like the monstrous sea-cat that pursues the narrator in one ghastly episode in the book. Its import begins to seem nihilistic.

So black in fact is this book (potatoes and eternity set in grim apposition), despite the high comedy of the characters resigning themselves to the fates literature has assigned to them, that it cast its shadow over O'Nolan's other major novels; for it alerts us as to how those more humorous works are also rooted in a dark vision of life. This is not to suggest, it must be stressed, that O'Brien was any kind of ambitious philosopher, employing narrative and story as Beckett had done to examine Cartesian and epistemological conundrums until he turned to a deconstructive interrogation of the very nature of tale-telling itself in the Trilogy. Rather, O'Brien, by contrast with his contemporary, lacked the kind of radically questioning mind that made Beckett's novels a searching engagement with the mystery of human existence. In its place was a settled conviction – the product, as Anthony Cronin has convincingly argued, of a conservative and unquestioned Thomistic Catholicism[21] – that the bleak truths about the sinful and cruel human condition were already fully available. There was nothing new under the sun, and certainly nothing new to be said about terrestrial life. Consequently, O'Brien's novels deal in futility, comic as that can be made to seem. Stories are seen to be versions of other stories in an achievement that makes pastiche a primary literary activity. Narrative ingenuity begins to seem an end in itself. And in as much as O'Brien's fiction has anything much to tell us, it is that life can be heartlessly savage, that sin leads to the repetitive torments of hell and that the pleasures of the text coexist with the indignities of the body and soul. For reading *The Poor Mouth,* with its physical privations and hardships, reminds us that *At Swim-Two-Birds,* for all its fanciful literary panache, is intimate with squalor, waste, bodily functions (vomiting or 'puking' are frequent) and a miasma of intellectual purposelessness. *The Poor Mouth*, with its frenetic stories of rural thievery and violence, also highlights evil as an abiding aspect of the human predicament, as perhaps the unnerving concomitant of this storyteller's indisputable success as a whimsical humorist. This we are certainly made to understand in the evacuated prose of *The Third Policeman*, as the narrator struggles to write an infernal language when 'there are no suitable words in the world to tell [his] meaning' (p. 116).

NOTES

1 E. M. Forster, *Aspects of the Novel* (1924; London: Edward Arnold, 1974), p. 17.

2 T. Kilroy, 'Tellers of Tales', *Times Literary Supplement* (17 March 1972), pp. 301–2.

3 This essay concentrates on five major novels by Beckett. It does not deal with the first novel Beckett wrote in French, *Mercier et Camier* (1946, published 1970 and in English 1974), which anticipated the concerns of the Trilogy: *Molloy* (in French 1951; in English 1955), *Malone Dies* (1951; 1958) and *The Unnamable* (1953; 1959).

4 S. Beckett, *Murphy* (1938; London: Pan Books, 1973), p. 16. Subsequent page references for quotations from this edition are given in the text.

5 S. Beckett, *Watt* (1953; New York: Grove; London: Evergreen, 1959), p. 247. Subsequent page references for quotations from this edition are given in the text.

6 For a sensitive analysis of the significance of translation in the production of the Trilogy, see L. Hill, *Beckett's Fiction: In Different Worlds* (Cambridge University Press, 1990), pp. 40–58.

7 L. Graver and R. Federman (eds.), 'An Interview with Beckett: 1956', in *Samuel Beckett: The Critical Heritage* (London: Routledge & Kegan Paul, 1979), p. 148.

8 Quoted in J. Knowlson, *Damned to Fame: The Life of Samuel Beckett* (London: Bloomsbury, 1996), p. 357. Knowlson usefully discusses Beckett's linguistic shift.

9 S. Beckett, *Dramatic Works and Dialogues* (London: John Calder, 1999), p. 26.

10 S. Beckett, *Three Novels* (New York: Grove Press, 1965), p. 28. Subsequent page references for quotations from this edition are given in the text.

11 For an excellent survey of the variegated critical response to Beckett's novels, see D. Pattie, *The Complete Critical Guide to Samuel Beckett* (London and New York: Routledge, 2000), to which I am indebted.

12 D. Lloyd, *Anomalous States: Irish Writing and the Post-Colonial Moment* (Dublin: Lilliput Press, 1993), p. 54.

13 *Ibid.*, p. 56.

14 B. O'Nolan published two further novels, *The Hard Life* (1961) and *The Dalkey Archive* (1964). They are much inferior to those considered in this essay, upon which his reputation as a novelist must depend.

15 Anthony Cronin makes this point in *No Laughing Matter: The Life and Times of Flann O'Brien* (London: Grafton Books, 1989), p. 106.

16 Flann O'Brien, *At Swim-Two-Birds* (1939; London: Four Square Books, 1962), p. 55.

17 As noted by A. Clissmann, *Flann O'Brien: A Critical Introduction to His Writings* (Dublin: Gill and Macmillan, 1975), p. 173.

18 Flann O'Brien, *The Third Policeman* (1967; London: Picador, 1974), p. 172.

19 Clissmann, *Flann O'Brien*, pp. 169–70.

20 For a study of the western island as cultural myth, see J. W. Foster, *Fictions of the Irish Literary Revival: A Changeling Art* (Dublin: Gill and Macmillan, 1987), pp. 94–113.

21 Cronin, *No Laughing Matter*, p. 106.

CHAPTER 9

Patrick Kavanagh: religious poet

Patrick Kavanagh possessed an unusually powerful intellect. This made him a caustic, even occasionally brutal, critic of his contemporaries and an acute commentator on Irish life, its social forms and its psychological deformations. The power and force of his poems *The Great Hunger, Lough Derg*, the knowledgeable intimacy with his own place in *Tarry Flynn*, are now recognised as among the most authentic reports from an indigenous Irish world which, since William Carleton opened its realities to inspection in the nineteenth century, had endured various forms of literary misrepresentation, exploitation and creative re-invention. In granting Kavanagh this intimacy with what is reckoned by many of his admirers as the literary authentic, a kind of critical consensus has developed which fails to take account of the subtlety and sophistication, the power indeed, of Kavanagh's mind as it operates on an area of experience other than the social and psychological: the religious.

To make such a claim, however, is to fly in the face of several attributes of his oeuvre which would tend to make such a claim seem difficult to defend. There is the somewhat pallid pietism of the early verses, with their shy, chaste Mariolatry and too ready acquiescence in religiose emotion:

> Here I wait
> On the world's rim
> Stretching out hands
> To seraphim.[1]

There is also the tiresome invective in his many *obiter dicta* against Protestantism which verge on the ignorance of mere sectarianism, as there is his simplistic identification of Catholicism with a true Ireland, which makes him seem at times as critically limited as any Irish Irelander or narrow nationalist possessed of stereotypes and myths of an essential Irishry.

It is difficult to take seriously as a religious thinker one who announces as gospel:

There is in this city a powerfully co-ordinated group of malicious mediocrities, mainly Protestant based, about which I have to explain. The real objection I have to the Protestant section here is not that – like the rest of the population – they are mostly fools and knaves; my objection is that they have not thrown up a single man, to my knowledge, who takes the dispassionate view without regard for his own petty interest. I presume it is a question of intelligence and the Protestant population being small, may be producing the percentage that is normal in the world.[2]

Yet despite these caveats, I believe that Kavanagh was a profoundly religious thinker whose analysis of Irish society proceeded from an instinctive yet seriously considered view of life rooted in his own deeply spiritual nature. In a country of rampant piety and theological ignorance, Kavanagh was that rare kind of individual, the religious thinker who probed his own faith in poems of shocking honesty and who sought to make that faith meaningful in daily existence. The result was that equally rare thing in Ireland: a body of imaginative writings which makes an original and compelling contribution to the history of religious thought that as yet has scarcely begun to receive its due.

These are large claims and I must attempt to justify them. Kavanagh's perennial and fundamental sense of the world was that daily life afforded the receptive, even passive soul the fullness of a created order. He shared the contemplative's disinclination to demand of life that it make rationally discernible sense or offer immediate, philosophically coherent meanings. Rather he apprehended a world that shared with the idea of divinity itself an unchanging givenness. He accordingly saw the world in a manner wholly at odds with contemporary progressive opinion, which Kavanagh loudly deprecated. Reality in Kavanagh's estimate might indeed be unspeakable, unwriteable, as indeed the mystical traditions of all religions have perennially told us is the case. In a powerful passage in the novel *By Night Unstarred* (unpublished in his lifetime), Kavanagh sought to represent the unrepresentable as follows:

The light of the intangible Truth had flashed across the hills to him and, that he knew, was something to be grateful for, something worth being born to misery for.

He had seen that light flash on the hills: it might be the sun going down or it might be nothing nameable at all. It was just the hint of the miracle of Creation that makes poets gasp …

Natural life, lived naturally as it is lived in the countryside has none of that progress which is the base of happiness. Men and women in rural communities can be compared to a spring that rises out of a rock and spreads in irregular ever-widening circles. But the general principle is static. Rural life is all background. Life in cities is not a spring but a river, or rather a watermain. It progresses like a novel, artificially. There is no progression in art; there is none in life. And a man coming from a circular static mood to the forward hurry of city life is at a disadvantage.[3]

Throughout his poetic career Kavanagh sought to produce an art which eschewed progression and which bore witness to the timeless stasis of a world which revealed itself as repeated patterns. Now it is easy enough to characterise such passages as the one quoted above as simple Romanticism (is Romanticism ever simple?), a sub-Wordsworthian, conventional summoning up of appropriate tropes to salute the visionary gleam. But in Kavanagh's career the impulse to suggest a timeless stasis, a weightless, immaterial, non-intrusive mode of consciousness is too pervasive to be dismissed as merely a Romantic affectation. Indeed its eschewal of the power of consciousness as a transformative agent in such poems as the famous 'Shancoduff' certainly sets it in a zone of feeling remote from the egotistical sublime. And with the exception of some of his love poems, there is in his writing little of that dramatisation of loss of vision which is a salient characteristic of the romantic mood in one of its most intense guises. By contrast, in poem after poem Kavanagh summons the moment into existence in the context of an eternal present tense which serves as a magnetic charge, attracting past and future to the still point of the poems' weightless immediacy. 'Peace' of 1943 is exemplary. The poem opens *in medias res* as if in the full instantaneity of the passing moments:

> And sometimes I am sorry when the grass
> Is growing over stones in quiet hollows
> And the cocksfoot leans across the rutted cart-pass
> That I am not the voice of country fellows
> Who are now standing by some headland talking
> Of turnips and potatoes or young corn
> Or turf banks stripped for victory.[4]

Note how the temporally situated voice of the poet ('And sometimes' with its unspoken shadow 'Other times') in the context of 'quiet hollows' is compared with a different order of voice, that of 'country fellows' who occupy in this poem of the war years with its references to the past ('Here Peace is still hawking') and hoped for victory an order of being which shares with the seasons a perpetual present tense, transcending all quotidian moments:

> Upon a headland by a whiny hedge
> A hare sits looking down a leaf-lapped furrow
> There's an old plough upside-down on a weedy ridge
> And someone is shouldering home a saddle-harrow.
> Out of that childhood country what fools climb
> To fight with tyrants Love and Life and Time.[5]

For all the ostensible nostalgia of this poem, its dominant note is a celebration of that sense of a composed, reposeful stasis in the order of things which, as his career progressed, was to become one of the poet's principal emotional and spiritual preoccupations. It was a state of being in the world to which the individual and art itself should aspire. It was consciousness of the challenging spiritual demands that this awareness involved which caused the poet to deprecate his own poem *The Great Hunger* for its lack of 'the nobility and repose' of poetry.[6] To discover what Kavanagh might have meant by such noble repose, the reader can turn to a poem like 'October', from the volume *Come Dance With Kitty Stobling* (1960), a later lyric where a timeless mode of consciousness rooted in an apprehension of the unchanging reality of the world is celebrated. 'The pattern of movement' on an October street in Dublin is 'Precisely the same' as broke the poet's heart decades before in a Monaghan adolescence.[7]

Through much of Kavanagh's poetry, this sense of the world arranging itself in repeated patterns that transcend normal time is mediated in a constant alertness to the cycle of the seasons and, in his early and middle years, to the liturgical year of the Christian Church. Both seasons and feasts, and their intertwining in his imagination, bear symbolic testimony to an unchanging endlessly repeated order of being. Nature herself, and this becomes more marked in his later poetry as his emotional involvement with ecclesiastical life waned, seems to participate in this sacramental reality. The colours of the year, particularly the yellow of autumn (the poem 'October' links here with 'Yellow Vestment' with its 'Water lilies waiting to be enchanted by a folk-song chanted' to make this explicit), seem to participate in a liturgically ordered world, with specific flowers – primroses, bluebells – emerging in their season like colours in the Church's own symbology.[8] As he writes in 'On Reading A Book On Common Wild Flowers',

> I knew them all by eyesight long before I knew their names.
> We were in love before we were introduced.
> Let me not moralize or have remorse, for these names

> Purify a corner of my mind;
> I jump over them and rub them with my hands,
> And a free moment appears brand new and spacious
> Where I may live beyond the reach of desire.[9]

It was of course very difficult for Kavanagh to reconcile this mystical sense of things with his equally intimate knowledge of the destructive aspects of religion in Irish rural life. In the 1940s the pressure of experience had stimulated the long poems in which he explored this problem most fully in such works as *The Great Hunger*, *Lough Derg* and *Why Sorrow*. In *Kavanagh's Weekly* (the periodical he produced with his brother Peter in the early 1950s and largely wrote himself), he was later to conclude of his own investigative efforts:

In Ireland we still have a strong Catholic religion, at least on the surface, but how deeply that religion influences men's minds is another question. Out of our own experience we cannot say that we found it influenced men on any fundamental issue. When we listened to men being themselves it was not religion that spoke but money and materialism in general.[10]

The Great Hunger is the work which addresses the quality of Irish faith most searchingly. As Antoinette Quinn has argued in her authoritative study of the poet, *Patrick Kavanagh: Born-Again Romantic*, this poem is a 'prophetic condemnation of rural Ireland … inspired by an intensely Christian interpretation of the holiness of human life'.[11] And she accurately identifies its theology as Joannine and the doctrine of the Incarnation as its central religious point of reference: 'Christ's incarnation is here envisioned not as some far off divine event but as a present meta-physicality, a quickening spirit that sanctifies the flesh.'[12] This directs us in Quinn's reading of the poem to the poet's sense of immanence in the bits and pieces of daily life ('Primroses and the unearthly start of ferns / Among the blackthorn shadows in the ditch'[13]) which a peasant Catholicism denies, as it neglects in a frightened puritanism the spirituality of the created order made manifest in the cycle of the seasons and the fertility of nature and the animal world. But Quinn does not take us quite far enough, to the point where the poem addresses in complex detail the doctrine of Incarnation (summoned to mind in the Joannine parody of the opening lines), and where the nature of Maguire's faith is examined directly. This occurs in cantos six and seven of the work, and they bear close analysis.

The season is May. Maguire dreams of 'Health and wealth and love'.[14] He watches children, whom he will never have, 'Picking up a primrose here and a daisy there – / They were picking up life's truth singly.'[15] By contrast, and here is his religious error, Maguire 'dreamt of the Absolute envased bouquet – / All or nothing'.[16] He hopes for absolute health, wealth and love, so that his dreams become 'Three frozen idols of a speechless muse'.[17] His sin is that of idolatry and a consequent misinterpretation of the doctrine of the Incarnation, symbolised in the Eucharist. For as the voice of the poet advises, 'in a crumb of bread the whole mystery is'.[18] So Maguire is admonished:

> He read the symbol too sharply and turned
> From the five simple doors of sense
> To the door whose combination lock has puzzled
> Philosopher and priest and common dunce.[19]

Maguire in the narrow fields of Monaghan is a closet idealist as well as closet masturbator, who turns in his sexual frustration to an idolatrous hope for perfection and a sinful denial of God present in the 'bits and pieces of Everyday'.[20] We see him sitting watching an 'evening / Too beautifully perfect to use'.[21] The consequences of such spiritual error are manifest in the next canto, number seven, as he listens to his mother's lie told it seems to restrain what she fears may be an unbridled sexuality which she and the priesthood believe requires the curb of conscience. In fact he lives in life-denying mystical aspiration for a transcendence from which he as a peasant must feel excluded. The women who desire him will never be satisfied in 'A metaphysical land / Where flesh was a thought more spiritual than music / Among the stars – out of reach of the peasant's hand'.[22] I read this enigmatic assertion as follows. Maguire as idealist falsely believes that in a true spirituality flesh would be transformed into something as insubstantial as thought, more spiritual even than the music of the spheres. Maguire is the absolutist, a Platonist who wishes for pure form, the idea of beauty rather than its flawed fleshy manifestation in the real world. He denies the central truth of the Incarnation with its implication that Word becoming flesh made sacred the stuff of our daily existence, that life is sacramental, with the Mass the key sign of that truth. And as a consequence of this theological misinterpretation, wrought of a troika of forces represented by a widowed mother, complicit church and grim economic necessity, Maguire develops his perversely ascetic, masochistic version of Christianity. So the question asked later in the poem is not a simply droll one: 'was he then a saint? / A Matt Talbot of Monaghan'.[23]

Through the poem, as we follow Maguire in the stages of his life and the slow atrophy of his powers, we are made aware of that ordinary life which he has rejected. The earth brings forth its flowers and fruits in their seasons. The natural world is one of teeming foison. Work, though cruelly arduous, is also sensuously satisfying; daily life can release signs of vitality:

> The yellow buttercups and the bluebells among the whin bushes
> On rocks in the middle of ploughing
> Was a bright spoke in the wheel
> Of the peasant's mill.[24]

And the swift, earthy demotic of the talk, wonderfully caught in the poem's own twists and turns of tone, its blend of portentous statement and sharp, ironic commentary, its metaphoric and metonymic amplitude, also suggest all the idealist is driven to disregard in the idolatrous worship of the Absolute.

Kavanagh, *The Great Hunger* gives us to understand, was deeply engaged by the idea of incarnation, reading it as a theological substantiation of his own instinctive sense of the holiness of things. The poem is therefore a remarkable study of the destructive impact on individual and collective life of what he sensed was an Irish perversion of a creed which could be profoundly life-enhancing.

Whether Kavanagh continued, as he grew older, to view the Christian faith as capable of giving doctrinal shape and theological endorsement to his own thoughtful spirituality is a question which as yet has not been fully addressed by his critics, though Quinn comes close in her study when she advises 'Although he described the poet as a "theologian" in "From Monaghan to the Grand Canal", Kavanagh was not "steel'd in the school of old Aquinas" and his relationship to Christianity was closer to Shakespeare's or Cervantes' than to Dante's.'[25] She recognises too that 'the mystical experience most frequently described in Kavanagh's poetry is the mental state in which poetry originates, a state often portrayed through Christian imagery'.[26] What her treatment of the late work indicates is that Kavangh increasingly came to worship in a non-dogmatic, non-credal fashion the creative impulse itself, and the state of waiting for the spark from heaven to fall, as in, for example. 'Having Confessed'. What for me adds a real complexity and interest to these late poems, which might otherwise remain simply expressions of a rather too easily won quietism of feeling, a slightly self-satisfied identification of a Mucker fog with the cloud of unknowing, is that the poet felt compelled to explore his mystical experience of the world in a series of extraordinary sonnets. In modern literature a tendency to highlight special

moments of intensified perception or awareness is, certainly, ubiquitous. Out of the random disorder of contingent reality some moments
can seem charged with special significance, like Pateresque pulsations,
to be saluted in tones and suggestions of the exquisite deriving from
Pater's sceptical melancholy, or from a Hardy-like stoicism. Stephens,
Frost, MacNeice, T. S. Eliot all would supply exemplary instances. In
these poets' works the heightened moment simply occurs, in a waste of
moments. In Eliot: 'Ridiculous the waste sad time / Stretching before and
after'; on a walk around a lake in Stephens; in Frost with an ambiguous
pebble of quartz in a pool; when someone 'stopped the moving stairs' in
MacNeice. In Kavanagh's poems of 'spots in time' the use of the sonnet
form suggests that the moment of revelation is not simply a random mystical experience of a customarily secularised consciousness, as it is even
in T. S. Eliot. Rather, it seems a true gift vouchsafed to the artist who
has sought to apprehend reality according to a deep sense of the metaphysical and moral implications of pattern and order themselves. 'I am
very fond', Kavanagh stated in a lecture at University College, Dublin,
'of the sonnet form, and not merely because it has been the most popular form for the the expression of love but because its strict rules, which
like the other rules Shakespeare broke so wonderfully, forces the mind to
moral activity, but is not itself forced.'[27] What I believe occurs in a small
number of remarkable later poems by Kavanagh is that the pattern of
life, a life in which pattern implies an unchanging stasis which the poet
sensed he had known in the Monaghan countryside, is paradigmatically
realised in the composure and vision of such works as the Canal Bank
poems and 'The Chest Hospital'. In these poems the sonnet form holds
the charged moments which they greet in a force field of moral and religious energies, that is energies which are productive of an act of worship
directed towards the good and the beautiful. And such an orientation of
the mind and heart, as the mystics of many traditions have instructed
us, is the beginning of wisdom, the source of all religious truth. 'I can
still see', Kavanagh stated in 1956 'that life and those houses with their
gables to the road. In front of the house in the yard, or as it was called,
the street, stood a tub which was used for washing the potatoes for the
dinner. If I walked into a house the pattern was the same throughout all
that area; and just now the item of furniture which evoked the whole
scene for me is the salt-box, a box like a small bin with a sloping door
like the top of a desk, and this salt-box hung beside the fire to keep the
salt dry. Nothing in that life has changed in a hundred-and-fifty years
since the time of Carleton.'[28]

For Kavanagh the poetic equivalent of such a glimpse of visionary stasis, which his memory treasures in details drawn as if from some Dutch still life of the seventeenth century, is the nobility and repose of true poetry, of a formal art which snatches out of time the passionate transitory and makes it the stuff of such an indisputably religious and persuasive sonnet as 'Question to Life', with its rhapsodic injunction:

> So be reposed and praise, praise praise
> The way it happened and the way it was.[29]

NOTES

1 P. Kavanagh, *Collected Poems* (London: MacGibbon and Kee, 1964), p. 8.
2 P. Kavanagh, *November Haggard: Uncollected Prose and Verse of Patrick Kavanagh*, ed. Peter Kavanagh (New York: Kavanagh, 1971), p.75.
3 P. Kavanagh, *By Night Unstarred: An Autobiographical Novel*, ed. Peter Kavanagh (The Curragh, Ireland: Goldsmith Press), pp. 131–2.
4 Kavanagh, *Collected Poems*, p. 31
5 *Ibid.*
6 P. Kavanagh, *Collected Prose* (London: MacGibbon and Kee, 1976), p. 21.
7 Kavanagh, *Collected Poems*, p. 159.
8 *Ibid.*, p. 157.
9 *Ibid.*, p. 137.
10 Kavanagh, *Collected Prose*, pp. 151–2.
11 Antoinette Quinn, *Patrick Kavanagh: Born-Again Romantic* (Dublin: Gill and Macmillan, 1991), p. 124.
12 *Ibid.*
13 Kavanagh, *Collected Poems*, p. 38.
14 *Ibid.*, p. 41.
15 *Ibid.*
16 *Ibid.*
17 *Ibid.*, p. 42.
18 *Ibid.*, p. 41.
19 *Ibid.*
20 *Ibid.*, p. 42.
21 *Ibid.*
22 *Ibid.*
23 *Ibid.*, p 49.
24 *Ibid.*, p. 45.
25 Quinn, *Born-Again Romantic*, p. 389.
26 *Ibid.*, pp. 389–90.
27 Kavanagh, *November Haggard*, p. 65.
28 *Ibid.*, p. 70.
29 Kavanagh, *Collected Poems*, p. 164.

CHAPTER 10

MacNeice's Irelands: MacNeice's islands

An island means isolation; the words are the same. We expect in
an island to meet with insular vices. What is shocking is to find an
island invaded by the vices of the mainland.

Louis MacNeice, *I Crossed the Minch*

The question of Louis MacNeice's Irishness can still generate controversy in Ireland. It may now be fairly widely accepted that MacNeice was
one of the most accomplished of the post-Yeatsian generation of poets,
but this Oxford-educated and London-domiciled, displaced Northern
Irishman is still sometimes disallowed a role in the intellectual life of the
Ireland of his day. As long ago as 1974 the poet Derek Mahon opined that
he had played no role in the country's intellectual life and seemed unwilling, even as late as 1985 in an interview with myself as editor of the *Poetry
Ireland Review*, to retract.[1] And in 1987 Denis Donoghue, reviewing a
volume of MacNeice's selected criticism in the *London Review of Books* (23
April), was able to use the original Mahon *obiter dictum*[2] as a stick to beat
those of us who think that the statement requires at the least substantial
qualification if it cannot be completely contradicted.

There is, of course, lots of evidence to support the Donoghue line.
In Armitage and Clark's less than fully dependable bibliography of
MacNeice's work,[3] we find that MacNeice in the course of a prolific
poetic career published in only two Irish periodicals: in *The Bell*, when
he was poetry editor, and once in *Lagan*, the Northern Irish annual associated with the Ulster regionalist movement of the 1940s. For the rest,
he sent his new poems out to the English periodicals and apart from
his short collection *The Last Ditch*, published in Dublin in 1940 by the
Cuala Press, for which the Yeats sisters were responsible, he looked to
Fabers when he sought volume publication. A Dublin rhyme summed it
up: 'Let him go back and labour / For Faber and Faber'. Except for the
possibility that he might have been appointed to the Chair of English

Literature in Trinity College, Dublin, when it fell vacant in 1939, he does not seem ever to have seriously contemplated living as an adult in Ireland. While he had a small circle of friends whom he visited in the North, he had far fewer contacts with the writers, artists and littérateurs who constituted the intellectual life of independent Ireland than had, for example, his friend W. R. Rodgers, whose work on Irish literary portraits for the BBC brought him together with most of the leading figures in Dublin in the period.[4]

The problem was, of course, that MacNeice was born too late to play the sort of role he might have done in the pre-independence quickening of intellectual life that we know as the Irish Literary Revival. This flowering had attracted his own future editor, the Banbridge-born E. R. Dodds, who had tried to learn Irish in the Gaelic League in Dublin and had served with Yeats on the committee to save the Lane bequest for Ireland. Dodds had also made a close friend of the scholar, republican and translator Stephen MacKenna, until marriage, employment and disillusionment at the violence of 1916 took him to the England where, in a career as a classics don in Birmingham and Oxford, he was increasingly to lose touch with the Ireland where he had spent a heady youth, when being an Irish poet had not seemed impossible.[5] By the time MacNeice himself was an Oxford undergraduate, Ireland was already establishing compulsory Gaelic in the schools and was on the way to banning books. About the former of these post-revolutionary enterprises, MacNeice took the attitude characteristic of most people of his class and background. In *I Crossed the Minch* (1938), he expressed sorrow that he knew no Gaelic as he headed for the Scottish islands to write a book about them, hoping that the Celt in him 'would be drawn to the surface by the magnetism of his fellows'.[6] But in *Autumn Journal*, he advises contemptuously of the Irish Free State's efforts to make the Irish form of the language available to Irish schoolchildren: 'let them fumble their sums in a half-dead language'.[7] And in his 'Alphabets of Literary Prejudices', published in 1948, he opines that 'Gaelic is a fine Language but the Gaelic League in Ireland is barking up the wrong flagpole. Eire having won her rightful independence, should be able to drop this propaganda which nearly all her citizens see through. When will well-known Irish writers who publish nothing but English stop preaching nothing but Irish?'[8]

It was not simply censorship and compulsory Irish, however, that MacNeice found distasteful about independent Ireland. An unpublished play, written in 1934 and performed in Birmingham, suggests that he thought 1930s Ireland ripe for Fascism, for this burlesque-like work has a woman declare herself dictator of Ireland complete with propaganda corps and enemies of the people. The leaderene raises revenue in this dramatic *jeu d'esprit* by the export of a drink brewed from seaweed. That MacNeice was in fact alert to the reactionary forces at work in Ireland in the 1930s is more convincingly evidenced by his reference to James Connolly in 'Eclogue From Iceland', where he has the Irishman Ryan, one of the three participants in the eclogue's debate, celebrate the socialist and 1916 martyr, declaring 'there was Connolly / Vilified now by the gangs of Catholic action'.[9] Yet this is one of the very few references in his 1930s poetry that shows MacNeice with any very clear picture as to what was actually going on in the Ireland that he rejected in a series of poems. And it is this sense that the Ireland he dismissed bore scant resemblance to the Ireland painfully establishing itself in the post-independence period that perhaps accounts for the coolness with which MacNeice was regarded by many of his Irish contemporaries and which still results in charges of the kind Donoghue laid against him. 'Valediction' and section XIV of *Autumn Journal* are the key texts.

Both of these long complex poems have their say on the North, about which MacNeice was emotionally much more convincing than about the South of Ireland. For the North he felt a profound distaste of the angry, pained kind we meet also in his poem 'Belfast'. But both poems seem to suggest, almost by extension, that the fixity of life he found so repugnant about the North was also characteristic of the South, even if it expressed it in a different fashion. The North is frozen, in his 1930s poems about it, in a condition for which its native basalt is an appropriate metaphor. It is a land of 'callous lava cooled to stone'.[10] The South, softer, romantic, lost in the past, a land of postcard images, is a place of drug-dull fatalism (a national stereotype which goes back to the Bishop Berkeley of *The Querist*) in which he can only imagine participating in terms of 'gesture' or of what he calls 'each imposture'. And crucially, in 'Valediction', he indicts the country for intellectual inadequacy of a definitive kind:

> The land will remain as it was,
> But no abiding content can grow out of these minds
> Fuddled with blood, always caught by blinds …[11]

And we remember that the single Irish intellectual whom Ryan *had* been able to extol along with the revolutionary Connolly in 'Eclogue From Iceland', written in 1936, was Dodd's friend and hero Stephen MacKenna, who in MacNeice's version of his career

> Spent twenty years translating Greek philosophy
> Ill and tormented, unwilling to break contract,

> A brilliant talker who left
> The salon for the solo flight of Mind.[12]

Dodds had edited *The Journal and Letters of Stephen MacKenna* with a memoir in 1936, and it was probably from this that MacNeice derived his impression of MacKenna as the Irish outsider, the quixotic Irish patriot who worked through ill health and penury to produce his famous translation of Plotinus. For MacNeice, he seems to have been the solitary exception which proved the rule enunciated in 'Valediction' in 1934 – no abiding content can grow out of Irish minds. Indeed the lines show the direct influence of Dodds, who had cited in his memoir a review of the translation by AE. AE had written of MacKenna's sentences that 'they keep their upward flight like great slow-moving birds',[13] a mode of thought quite different from that attributed by Ryan in the eclogue to his fellow-countrymen, who shoot 'straight in the cause of crooked thinking'.[14]

In *Autumn Journal*, Ireland is reckoned a country in thrall to intransigent forces of one kind or another – in the grip of single purposes founded on a jumble of opposites. It is a reality governed by atavism, irrationality, where one faction is as bad as the other. This sense of things emerges most vigorously in the poem during the opening lines on the North, where MacNeice writes

> And one read black where the other read white, his hope
> The other man's damnation:
> Up the Rebels, To Hell with the Pope,
> And God Save – as you prefer – the King or Ireland.[15]

The entire passage oddly blends denunciation of Northern intransigence with images of Ireland as a whole, of the kind he had used in 'Valediction'. These are snapshots, even cinematic shots, employed to create an impression of Ireland's intractable political imbroglio: 'The landowner shot in his bed / … the angry voices / Piercing the broken fanlight in the slum'.[16] Such images are juxtaposed with others that suggest the hold of Ireland in her feminine and mysterious guise, which prompts the poet to reflect, in the most analytic section of the poem, on the question he poses himself: 'Why do we like being Irish?' Firstly, he says, 'It gives us a hold on the sentimental English',[17] begging two questions – what is meant by 'us' in this context and are the English sentimental? But more positively he evokes the virtues of the small community:

> And partly because Ireland is small enough
> To be still thought of with a family feeling,
> And because the waves are rough

That split her from a more commercial culture:
And because one feels that here at least one can
Do local work which is not at the world's mercy
And that on this tiny stage with luck a man
Might see the end of one particular action.[18]

Only to deny their validity with real bitterness: 'It is self-deception of course; / There is no immunity in this island either'.[19] One wonders, immunity from what? But that is unresolved as the poet launches into a lengthy denunciation of the South's political and economic culture, which echoes the passage on the North in its assumption that Ireland is characterised by a deadly tendency to generate sterile and somehow unreal oppositions – in the North Orange and Green, in the South patriots and traitors, sheep and goats.

For the rest, the analysis is variously superficial, disdainful and even contradictory: an absurdity like the censorship of books is equated with urban renewal; Ireland's economy is dismissed as 'A cart that is drawn by somebody else's horse / And carrying goods to somebody else's market'.[20] Written at the end of a six-year period in which Ireland had attempted a painful self-sufficiency, with an economic war fought against Britain, this is woefully inadequate – even a gratuitously offensive slur. Combined with scorn, it becomes readily apparent why the poem's perspectives can still stir local feeling:[21] 'Let them grow beet-sugar; let them build / A factory in every hamlet'.[22] (MacNeice's Church of Ireland clergyman father had served briefly in County Waterford, a centre of sugar-beet production.) Of course to read the poem in this way is to read it too literally; it is the expression of a mood not a documentary report. Yet the documentary techniques of the poem itself, its cinematic and photographic realism, its easy evocation of social reality, all incline a reader to take it seriously as rapportage, and as such to enter objections. In doing so, one may be not only forgetting that *Autumn Journal* is a poem but may be missing the ambivalence of feeling in this section. For there is real disappointment present in the passage I have quoted. And to understand this is to allow MacNeice a more intimate involvement with independent Ireland than anything I have highlighted so far might suggest.

The hint that something more complex than ignorant dismissal is at work in this passage is in the line 'There is no immunity in this island either.' A careless reading might assume that by 'this island' he means Ireland as compared to the neighbouring island of Britain, forgetting that MacNeice had been much concerned with islands in the years before he wrote *Autumn Journal* – with Iceland, with the Hebrides. He had even written about London Zoo as if it were a kind of island in the seas of metropolitan life, in his book *Zoo* (1938). And passages in his book about the Hebrides, *I Crossed the Minch* (1938), suggest that in *Autumn Journal* it is those islands he has in mind as he writes about the south of Ireland. In the prose text his ambivalence of feeling about such small communities is much more obvious than it is in the passage from the poem which I have criticised.

In the Hebrides MacNeice is able to recognise the validity of nationalism:

Scotland as a whole will never again regain a vital self-consciousness of her unity and individuality, but such a thing is still just possible for the Gaelic-speaking islands as a group in separation from the mainland. Their traditional language needs no artificial cultivation, their population is small enough to allow a genuine community feeling, their social life is still homogeneous (though commercialisation may soon drive rifts through it), lastly the sea still separates them from their neighbours.[23]

So stimulated, he turns to Ireland and her nationalism:

Nationalism of the Irish type is often regarded as reactionary. With the World revolution and the Classless Society waiting for the midwife, why take a torch to the stable to assist at the birth of a puppy? Even if the puppy is pedigree. On this question I am unable to make up my mind. When I am in Ireland I find myself becoming Nationalist. If I lived in the Hebrides, I should certainly plump for the puppy.[24]

There is in all of this, one realises, a deep concern for the survival of local communities and a terrible suspicion that what he calls 'commercialisation', and what others in the 1930s would have identified as capitalism, will render such concern vain. Economic independence seems even more absurd in the Hebrides than it does in Ireland; but his remarks on the future of the islands do cast a softening light on the harsh strictures of the passage in *Autumn Journal*.

It would be absurd to suggest that the Hebrides should attempt to be self-supporting – economically independent. (No-one, as far as I know, has yet introduced into the Hebrides the bogey of beet-sugar with its accompanying chorus of rats [MacNeice seems to have had a thing about beet-sugar].) Some compromise, however, should be possible which would preserve the islands' social and cultural independence. Economically they should be allowed to adjust to their bigger neighbours without kowtowing to them.[25]

In writing about the Hebrides, therefore, MacNeice was able to achieve a balance and dispassionate good sense that tended to escape him when he wrote of Ireland, where the intensity of his feelings produced what he admitted were present in the work: 'overstatements ... e.g. in the passages dealing with Ireland'.[26] In *I Crossed the Minch*, it was possible to see an Ireland in miniature on the Hebridean isles and to contemplate the social and economic life of both without the bitterness and anger which disturbed the poet as he inspected his native land directly. On the Hebrides, MacNeice can ponder the claims of the local, island community, as against those of the developing international order, without rancour; 'A world society must be a federation of differentiated communities, not a long line of robots doing the goose-step':

> Are the family, the local community, the clique community of ideas, personal relationships, even persons themselves, to be jettisoned in order that Collective Man may keep floating? I think not ... It is an admirable hope that the peoples of the world shall understand one another and that one man shall understand his neighbour but not if there is nothing to understand. Any development means differentiation.[27]

Independence and local culture on the Hebrides are not associated with reactionary ideas in the way they are in *Autumn Journal*, where the poet dismissively advises 'Let the round tower stand aloof / In a world of bursting mortar'.[28]

So MacNeice's attitude to islands in these various texts is markedly ambivalent. He was attracted by much in island life; but there was something he distrusted about islands, as well as finding in them images of possible social life, paradigms of a coherent international order. They represented evasion, escapism, an unwillingness to confront responsibility. In Iceland, which he visited with W. H. Auden in 1936, it was a relief to discover what he called in 'Letter to Graham and Anna' 'The necessity of the silence of the islands',[29] yet he also realised that this was an interlude:

> Here is a different rhythm, the juggled balls
> Hang in the air – the pause before the soufflé falls ...
> Here we can practise forgetfulness ...[30]

His poem 'On Those Islands', with which *I Crossed the Minch* concludes, is richly celebratory of Hebridean life, but in a hypnotic manner situating the islands as a mysterious place apart. The repeated phrase 'On those islands', running through the poem, has an oddly narcotic effect as if the place fulfils the dream of 'Postscript to Iceland': 'In that island never found / Visions blossom from the ground.'[31] They remain, however, visions, unreal and tantalising in equal degree, a dream-fantasy of community and belonging, of the kind MacNeice could never allow himself in relation to the Ireland whose claims on him were all the more immediate. Of her he felt driven to write in *Autumn Journal*:

> She is both a bore and a bitch;
> Better close the horizon,
> Send her no more fantasy, no more longings which
> Are under a fatal tariff.[32]

Tariffs had, of course, played their part in the economic war (it was sometimes known as the Tariff War) that concluded in 1938 between Britain and Ireland with the return of the Treaty ports. Tariffs had helped to maintain that isolation in Ireland that MacNeice both admired and distrusted in the islands he visited and wrote about in the 1930s. Within months of the publication *of Autumn Journal*, it was more than tariffs which separated the citizens of southern Ireland from those of the United Kingdom. For MacNeice, Irish neutrality in the Second World War was a surrender to the temptation that islands inevitably suffer – myopic self-regard. Writing in 1954 in a review of *The Letters of W. B. Yeats*, he offered the acerbic comment that 'Vacillation between would-be fascism and neutrality (encouraged by an ignorance of history) may well be characteristic of Yeats but is also characteristic of his country.'[33] In Dublin in 1939, when war was declared, he had been appalled at how little the fact seemed to concern the local literati. And in 1943 he published 'Neutrality', which indicts Ireland for callous disregard of her neighbours' fate in the Battle of the North Atlantic. Significantly the poem begins: 'The neutral island facing the Atlantic, / The neutral island in the heart of man.'[34] Ireland is an island behaving the way islands do. For the ideal of the island is a kind of evasive innocence, an archaic dream of origins and independence.

The war ended, a visit to Ireland by MacNeice resulted in a cluster of 'Irish' poems in the volume of 1948, *Holes in the Sky*: 'Garrick Revisited', 'Slum Song', 'The Strand', 'Last Before America'. The tone now, however, is more dispassionate, more like, indeed, the tone employed in the descriptions of the Hebrides in *I Crossed the Minch*:

> At night the accordian melts in the wind from the sea
> From the bourne of emigrant uncle and son, a defeated
> Music that yearns and abdicates; chimney-smoke and spindrift
> Mingle and part as ghosts do. The decree
> Of the sea's divorce is final.[35]

But the attraction of islands remains for the poet who can now contemplate his own country as

an image
For those who despise charts but find their dream's endorsement
In certain long low islets snouting towards the west
Like cubs that have lost their mother.[36]

And *Holes in the Sky* also contains the complex meditative poem on the island sensibility, 'No more sea', with its echoes of and allusions to earlier poems. The poem evokes the silence of islands, which of necessity he had admitted in his 'Letter to Graham and Anna', while the phrase 'a fossil / Mind in its day both its own king and castle'[37] reminds us that in section XVI of *Autumn Journal* he had excoriated an island 'assumption that everyone cares / Who is the king of your castle.'[38] Now in a world that seems to be moving towards some universal dryness of the spirit, towards drab uniformity, to live as an islander 'embroiled with ocean'[39] has its own symbolic attractions. Thereafter in MacNeice's poetry, Ireland (in such poems as 'Western Landscape', 'Donegal Tryptich', 'Prologue' to *The Character of Ireland*) is associated with water, movement, an imaginative alternative to the increasingly homogeneous culture of a mass society. His immediate involvement with the island on which he had been born became, it is true, after this poetic re-entry, a matter of occasional visits and even more occasional poems (apart from his brief poetry editorship of *The Bell* in 1946 and 1947).[40] But an imaginative preoccupation with island possibilities, which remained with him to the end of his life, often brought Ireland to mind. And what he termed in his poem 'The Island', in *Ten Burnt Offerings*, 'the slow concord of an island'[41] was something he recognised as an alternative to the increasingly dehumanised mass society he came to detest in post-war Britain. If MacNeice's Ireland had never quite achieved such slow concord, his poetic analysis of the island condition, its weaknesses and its possible strengths, seems to me a significant contribution to the intellectual life of an island country – a contribution which, in a period of renewed national conflict and international restructuring, warrants attention.

NOTES

1 See *Poetry Ireland Review*, 14 (Autumn 1985), 19. Though in response to a questioning of this view, Mahon admitted that his generation of poets from the north of Ireland had made MacNeice part of Ireland's intellectual history and that 'he deserves to be more widely read in Ireland; and in England for that matter'.

2 See Derek Mahon, 'MacNeice in England and Ireland', in T. Brown and A. Reid (eds.), *Time Was Away: The World of Louis MacNeice* (Dublin: Dolmen Press, 1974), pp. 113–22.

3 C. M. Armitage and Neil Clark, *A Bibliography of the Works of Louis MacNeice* (Edmonton: University of Alberta Press, 1973).

4 See W. R. Rodgers, *Irish Literary Portraits* (London: BBC, 1972).

5 See E. R. Dodds, *Missing Persons* (Oxford: Clarendon Press, 1977).

6 Louis MacNeice, *I Crossed the Minch* (London: Longmans, Green and Co., 1938), p. 3.

7 E. R. Dodds (ed.), *The Collected Poems of Louis MacNeice* (London: Faber and Faber, 1966), p. 133.

8 Originally published in *Windmill*, 51 (March 1948); see A. Heuser (ed.), *Selected Literary Criticism of Louis MacNeice* (Oxford University Press, 1987), pp. 143–4.

9 Dodds (ed.), *Collected Poems*, p. 45.

10 *Ibid.*, p. 52.

11 *Ibid.*, p. 53.

12 *Ibid.*, p. 45.

13 Quoted in E. R. Dodds (ed.), *Journal and Letters of Stephen MacKenna*, with a memoir and a preface by Padraic Colum (London: Constable, 1936), p. 40.

14 Dodds (ed.), *Collected Poems*, p. 41.

15 *Ibid.*, p. 132.

16 *Ibid.*

17 *Ibid.*

18 *Ibid.*, p. 133.

19 *Ibid.*

20 *Ibid.*

21 Edna Longley has argued that this section on Ireland in the context of *Autumn Journal* as a whole serves a thematic purpose by highlighting the inadequacy of impassioned political commitments, thereby giving enhanced credibility to the liberal humanism of the work's overall stance. She states that 'By embodying the deadly alternative to liberal or tragic "doubt", MacNeice rescues it from charges of weakness'; Edna Longley, *Poetry in the Wars* (Newcastle upon Tyne: Bloodaxe, 1986), p. 90. This, of course, says nothing about the adequacy of MacNeice's assessment of Ireland's *res publica*, whatever the poetic significance of the passage in question.

22 Dodds (ed.), *Collected Poems*, p. 133.

23 MacNeice, *Minch*, p. 10.

24 *Ibid.*

25 *Ibid.*, p. 12.

26 MacNeice, 'Note' to 'Autumn Journal', in Dodds (ed.), *Collected Poems*, p. 101.

27 MacNeice, *Minch*, p. 101.

28 Dodds (ed.), *Collected Poems*, p. 133.

29 *Ibid.*, p. 62.

30 *Ibid.*, pp. 63–4.

31 *Ibid.*, p. 74.

32 *Ibid.*, p. 134.

33 Louis MacNeice, 'Endless Old Things', review of *The Letters of W. B. Yeats*, ed. Allan Wade in Heuser (ed.), *Selected Literary Criticism*, p. 190.

34 Dodds (ed.), *Collected Poems*, p. 202.

35 *Ibid.*, p. 226.

36 *Ibid.*, p. 227.

37 *Ibid.*

38 *Ibid.*, p 134.

39 *Ibid.*, p. 228.

40 *The Bell* was founded by Seán O'Faoláin in 1940 as a political and cultural monthly review. MacNeice took over the job of poetry editor from Geoffrey Taylor. During MacNeice's time with the journal the general editorship changed hands, passing to Peadar O'Donnell, a socialist and activist with whom MacNeice might have been expected to share a good deal as a fellow northerner (O'Donnell was a Donegal man). Whatever the reason, this one occasion when MacNeice might have played a direct part in the intellectual life of the country was a good deal less than a full success. A check through the files suggests that MacNeice lacked the contacts and the interest to make his editorship a vital one. There were months when no poems were published at all; and few of the poems which did in fact appear, apart from MacNeice's own and one or two by W. R. Rodgers and Roy McFadden, are in any way memorable (although MacNeice did publish Patrick Kavanagh's poem on Jim Larkin, a nice moment of contact between two contrasting Irish minds). MacNeice's involvement with *The Bell* petered out in May 1947.

41 Dodds (ed.), *Collected Poems*, p. 30.

Louis MacNeice and the Second World War

For Louis MacNeice, as for so many, 1939 was a year of journeyings. Hitler's invasion of the Sudetenland and the feeble response of the international community, as well as the involvement of the great powers in the Spanish Civil War and the horrors of *Kristalnacht*, had alerted the world to the imminence of a major conflagration in Europe. So last holidays abroad were enjoyed before once again the lights would go out all over the Continent, and hurried exiles were arranged as individuals and families sought sanctuary in regions and countries which might escape the nightmare to come. Urgent messages were carried from country to country in the hope that the disaster might be averted. It was, in Cyril Connolly's words, 'Closing time in the gardens of the west'. For many writers, accustomed to easy travel in a decade in which air as well as railway transport had made the crossing of international borders a natural thing, the prospect of being unable to enjoy such freedom was a fact which began to concentrate their minds in precise ways. Ezra Pound travelled in 1939 to his native United States in a vain attempt to influence governmental economic policy but chose to return to Italy to the tragic fate which awaited him there. Francis Stuart would wait a year before, in 1940, his dark angel would take him to Berlin and a complicity with the regime there that none of his subsequent writings nor the special pleadings of his apologists have quite been able to expunge. By contrast, Samuel Beckett heard the declaration of war in the Dublin suburb of Foxrock where he had spent the summer and hurried back to Paris, preferring, as he said, France at war to Ireland at peace, where he would eventually be honoured by the French Government for distinguished war service in the resistance to the Nazi tyranny. Louis MacNeice was also on holiday in Ireland on 3 September 1939. He spent the following day at the All-Ireland Hurling final between Cork and Kilkenny (in his record of the match MacNeice mistakes Kilkenny for Kerry).

I was alone with the catastrophe, spent Saturday drinking in a bar with the Dublin literati; they hardly mentioned the war but debated the correct versions of Dublin street songs. Sunday morning the hotel man woke me (I was sleeping late and sodden), said, 'England has declared war'. Chamberlain's speech on a record was broadcast over and over again during the day. I went to Croke Park in the afternoon to watch the All-Ireland hurling final – Cork in crimson against Kerry in orange and black. Talk of escapism, I thought ... There was a huge crowd of Gaelic Leaguers, all wearing their *fáine,* one-minded partisans.[1]

Escapism of course was much on MacNeice's mind in September and October of 1939. In January his friend W. H. Auden had emigrated to the United States with Christopher Isherwood. Furthermore, MacNeice himself had decided to abandon his lectureship in Classics at Bedford College in London, and America was beckoning. There was too the possibility of a chair in English literature in Trinity College, Dublin, which had just become vacant. About this MacNeice wrote in September to his friend and mentor, the classical scholar E. R. Dodds, 'I dare say this will scandalise you as being a kind of escapism but I can't really see that I should be doing any more for civilisation by what they say the intellectuals must do – propaganda work.'[2]

For MacNeice, of course, the decision about what he might do in the imminent war was complicated by his Irish nationality. For although throughout the 1930s he had written deprecatingly in his poetry about much that irritated and repelled him in Ireland north and south, MacNeice had no doubt that his patrimony was an Irish one. The MacNeices hailed from the west of Ireland and his father had even served in the Church of Ireland in County Waterford in the 1930s, further complicating his son's Northern Irish provenance. And his mentor Dodds (who had given him his first job in Birmingham), a Banbridge Protestant who had acted as secretary to Yeats in the Lane Committee in Dublin and had edited the *Journal and Papers of Stephen MacKenna*, was an Irish Nationalist of marked individuality. Indeed, in 1914 he had decided that 'this was not my war'.[3] And while the Rising of 1916 was not his rising either – 'Its price was in my view too high'[4] – he remembered in his memoirs, reflecting on Yeats's 'celebrated palinode':

I could not remain unaffected by the surge of sympathy which that poem immortalizes. It was impossible to withhold one's admiration from the heroic dreamers in the Dublin Post Office. And after the executions any notion of again putting on a British uniform, even in the harmless capacity of a hospital orderly [in which role Dodds had briefly acted in Serbia in 1915], became invincibly repugnant. If, as was threatened, an attempt were now made to impose conscription on the Irish people against their will, I was, like many others, determined to resist by force if I had no other option.[5]

In 1939 it is almost certain that MacNeice would have felt as an Irishman that it was not necessarily incumbent upon him to enlist in the British forces to fight against Germany. In 1941 he was to write after he had decided to return to London from the United States, 'I have never really thought of myself as British; if there is one country I feel at home in, it is Eire.'[6] Dodds, his older friend, would have understood, whatever his English contemporaries might have felt. For Dodds had remained in Oxford as a student until 1917, stubbornly expressing sympathy for the rebels of 1916 in the midst of world war. When he graduated in 1917, he took a post as a teacher in Kilkenny College and then at the High School in Dublin where he remained until 1919. It is this context of Irish Nationalist scruple about service in the King's uniform that gives meaning to MacNeice's letter to Dodds in October 1939 from Dublin, where he ponders the possibility of enlistment:

Down here one gets quite de- (or dis)orientated. It all sounds like a nightmare algebra which you have to change back into people being killed. It is all very well for everyone to go on saying 'Destroy Hitlerism' but what the hell are they going to construct? I am now falling into a sort of paradox which is: – if the war were a rational war leading somewhere, I should want to stay out of it in order to see where it led to: but if it is a hopeless war leading nowhere, I feel half inclined to take the King's shilling & escape – more likely than not – the frustration to come.[7]

As Irishman he reckons he has a perfectly honourable choice in the matter. No Englishman could justifiably censure him for disloyalty in not rallying to the colours. Indeed, he understands that from the nationalist point of view the war is England's war. By November 1939 we find him writing in even more troubled terms to Dodds from Belfast on precisely the issue that had confronted Dodds in 1914: 'the tiresome corollary of this from my point of view is that, *if it* is my war, I feel I ought to get involved in it in one of the more unpleasant ways'.[8]

In the new year (1940) it was not yet his war and he set out for America and a teaching post at Cornell. In Peter McDonald's words, 'to all appearances he had joined Auden, Isherwood and the rest in "escapism"'.[9] But of course he had not, as McDonald in his excellent study of MacNeice from which I have quoted these extracts from the poet's correspondence, understands, even if he fails fully to grasp how for MacNeice, the Irishman, the question of whether the war was his war was a very real one.

There was, however, something in what Ireland represented for MacNeice that he knew he must resist. In the sequence poem that appeared in 1940 as 'The Coming of War' in *The Last Ditch* (the only book by MacNeice to be published in Ireland, through the good offices of the Yeats family's Cuala Press), and which reappeared in edited form as 'The Closing Album' in *Plant and Phantom* in 1941, the poet names that intangible something 'Forgetfulness'[10] ('Cushendun'). He could, he feels, hide his 'head / In the clouds of the west' ('Running away from the war').[11] Yet even in Ireland war intrudes – 'But Mars was angry / On the hills of Clare' ('O the Crossbones of Galway')[12] – and the country offers only a tantalisingly beautiful but essentially deceptive haven from responsible action and 'doom all night … lapping at the door' ('Why, now it has happened')[13] or at best a place that gave him 'time for thought' ('Dublin').[14] Ireland therefore represented for MacNeice in the war years an image of an impossible condition in which history and its demands could somehow be avoided, a state of mind and feeling in which the self could indulge in a lotus-like forgetfulness of real, complex issues of loyalty, duty, responsibility. I therefore think it wrong to read his often-quoted poem of 1942 'Neutrality', too literally. Certainly the death of MacNeice's close friend Graham Shepard on a convoy in the North Atlantic gives an edge of real bitterness to its final stanza where the poet advises a neutral island:

> look eastward from your heart, there bulks
> A continent, close, dark, as archetypal sin,
> While to the west off your own shores the mackerel
> Are fat – on the flesh of your kin.[15]

However, it seems unlikely that the man who in 1939 and 1940 could agonise in his letters to Dodds over the question as to whether the war was his war could completely fail to understand Ireland's neutrality in the conflict. Certainly in 1941 he insisted, after a three-week stay in Ireland, 'I have no wish now to bring up the undying (though chameleonic) Irish Question but I would ask you to remember that the feeling in Eire is now predominantly pro-British (though still opposed to participation in the War), that the pro-German minority is extremely small and that De Valera's position is agonizingly difficult. Those who propose the application of the strong hand to Eire are forgetting their history …'[16] Accordingly, in 'Neutrality', he associates 'The neutral island facing the Atlantic' with a human *universal*, 'the neutral island in the heart of man', and both with the archaic mythical landscapes of an imagined west which represents a powerfully attractive narcotic when the challenges of reality are too great:

> Look into your heart, you will find a County Sligo,
> A Knocknarea with for navel a cairn of stones,

You will find the shadow and sheen of a moleskin mountain
And a litter of chronicles and bones.
Look into your heart, you will find fermenting rivers,
Intricacies of gloom and glint,
You will find such ducats of dream and great doubloons
   of ceremony
As nobody to-day would mint.[17]

The topography and the allusions here are obviously Yeatsian. MacNeice deems Yeatsian Romanticism, its aristocratic celebration of ceremony, as complicit with a kind of escapism which must be resisted, however appealing it may be. Indeed, the stanzas I have quoted are compact of nostalgia and a recognition that there is something deathly about such solipsistic imaginative self-regard in face of war. It is an all-too-human temptation, to be fiercely resisted.

This poem is, of course, only one aspect of MacNeice's complex response to Yeats whose poetry and achievement he confronted in his book *The Poetry of W. B. Yeats,* which he began working on in 1939 and completed during his time at Cornell in 1940, at the same period as he was wrestling with the moral and personal demands of the war.

Journeying to the United States the poet remembered, in the long autobiographical essay he wrote in the months immediately following his return to London, how 'for five months' he had been 'tormented by the ethical problems of the war. In Ireland most people said to me "What is it to you?" while many of my friends in England took the line it was just power politics.'[18] America, like Dublin in 'Running Away from the War', gave him 'time for thought': 'I thought I could think things out there, get myself clear before I went into the maelstrom.'[19] Indeed, the fact that MacNeice titled his autobiography (which was published posthumously, since he decided at the time not to publish a work which might have offended his father and stepmother) *The Strings Are False* suggests that MacNeice himself saw this work as a kind of prelude to battle. For in Act IV, Scene iii of Shakespeare's *Julius Caesar,* in Brutus's tent before the battle of Philippi, Brutus's boy Lucius, a musician, stirs in his sleep after Brutus has seen the ghost of Caesar. He murmurs, 'The strings, my lord, are false.' Indeed the whole structure of the work as we have it suggests that MacNeice reckoned his essay a study of the moment before the outbreak of conflict. It opens with the poet aboard ship, returning to England, and ends at the moment he had left for America on an earlier, short visit at Easter 1939, before war had been declared.[20] And a protracted central section deals with his stay in Barcelona during the siege, just before the final struggle for the city had begun. *The Strings Are False* is therefore an account of an entr'acte in which the poet had sought 'clarification', which, as he insists, 'may be too much to demand of most people but a writer must demand it of himself'.[21]

Not that the essay arrives at any great clarity: 'It is, as I said, the same boat that brought me over. That was in January 1940 and this is December 1940. But before all that? I am 33 years old and what can I have been doing that I still am in a muddle?'[22] But he had decided that England was the place to be since, as he reported in a letter to his father, he 'thought [he] was missing history'.[23] And in *Horizon* in 1941 he confessed:

While I was in America I felt a very long way from Europe, though not so far away as I felt during the autumn of 1939 in Ireland... From June on I wished to return, not because I thought I could be more *useful* in England than in America, but because I wanted to see these things for myself. My chief motive thus being vulgar curiosity, my second motive was no less egotistical; I thought that if I stayed another year out of England I should have to stay out for good, having missed so much history, lost touch.[24]

In reacting in this way MacNeice displayed an acute artistic self-awareness. For his surest achievement of the 1930s had been *Autumn Journal*, an intimate, immediate response to an historic moment. As artist he could not afford to miss history. And his writings in the next four years indicate how wisely he had acted, for the war years were to be one of the most productive, creative periods of MacNeice's life, when his work expressed a complex, rich view of the world. It was a view that his critical engagement with Yeats's poetry did much to stimulate.

For MacNeice, Yeats's poetry posed a very special challenge. Throughout the 1930s he had espoused in his published essays and reviews a critical position that deemed poetry to be a matter of communication, which was of necessity about something, and if it was to be of social utility, as the poet believed it should be, that something had to be significant. Yeats's poetry with its magic, Irish Nationalism and aestheticism seemed to fly in the face of such prescriptions; yet MacNeice could not deny that if he were 'making a general anthology of shorter English poems, I should want to include some sixty by W. B. Yeats. There is no other poet in the language from whom I should choose so many ... I like rereading Yeats more than I like rereading most English poets.'[25] So this demanded some explanation in view of MacNeice's earlier critical nostrums. War is the defining reality as MacNeice shifts his ground. 'I had', he tells us in chapter 1 of his study of the recently dead Yeats, 'only written a little of this book when Germany invaded Poland':

On that day I was in Galway. As soon as I heard on the wireless of the outbreak of war, Galway became unreal. And Yeats and his poetry became unreal also. This was not merely because Galway and Yeats belong in a sense to a past order of things. The unreality which now overtook them was also overtaking in my mind modern London, modernist art and Left Wing politics. If the war made nonsense of Yeats's poetry and of all works that are called 'escapist', it also made nonsense of the poetry that professes to be 'realist'... For war spares neither the poetry of Xanadu nor the poetry of pylons. I gradually inferred, as I recovered from the shock of war, that both these kinds of poetry stand or fall together. War does not prove that one is better or worse than the other; it attempts to disprove both. But poetry must not be disproved. If war is the test of reality, then all poetry is unreal; but in that case unreality is a virtue. If, on the other hand, war is a great enemy of reality, although an incontestable fact, then reality is something which is not exactly commensurable with fact.[26]

Yeats's poetry, like the challenge of war, provoked a crisis of faith in which the problem of value became central in MacNeice's mind. It was no longer a question, in the face of war, of whether Yeats's poetry was more or less valuable than that by MacNeice's exact contemporaries, but whether poetry itself was of any value. And bound up with the question of the value of poetry was the even more fundamental question as to the value of human life itself. This becomes a recurrent theme in the poet's writings during the war in a body of work which, including graphic prose accounts of the Blitz on London, radio plays and poems, constitutes one of the most impressive records we possess of Britain at war (Henry Moore's series of sketches of the underground world during the bombings come to mind as an equivalently memorable achievement) – a body of Irish writing to be compared surely with Francis Stuart's record of his Berlin years.

For MacNeice, the war as he experienced it most directly in the Blitz was a great force of negation, a terrifying unleashing of elemental energies that would destroy everything which makes human life livable. In 'The Morning After the Blitz', in May 1941 he wrote of a bombing raid as being 'like the banging of all the tea-trays and the loosing of all the fireworks and the rumbling of all the tumbrils and the breaking of all the oceans in the world. Just one long drawn-out lunatic symphony.'[27] Yet even pure destruction, what he called in his poem 'Troll's Courtship' 'utter negation in a positive form'[28] could be oddly exhilarating, as if the destruction of London clarified issues in a demanding, exacting way: 'When the All Clear went I began a tour of London, half appalled and half enlivened by this fantasy of destruction. For it was – if I am to be candid – enlivening.'[29] It was also compellingly dramatic. This is MacNeice's extraordinary description of a raid on 10 May 1941 when the poet watched the city burning from the dome of St Paul's, which had narrowly escaped a direct hit:

When the day came up and the planes had gone, London was burning still; you could stand on top of the dome and warm your hands at it. I had never before realized the infinite variety of fire – subtleties never attained by any Impressionist painter. These fires were a wedding of power with a feminine sensuous beauty. A glowering crimson power mottled with black; a yellow liquid power – a kind of Virgin Birth – which is sheer destruction; a cracking, a hissing, and an underground growling. But up above were the softest clouds of smoke – soft as marabou – purple and umber and pink and orange which spread out and shaded off to blue. Looking at these fires from above I got them in perspective. When the fire takes over a new building, first of all it is the building that is on fire, but later it is the fire that is the solid object, the building is just a gimcrack screen that the fire has folded around itself.[30]

These experiences were the basis of three of MacNeice's most memorable war poems 'Brother Fire', 'The Trolls' and 'Troll's Courtship'. They share with the prose descriptions a chill ecstasy, as if the overwhelming experience of mass destruction had induced an elevation of mood for which mythical, metaphysical and religious categories are the only possible means of representation. Tonally these poems are remarkable for their insouciant courting of nihilism, a debonair zest for a terror which is stripping reality of its essences and imposing absolute demands on a consciousness for which the issue of value is all that remains when 'Brother Fire' has done his worst. After the raid on 10 May, which MacNeice watched from the cathedral, he wrote:

All the same I know we should ask ourselves every so often whether, living in these conditions, we are still seeing straight. I find that I vacillate as to the answer; sometimes I say to myself 'This is mere chaos, it makes no sense' and at other times I think 'Before I saw wartime London I must have been spiritually colour-blind.' There is plenty of degradation – the cheapness inevitable in a world that involves so much short-term propaganda – and plenty of squalor, but there is also an exaltation and, when I say that, I do not mean anything in the nature of Rupert Brooke heroics or last ditch bravado, I mean something much bleaker and, in one sense, humbler, something like the feeling you get on top of a mountain on a cold, grey day… There is, in some quarters, an understandable swing-back to religion but the revival of religion (with its ordinary connotations) is something I neither expect nor desire. What *is* being forced upon people is a revival of the religious sense. And after the hand-to-mouth ethics of nineteenth-century liberalism and the inverted and blinkered quasi-religion of Marxism and the sentimentality of the cynical Lost Generation – after all that, we need all the senses we were born with; and one of those is the religious.[31]

So in 'Brother Fire' he addresses, with Franciscan humility, the principle of negation at work in the fires looting the city, reckoning it a force of purgation and spiritual renewal: 'Which gluttony of his for us was Lenten fare'. Fire is that by which 'were we weaned to knowledge of the Will / That wills the natural world but wills us dead'.[32] The fire is simultaneously creator and destroyer, an elemental energy sometimes contained in the grates where the folkloric dogs stand guard, sometimes 'having his dog's day / Jumping the London streets with millions of tin cans / Clanking at his tail'. 'O delicate walker' apostrophises the poet,

> babbler, dialectician Fire,
> O enemy and image of ourselves,
> Did we not on those mornings after the All Clear,
> When you were looting shops in elemental joy
> And singing as you swarmed up city block and spire,
> Echo your thoughts in ours? 'Destroy! Destroy!'[33]

For MacNeice the question of the value of poetry and of life itself, so keenly pressed by the experience of the London Blitz, involved him in the philosophic problem of reductionism. As MacNeice was agonising about where he should spend the war and after he had plunged into a life in England of intense work – producing articles, features for the BBC, developing the genre of radio drama – he was also brooding, in a way he had not done since his undergraduate years in the 1920s, on essentially metaphysical problems, now given an immediate edge by the possibility of his own death. War, it seems, raised the question of value in power-ful yet precise terms. It seemed an undeniable, determining force beside which poetry and human feeling, life itself, were insubstantial, tenuous things. War, in the most cruel fashion possible, seemed to confirm what the 1930s poets in general had tended to believe in a rather superficial manner, that forces as great as the *Zeitgeist*, history, the dialectic, the iron laws of natural selection and biology, were the determinants of individual consciousness, which deluded itself that it possessed meaningful auton-omy. War made such theorising all too real as society was caught up by a process over which the individual seemed to have no control whatsoever. So MacNeice writes of a conscript in the poem of that name, as one who is, apparently, wholly determined:

Being so young he feels the weight of history
Like clay around his boots; he would, if he could, fly
In search of a future like a sycamore seed
But is prevented by his own Necessity,
His own yet alien, which, whatever he may plead,
To every question gives the same reply.[34]

The conscript is not the only figure in the poems of the war years caught in his own necessity. MacNeice writes of character types in 'Bottleneck', 'The Mixer', 'The Libertine', 'The Satirist', as figures for whom character is destiny. He writes compassionately too of the victims of the war itself, refugees especially, cast up on foreign shores by the inevitable tides of war. One of his key images of these years, in the poetry and the prose, is the Atlantic crossing, a tunnel which ships enter and must negotiate if they are not to perish: as 'Convoy' has it, 'No Euclid could have devised / Neater means to a more essential end'.[35] Nature, in 'Explorations', also reminds of determinism and ineluctable law:

The whale butting through scarps of moving marble,
The tapeworm probing the intestinal darkness,
The swallows drawn collectively to their magnet
These are our prototypes …[36]

'And yet', continues this poem. It is that 'and yet' which philosophically concerns MacNeice in the war years. Poetry and life may be explicable in terms of determining forces, but MacNeice recurrently resists the idea that to explain something is to explain it away. A phenomenon cannot be reduced to its causes. The challenge war presented to Yeats's work and by extension to all poetry demanded that MacNeice develop a philosophy of life and death that could sustain art and existence through the ultimate crises they faced. To satisfy MacNeice's intelligence, such a view had to resolve the philosophic dilemmas posed by reductionism and determinism. Consequently, in the Preface to *The Poetry of W. B. Yeats*, MacNeice worries about the relationship of poetry to life, introducing his anti-reductionist concerns:

We still tend to think that, because a thing is in time, its value can only be explained by an abstraction from the thing of some supposedly timeless qualities; this is to explain the thing away. That a rose withers is no disproof of the rose, which remains an absolute, its value inseparable from its existence (for existence is still existence, whether the tense is past or future) … Life – let alone art – cannot be assessed purely in terms of utility. Food, for example, is useful for life but what is life useful for? To both the question of pleasure and the question of value the utilitarian has no answer. The faith in the *value* of living is a mystical faith.[37]

In chapter 1, 'Introductory', he expands at length on this perception, responding to critics who 'often tend to write as if a condition were the same thing as a cause'.[38] Again he offers a definition of life and crucially of poetry which rescues them from reductionist and utilitarian explanation: 'Life for living creatures is not something which you merely have or have not; it is something plastic; it *is* what you make it. The sense of values governing this conscious or unconscious creation of life (presumably unconscious among the lower animals, partly conscious among human beings) is not utilitarian, it can only be described as mystical.'[39]

This outlook, developed as he was working on his book on Yeats, finds frequent expression in MacNeice's poems of the war years, making them by and large more positive in overall tone, more celebratory than anything he had produced before. There is much to fear, much to deprecate in a world at war, but even the conscript is allowed the possibility:

> though on the flat his life has no
> Promise but of diminishing returns,
> By feeling down and upwards he can divine
> That dignity which far above him burns
> In stars that yet are his and which below
> Stands rooted like a dolmen in his spine.[40]

'Prospect' expresses with lyrical élan this new mystical response (there is nothing like it in the pre-war poetry) to life:

> Though Nature's laws exploit
> And defeat anarchic men,
> Though every sandcastle concept
> Being *ad hoc* must crumble again,
> And though to-day is arid,
> We know – and knowing bless –
> That rooted in futurity
> There is a plant of tenderness.[41]

What saves MacNeice's anti-reductionist stance from sentimentality in the poems he wrote in the early 1940s is the fact that he combines this positive note with an immediate, almost existential awareness of the fact of death. It is the mystery and glory of consciousness which makes humankind unique for MacNeice; it is hoping and despairing that makes us 'the final / Anomaly of the world' ('Explorations'[42]). And in these years, death as the end of consciousness was a daily present possibility for the poet and his friends as it was for all the citizens of London. The shutter could fall 'Congealing the kaleidoscope at Now' ('The Casualty'[43]) as it did in mid-Atlantic for Graham Shepard, for whom he wrote the powerful elegy from which this phrase comes. Death as intimate reality in the war years gave a zest and intensity to life that informed the experience of conscious existence with an almost religious quality. Critics have noted a similar mystical empiricism as an effect of desperate conditions in Francis Stuart's *Black List, Section H*. MacNeice, in a posthumously published meditative manuscript written in 1941, brooded on the knowledge of death which the war had brought:

Death in its own right – as War does incidentally – sets our lives in perspective. Every man's funeral is his own, just as people are lonely in their lives, but Death as a leveller also writes us in life. & Death not only levels but differentiates – it crystallizes our deeds.

   We did not need a war to teach us this but war has taught us it. Before the war we wore blinkers. Applied science, by increasing comfort & controlling disease, had – geared to a 'liberal' individualism – encouraged us to think of death as a pure negation, a nuisance. But applied science, by shattering a town overnight, by superimposing upon ordered decay a fantastic but palpable madness, has shown us the integral function of death. Death is the opposite of decay; a stimulus, a necessary horizon. & this will affect our conception of Freedom.[44]

In 'Prayer in Mid-Passage', written about 1943, MacNeice draws on such thinking to produce one of his most haunting poems, which links the trope of a sea voyage, the Atlantic Tunnel, with the Dantesque moment of mid-life crisis (the poet was thirty-five in 1943). He addresses his own death as the source of the faith which allows him to break silence with meaningful song in the midst of war:

> We were the past – and doomed because
> We were a past that never was;
> Yet grant to men that they may climb
> This time-bound ladder out of time
> And by our human organs we
> Shall thus transcend humanity.
> Take therefore, though Thou disregard,
> This prayer, this hymn, this feckless word,
> O Thou my silence, Thou my song,
> To whom all focal doubts belong
> And but for whom this breath were breath –
> Thou my meaning, Thou my death.[45]

NOTES

1 L. MacNeice, *The Strings Are False* (London: Faber and Faber, 1965), p. 212.
2 Quoted in P. McDonald, *Louis MacNeice: The Poet in His Contexts* (Oxford: Clarendon Press, 1991), p. 97.
3 E. R. Dodds, *Missing Persons* (Oxford: Clarendon Press, 1977), p. 39.
4 *Ibid.*, p. 67.
5 *Ibid.*
6 L. MacNeice, 'The Way We Live Now', in A. Heuser (ed.), *Selected Prose of Louis MacNeice* (Oxford: Clarendon Press, 1990), p. 82.
7 McDonald, *Louis MacNeice*, p. 98.
8 *Ibid.*, p. 99.
9 *Ibid.*
10 E. R. Dodds (ed.), *The Collected Poems of Louis MacNeice* (London: Faber and Faber, 1966), p. 165.
11 L. MacNeice, *The Last Ditch* (Dublin: Cuala Press, 1940), p. 7.
12 *Ibid.*, p. 10.
13 *Ibid.*, p. 11.
14 *Ibid.*, p. 5.
15 Dodds (ed.), *Collected Poems*, p. 15.
16 Heuser (ed.), *Selected Prose*, p. 116.
17 Dodds (ed.), *Collected Poems*, p. 202.
18 MacNeice, *Strings Are False*, p. 21.
19 *Ibid.*
20 *The Strings Are False*, it must be admitted, is a document over whose publication the author had no control. It has been produced by E. R. Dodds from the textual remains of a work in progress, who adjudicated between two drafts. It is not certain, though I believe it probable, that the first three chapters would have remained at the beginning of the work, if MacNeice himself had completed it for publication. Dodds reports: 'Louis's final intention may have been to transfer the substance of chapters i and ii (which were still in rough draft) from the beginning of the book to their chronological place at the end, either omitting chapter iii or perhaps using part of it as an introduction. But that plan would have involved considerable rewriting, which was never done. I have accordingly left chapters i to iii where they stand in B [one of the drafts]. They introduce Louis at a pause in his life, isolated in a temporary limbo between two worlds, looking back over his past and forward to a future which for him as for all British subjects was in 1940 dark and uncertain' (*Strings Are False*, p. 12). Dodds derived the title for the book from a typescript of chapter xxxii of the work, 'evidently designed for separate publication in some journal, which bears the superscription "A Visit to Spain: Easter 1936 (excerpted from a book, now in preparation, entitled *The Strings Are False*"' (*Ibid.*, p. 11). In my view the title suggests, with its reference to the eve of battle, that Dodds did right to structure the work as he did. That impression would have been significantly lessened had he or MacNeice moved the first two chapters to the close of the work.

21 MacNeice, *Strings Are False*, p. 21.
22 *Ibid.*, p. 35.
23 Quoted in W. T. McKinnon, *Apollo's Blended Dream* (London: Oxford University Press, 1971), p. 32.
24 L. MacNeice, 'Traveller's Return', in Heuser (ed.), *Selected Prose,* p. 83.
25 L. MacNeice, *The Poetry of W.B. Yeats* (London: Oxford University Press, 1941), p. 1.
26 *Ibid.*, pp. 1–2.
27 L. MacNeice, 'The Morning After the Blitz', in Heuser (ed.), *Selected Prose*, p. 117.
28 Dodds (ed.), *Collected Poems*, p. 199.
29 MacNeice, 'The Morning After the Blitz', p. 117.
30 L. MacNeice, 'London Letter [5]: Reflections from the Dome of St Paul's', in Heuser (ed.), *Selected Prose*, pp. 133–4.
31 *Ibid.*, pp. 135–6.
32 Dodds (ed.), *Collected Poems*, p. 196.
33 *Ibid.*
34 *Ibid.*, p. 203.
35 *Ibid.*, p. 200.
36 *Ibid.*, p. 194.
37 MacNeice, *The Poetry of W. B. Yeats*, pp. vii–viii.
38 *Ibid.*, p. 9.
39 *Ibid.*, p. 10.
40 Dodds (ed.), *Collected Poems*, 203.
41 *Ibid.*, p. 213.
42 *Ibid.*, p. 195.
43 *Ibid.*, p. 245.
44 'Broken Windows or Thinking Aloud', in Heuser (ed.), *Selected Prose*, p. 142.
45 Dodds (ed.), *Collected Poems*, p. 212.

CHAPTER 12

MacNeice and the puritan tradition

In 1935 MacNeice, in his essay 'Poetry Today', declared that 'Whatever the "true function" of poetry is, there is something idolatrous or fetishistic about our pleasure in it.'[1] It was a daring admission in a decade when poetry was widely reckoned only admissible if it served some obviously ethical function. In contrast to the prevailing political puritanism of the period, MacNeice was unwilling to deny that poetry gives pleasure, and he knew that this fact to the puritan mind must seem a kind of idolatry, a worshipping of a false god, the making of a fetish of something insignificant and unworthy. However, for MacNeice the matter is, in the end, quite simple: 'poetry *qua* poetry is an end and not a means; its relations to "life" are impossible to define; even when it is professedly "didactic", "propagandist" or "satirical" the external purport is, ultimately, only a conventional property, a kind of perspective which many poets like to think of as essential'.[2]

MacNeice in his twenties and early thirties, when he wrote his most searching essays on the role of poetry in such articles as the one quoted above, 'Subject in Modern Poetry' and in his book *Modern Poetry: A Personal Essay* (1938) was well-equipped to resist all those who would have made poetry subject to ethics or even to political necessity. For as an Ulsterman, he well understood that the impulse of the puritan sensibility is to suspect art and the pleasure it affords. And the poet who had escaped the utilitarian 'Attempts at buyable beauty' of Belfast (excoriated in the poem of that name) was unlikely to submit to any dogma which would have reduced poetry to a merely functional activity in the service of ideology. In his recollective account of his youth, 'When I Was Twenty-One', published in 1961, he recalled a need felt in his early manhood to 'escape from the puritanism and mud of my Ulster surroundings to the honey-coloured finials and gilded understatements of Oxford'.[3] This polarity between a puritanical Ulster and the escapist attractions of sensuous immediacy governs almost all of MacNeice's autobiographical prose writings about his childhood, even if, as in *Zoo*, he remembers to submit a recantation:

A harassed and dubious childhood under the hand of a well-meaning but barbarous mother's help from County Armagh led me to think of the North of Ireland as prison and the South as a land of escape. Many nightmares, boxes on the ears, a rasping voice of disapproval, a monotonous daily walk to a crossroads called Mile Bush, sodden haycocks, fear of hell-fire, my father's indigestion – these things, with on the other side my father's Home Rule sympathies and the music of his brogue, bred in me an almost fanatical hatred for Ulster. When I went to bed as a child I was told: 'You don't know where you'll wake up.' When I ran in the garden I was told that running was bad for the heart. Everything had its sinister aspect – milk shrinks the stomach, lemon thins the blood. Against my will I was always given sugar in my tea. The North was tyranny.[4]

What stimulates MacNeice to second thoughts about Ulster in this extract from *Zoo* is a weekend in Belfast which 'was all sunshine'. 'I could not', admits MacNeice, 'remember Belfast like this, and the continuous sunshine delighted but outraged me. My conception of Belfast, built up since early childhood, demanded that it should always be grey, wet, and repellent and its inhabitants dour, rude and callous.'[5] That delight in the unexpected sunshine in the city alerts us to a characteristic of MacNeice's sensibility – its instinctive relish for the pleasure of sensory experience set against the rigours of a puritan sense of life. It is almost as if the memory of Belfast which the poet carried with him is the energising spring which releases a new vision of the place he had hitherto known only under the guise of tyranny. So where he had recently written of

> ... the end of the melancholy lough
> Against the lurid sky over the stained water
> Where hammers clang murderously on the girders
> Like crucifixes the gantries stand[6]

now he evokes Belfast Lough in a passage of delighted sensuous zest:

As we went faster, crinkling the water a little, the reflections squirmed like tadpoles, the double reflections from the sheds regularly and quietly somersault-ing. Two cranes facing each other conferred darkly. In the widening channel the lines of reflected lights behind us stretched in uncertain alleys like the line of floating corks set out for swimmers. A black motor-boat cutting across them threw out shooting stars behind it. A buoy skated rapidly backwards winking periodically red. Then the cranes and quays fell away and the channel opened into the lough – a single line of lights on each side – like a man stretching his arms and drawing a breath. Cassiopeia was tilted in her deck-chair over Antrim; Arcturus over Down.[7]

It is impossible, in this little prose poem of dark and light, not to respond to the images of pleasurable expansion and enlargement of vision which it exploits. The relish of the occasion is physical, somatic, sensuous. Note 'squirmed', 'somersaulting', 'stretched', 'swimmers', 'skated', 'winking', 'drawing breath'.

It is in two-and-half terrible pages, which are given as section seven of *The Strings Are False* (MacNeice's unfinished autobiography), that this juxtaposition between what the poet, at the head of the immediately succeeding section, calls 'puritan repression' and sensuous delight is most deliberately represented in MacNeice's work. There we are told of the death of Louis's mother, of the dark night terrors which followed as his father mourned his wife, of the boy's guilt and the steady encroachment of religion. Set against such a backdrop of gloom and shadow, the sensory brilliance of the visible world is in recollection surprisingly vital:

> That Christmas we got a great many presents; they were marshalled on the nursery hearthrug by the crackling of the early morning fire. Everything was gay with colour, there were coloured chalks and coloured wooden rattles and striped tin trumpets and tangerines in silver paper, and a copy of the *Arabian Nights* with princesses in curly shoes and blue-black hair.[8]

And MacNeice was always to be responsive to a world of surprising sensation that must be rendered in terms of a strongly verbal lexicon. The 'crackling' fire of this passage finds frequent echo in the poetry as in the grass which 'boils with grasshoppers' (p. 230) in 'The Cyclist' or 'the rumpled / Tigers of the bogland streams' which 'Prowl and plunge through glooms and gleams' (p. 446) in Poem I of 'Donegal Triptych', or the coffee which 'leaps in a crystal knob / Chugs and glints while birds gossip' (p. 488) in 'Country Week-End'. But what of course this passage most precisely brings to mind, with its tangerine and evocation of the exotic range of epicurean possibility, is one of MacNeice's most remarkable poems, the sensationally intense aperçu 'Snow', with its snow, pink roses, fire and tangerine. The poem as a celebration of the pleasures of perception and of the senses which make that possible is the delighted response of a poet who knows such things arrive of a sudden, excess given added spice by our customary expectation of altogether less. For the poem expresses pleasure unburdened by guilt, is even perhaps self-consciously ostentatious about so doing, but is also, in its insistent comparative tone, aware how freakish (only after a snowfall, when snow and roses are collateral?) is the possibility of such drunken zest.

MacNeice is in fact a considerable poet of pleasure. He is certainly no mere hedonist, but he unabashedly relishes the gifts of sight, sound, texture, smell and taste as they make life livable. He is especially exhilarated by the effects of sunshine on water ('The dazzle on the sea', p. 86), the mayfly's 'dance above the dazzling wave' (p. 14), but he is attentive too to moments of bodily sensation and sexual impulse. In 'The Stygian Banks', for example, he remembers how 'Munching salad / Your child can taste the colour itself – the green – /And the colour of radish – the red' (p. 264). In Poem I of 'Trilogy for X', images of wind and of trains evoke a powerful, intimate physical passion:

> But now when winds are curling
> The trees do you come closer,
> Close as an eyelid fasten
> My body in darkness, darling;
> Switch the light off and let me
> Gather you up and gather
> The power of trains advancing
> Further, advancing further. (p. 89)

Nor does MacNeice neglect the lesser pleasures of drink, bawdy talk, gossip, habitual satisfactions – what he identifies in his late poem 'Memoranda to Horace' as 'the tangles' (p. 542). Few twentieth-century poets could have written with such enthusiasm of sociability, with booze and crack:

> In the road is another smile on the face of day.
> We stop at random for a morning drink
> In a thatched inn; to find, as at a play,
> The bar already loud with chatter and clink
> Of glasses, not so random; no one here
> But was a friend of Gwilym's. One could think
> That all these shots of whisky, pints of beer,
> Make one Pactolus turning words to gold
> In honour of one golden mouth, in sheer
> Rebuttal of the silence and the cold
> Attached to death ... (p. 412)

Few others could have responded with such vital pleasure to a glass of water on a wiltingly hot day: 'tower of liquid light .../ Which the sun coins and cool from ice / It spears the throat like an ice-cold sun' ('Our Sister Water', p. 301).

MacNeice is constantly alert in his poetry to the palpable givenness of the material world in which he takes such pleasure. He is a poet for whom things exist undeniably distinct from the poet's designs upon them – beautiful, attractive, desirable, pleasure-giving in their own right. In 'Train to Dublin', he salutes 'the incidental things which pass / Outward through space exactly as each was' (p. 28) and his poetry is rich in the quiddity of a world of such inscapes. It was indeed a capacity for responding to things as well as people that MacNeice admired in his friend Graham Shepard of whom he wrote in his fine elegy 'The Casualty': 'For above all that was your gift – to be / Surprised and therefore sympathetic, warm / Towards things as well as people' (p. 247); the poem accordingly evokes the dead man in a proliferation of brilliant and precise visual as well as emotional epiphanies – 'here the Wiltshire sleet / Riddles your football jersey – here the sack / Of night pours down on you Provençal stars' (p. 247).

MacNeice, the Ulsterman in flight from a grim puritanism, found in the material world a pleasure that he allowed to inform his art. Of course he knew that poetry had to be more than a celebration of sensuous experience. But reading Hopkins's *Note-Books and Papers* in 1937, he noted that poet's 'voracity for objects'[9] and observed: 'his zeal in recording the visions of his bodily eye I find extremely refreshing and salutary'.[10] He found it so in a period when what he identified as a 'ruthless puritanism' had tended to make 'the human subject ... of supreme importance'.[11] MacNeice reflects plaintively of this situation: 'We might remember ... that man is a [living animal] as well as [citizen] and that quite a number of people have an organic sympathy with trees, mountains, flowers, or with a painting by Chardin.'[12]

Yet for all his willingness to admit pleasure to his poetry and to acknowledge that pleasure is certainly an aspect of poetry's attraction for us, MacNeice knew that art for pleasure's sake is as unproductive an aesthetic as *l'art pour l'art*. He shared his generation's suspicion of mere aestheticism. In 1936 he advised: 'Art for Art's Sake has been some time foundering. A masthead or two even now show above the water ... but on the whole, poets have ceased showing themselves off as mere poets. They have better things to do; they are writing *about* things again.'[13] And he evinced a distaste for a poetry that is all sensuous beauty and the indulgence of a life of sensation rather than thought in a remarkably grudging introduction he published to a selection of Keats's poetry in 1941. The times of course were urgent and furthermore MacNeice had been at work on his study of W. B. Yeats, published in the same year, so some of the elder poet's antagonism to Keats may have rubbed off on him. He does in fact argue that had Keats lived he might, like Yeats, have become less 'poetic'. Be that as it may, in a volume which includes C. S. Lewis on Spenser, Tillyard on Milton and Auden on Byron, all sympathetic advocates of their writers, MacNeice takes Keats on what he regards as his own terms as 'an adolescent writing for adolescents'.[14]

Keats's poetry draws from MacNeice the judgement that 'there is no such thing as a merely sensuous poet'[15] and an acknowledgement that even Keats was more complex than his most self-indulgent lines would suggest. He was, admits MacNeice, a 'mystic through the medium of the senses'.[16] MacNeice insists, 'few major poets, however, have lived by mysticism – or by the senses – alone'.[17]

MacNeice's curiously 'puritan' estimate of Keats may, I would like to argue, originate in more than his reading of Yeats or the exigencies of the hour in wartime London. For he himself, as he certainly knew when he penned his essay on Keats, had a good deal of the 'sensuous mystic' (his own term for Keats) in him. The man who in 1957 would write:

We cannot of course live by Keats's Negative Sensibility alone, we must all, in E. M. Forster's phrase, use 'telegrams and anger'; all the same what I feel makes life worth living is not the clever scores but the surrenders – it may be to the life-quickening urge of an air-raid, to nonsense talked by one's friends, to a girl on top of the Empire State Building, to the silence of a ruined Byzantine church, to woods, or weirs, or to heat dancing on a gravelled path, to music, drink, or the smell of turf smoke, to the first view of the Atlantic or to the curve of a strand which seems to stretch to nowhere or everywhere and to ages before and after the combustion engine which defiled it.[18]

was one who in 1940 had insisted in the preface to his study of Yeats, dated September 1940, 'The faith in the *value* of living is a mystical faith. The pleasure in bathing or dancing, in colour or shape, is a mystical experience.'[19]

MacNeice, I think, knew there was a Keatsian sensuous mysticism in his own attitude to life. He knew that his own first volume, *Blind Fireworks,* could be accused of sensuous excess and that he, as he puts it in 'Dedicatory Poem to *Collected Poems, 1925–48*', published in 1949, had been at one time 'content if things would image / Themselves in their own dazzle'.[20] Indeed one of the prevailing excitements of MacNeice's poetry and prose throughout his career is the way it can suggest consciousness being roused to pleasure by the world of material objects as they swim, unbidden, into awareness. This is 'Morning Sun' from March 1935:

> Yellow sun comes white off the wet streets but bright
> Chromium yellows in the gay sun's light,
> Filleted sun streaks the purple mist,
> Everything is kissed and reticulated with sun
> Scooped-up and cupped in the open fronts of shops
> And bouncing on the traffic which never stops. (p. 26)

This is 'Country Week-End' from the late 1950s:

> Wild grass in spate in a rainy wind,
> We have come from London to stay indoors
> With paraffin on our hands, our eyes
> Watching through glass the trees blown east.
> As if hypnotised, as if this wet
> Day were the sum and essence of days
> When such spinning shafts of steely water
> Struck to numb, or revive, the mind. (p. 490)

What inhibits the mystical streak in MacNeice and his epicurean delight in pleasure is his social awareness and commitment to communitarian social values. In his introduction to Keats's poetry, he cites that poet's famous assertion that 'A Poet is the most unpoetical of anything in existence, because he has no identity' only to comment: 'That a poet has no identity is a useful half-truth, for it counteracts the common opinion that a poet is someone hawking his own personality. Many poets, however, have had an identity as spokesman for a congenial community or for a tradition that was still functioning.'[21] This is entirely of a piece with the MacNeice of the final section of *Autumn Journal* who, in the face of the collapse of the Republican Government in Spain, the betrayal of the Czech Republic and impending war against Hitler, dreams of and prays for 'a possible land... / Where life is a choice of instruments and none / Is barred his natural music' (p. 152). It is a collective Utopia that the poet envisages, anti-capitalist, 'Where nobody sees the use / Of buying money and blood at the cost of blood and money' (p. 152). One senses that it is such a community that MacNeice as poet wished himself to serve as spokesman, when he considered how Keats was bereft both of community and tradition.

There has been a marked tendency for MacNeice's critics, and I include myself among their number, to underestimate his political and social commitments. Anxious to exonerate him from the charge that he worshipped with his naive generation the communist god which failed, MacNeice's critics have too readily identified his view of life with an unexceptionable liberal humanism, or just have not bothered to examine what his poetry is about – even when MacNeice's own essays tell us that poetry is always about something. Perhaps the depredations of Thatcherism in the United Kingdom (which would have appalled MacNeice) and the consequences of neo-liberal, free-market economics have made it possible to read him as a much more political poet than when he was reckoned by his contemporaries merely the voice of a conventional set of left-of-centre social opinions.

MacNeice, it must be remembered, although no Marxist, stated of his politics in 1942: 'distrust all parties but consider capitalism must go ... Would normally vote Labour in England, but think the Labour Party won't get anywhere till they have got rid of their reactionary leaders.'[22] In 1955, updating this biographical entry, which appears in a dictionary of modern literature, MacNeice was not moved to amend his earlier statement. Through his poetry and prose writings in the 1930s, although he is watchfully suspicious of the political nostrums of the comrades, there is a concern to address the social issues of the day – unemployment, human degradation in an industrial society, the challenge of fascism. What stirs him is the idea of community as he seeks to break out of the privileged cocoon his background and education have spun for him. It must be noted of MacNeice's work in general that he is one of those modern poets who do not scorn or patronise common life. This is a poet who can write a tender elegy for Florrie Forde (a music hall songster), can salute the quotidian satisfactions of pub games, sport, the world of domesticity, 'routine work, money-making or scholarship' (p. 76), cliché, small talk, the potency of cheap music, those songs that come to us 'off the peg' and 'made to measure' (p. 545) and can affectionately recall the lives of an illiterate gardener, an elusive, forgetful godfather and bear testimony to the quiet dignity of the men and women of unsung integrity who comprise, what he calls in one poem, 'The Kingdom':

> Under the surface of flux and of fear there is an underground
>   movement
> Under the crust of bureaucracy, quiet behind the posters,
> Unconscious but palpably there – the Kingdom of individuals. (p. 248)

His relish for the pleasures of life is tempered too by an awareness that much which makes life agreeable for the few in the modern world of luxury and comfort is bought at the expense of the poor and the industrial labour they must endure. In fact, MacNeice's impulse to delight in the presence of objects, things, sensations, to relish common life, coexists with a slowly intensifying distaste for mass production. More and more in the post-war period (as the consumer society replaced the austerity of the war economy and the welfarism of socialist reconstruction under Labour), he becomes assailed by a sense of meaning, vitality, being drained from things as they proliferate in the endless repetitive availability which is the motor of modern commerce. The alienation that he expressed with increasing bitterness as he grew older may have its sources in psychological, religious and metaphysical anxieties, but its significant social content must not be disregarded. This is a poet (the poet of 'Snow') who deprecates a world of 'Roses with the scent bred out, / In lieu of which is a long name on a label' (p. 522). In place of community has emerged a voracious capitalism which has made of citizens consumers of unreality, addicts of false consciousness. In 'New Jerusalem' from 1962 he advises in sardonic anger:

> Bulldoze all memories and sanctuaries: our birthright
> Means a new city, vertical, impersonal,
> Whose horoscope claimed a straight resurrection
> Should Stimulant stand in conjunction with Sleeping Pill.
> As for the citizens, what with their cabinets
> Of faces and voices, their bags of music,
> Their walls of thin ice dividing greynesses,
> With numbers and mirrors they defy mortality. (p. 529)

MacNeice's late poetry is in fact a poetry of pained revulsion at what modernity has done to the human potential of ordinary life. In this respect his work represents a striking break with the ethos of the literary Modernism which as a young man he could not have failed to have encountered as the definitive response to the century's modernity. Indeed, MacNeice himself admitted in the 1930s that 'the history of post-War poetry in England is the history of Eliot and the reaction from Eliot'.[23] It is a testament to the imaginative and ethical strength of MacNeice as an artist that his own poetry is an impressive reorientating of English poetry's fundamental concerns in the common life of a community rather than in the high culture, under threat from modernity, which was the source of so much Modernist imagining and anguish.

However, MacNeice was not a man to wear his beliefs on his sleeve. In 1953 he did respond nevertheless to a request by Ed Murrow to answer the question 'What do I believe?'. In this brief statement he insists that belief is a matter of values and is always belief in something. But he is at pains to insist that this is not merely a matter of individual whim. His sense of life is ineradicably communitarian:

Apart from the fact that, whether we want to or not, we have to live in communities, I think that human individuals are much more like each other than they are unlike each other. One may live on bread and another may live on meat but they all feel hunger when they're hungry. And on a much higher plane than that of hunger, I think that all human beings have a hankering for pattern and order; look at any child with a box of chalks. There are of course evil patterns or orders – which perhaps is the great problem of our time. What I do believe is that as a human being, it is my duty to make patterns and to contribute to order – good patterns and a good order. And when I say duty I mean duty; I think it is the turn of enjoyment, I believe that life is worth while *and* I believe that I have to do something *for* life.[24]

Notable here is the democracy of feeling, the lack of elitism, the recognition of duty and the relish for living. For this is a poet who values pleasure but who also wishes to live in a community for which he feels an obligation.

For MacNeice of course the question of community loomed ambiguously because of his nationality. I have written earlier of his complex relationship as an Irishman with both Irish communities north and south of the border and of his early interest in islands as metaphors of possible modes of community which might offer an alternative way of thinking about human order in an era of transnational capitalism.[25] What must, however, be said is that MacNeice only sporadically felt truly a part of any community and that when he did, it was an English one. So in my view much of the best recent criticism of MacNeice, has been somewhat Hiberno-centred. Furthermore, MacNeice's main influence as a poet has been marked in contemporary Irish poetry. I sense that as a result the English MacNeice has been rather neglected. I am thinking in this respect of the poet who experienced an English classical education and whose literary formation and preoccupations throughout his life were predominantly English.

The exact nature of MacNeice's classicism is, I hasten to add, as complex as his relationship with Ireland and intriguingly has its Irish aspect, not least through his friendship with E. R. Dodds. For MacNeice the classical world represented a literary resource that offered models of artistic integrity in evil times (Horace, whom he translated skilfully, on his Sabine farm was his imaginary confederate). He rejected the malign symbiosis of English classicism and imperial service (he was sufficiently concerned about the matter, we note, to include in his autobiographical entry to the dictionary of modern literature, cited above, the statement: 'Think the present English system of teaching the classics is bad').[26] He provided an acute diagnosis in *Autumn Journal* of a syndrome which combined a classical education with an elitist assumption of the English right to govern – 'the classical student is bred to the purple' (p. 126). But he made his knowledge of classical and English prosody the basis of some of his own metrical proficiency (strikingly evident in *Autumn Journal*), giving to modern English verse a tone of lucid, conversational communicability, which enabled him to forge an instrument of precise, sane, communal immediacy, colloquial and colourfully direct, urbane and elegant by turns. It was a tone admirably suited to broadcasting in the period when the BBC under the influence of Lord Reith took its public service duties completely seriously.

Radio in the war years and in their aftermath offered MacNeice (he was employed by the BBC from 1941 until 1960 and then as a freelance, until his death in 1963, restricting himself almost entirely to radio) the opportunity to work in a small community of creative people who hoped they might make a contribution to the cultural life of the general community. This was the period when the radio feature and the radio play were in the process of development and MacNeice became an accomplished practitioner in both forms. What characterised his radio work, I believe, was a capacity to deal in serious, even 'highbrow', matter, without patronising a popular audience. One senses, in his plays and features, that MacNeice knew the people for whom he was writing and could address his predominantly English, adequately educated, middle-class constituency in precisely the tones and emotional timbre they would find congenial.

In the period MacNeice was at work in the BBC, English public discourse, it must be remembered, was undergoing significant changes. To listen now to the speeches of politicians in the radio archives, to read their parliamentary effusions, to watch Pathé News films, is to be reminded that the English elite, in Church and State, addressed the commonality in the 1940s in a language of high-flown sentence, grandiloquent fustian and mannered reserve. Churchillian rodomontade was only possible because of the generally rhetorical verbal climate. By the early 1960s and the television age, such public discourse had come to seem impossibly pompous, bullying and ridiculously complacent. The Goons and, later, Monty Python put paid to it. By contrast, MacNeice as broadcaster employed a version of plain style – supple, judicious, not without its own colour and energy and its metaphorical suasions. In so doing he helped to make available a tone and a mode of address that might be termed the house style of the BBC in its heyday, a style remote from the imperial rumble of establishment authoritarianism or the crass *Sun-ese* of the contemporary sound-bite.

It was a style which increasingly came to prominence in MacNeice's own post-war poetry, in such pieces as 'Beni Hasan' (1955), or 'Figure of Eight' (1956) or 'Selva Oscura' (*c.* 1960). Cool, intelligent, elliptical, it disguises deep feeling in syntactical finesse. It assumes it will find a readership in a community of equally thoughtful individuals:

> A life can be haunted by what it never was
> If that were merely glimpsed. Lost in the maze
> That means yourself and never out of the wood
> These days, though lost, will be all your days;
> Life, if you leave it, must be left for good. (p. 512)

Among the sources for this communitarian style are the poets and prose writers of what might be termed an English puritan tradition. I mean poets such as Spenser and Herbert (both poets with beliefs, something to say, a message to communicate), whom MacNeice greatly admired; the tradition would also include the morality play *Everyman* (MacNeice noted its 'spare and undecorated and sometimes colloquial'[27] style) and the Bunyan of *Pilgrim's Progress,* whose plain-style quest romance with its double-level significance so influenced MacNeice's own remarkable parable, the radio play *The Dark Tower* (1946).

In writing in this way, MacNeice was engaging with a mode of English feeling and self-understanding which has its distinctively democratic aspects. MacNeice himself observed: '*Everyman,* like *Pilgrim's Progress* later, came from the people and was addressed to them.'[28] He was identifying too, in his frequent employment of quest motifs in poetry and drama, with a still potent English tradition which, from Langland and Malory onwards, had seen, in a myth of quest, an image of life lived purposefully and self-forgettingly. It was a way of feeling, English and communal, that found expression for example in the music of Vaughan Williams whose *Fantasia on a Theme of Thomas Tallis* (1910) had been adapted by the composer for a stirring wartime radio version of Bunyan's famous work. Williams had always associated his own composition with *Pilgrim's Progress* (like MacNeice he was also an admirer of George Herbert) and had welcomed the opportunity to blend his music with Bunyan's prose at a time of profound English national crisis. MacNeice must surely have had this important collaboration in mind, and have been aware of working in a specific tradition, when his own quest play, *The Dark Tower*, was given an added 'dimension'[29] by the music of that other composer of the English musical renaissance in the twentieth century, Benjamin Britten.

So the MacNeice who adapted the English classical tradition in which he had been trained to his own egalitarian, communitarian purposes, as a communicator also built on an English style and exploited an essentially puritan English tradition of writing and imagining to give his beliefs a valency in the public sphere of post-war British life. The resulting work and achievement were admirably consistent with the political and social commitments which MacNeice made as a man who believed, for all his valuing of sensory pleasure, that he was obligated to do something '*for life*'.[30]

NOTES

1 L. MacNeice, 'Poetry Today', in A. Heuser (ed.), *Selected Literary Criticism of Louis MacNeice* (Oxford: Clarendon Press, 1987). p. 12.

2 *Ibid.*, p. 41.

3 L. MacNeice, 'When I Was Twenty-One', in A. Heuser (ed.), *Selected Prose of Louis MacNeice* (Oxford: Clarendon Press, 1990), p. 222.

4 L. MacNeice, *Zoo* (London: Michael Joseph Ltd, 1938), p. 79.

5 *Ibid.*, p. 78.

6 E. R. Dodds (ed.), *The Collected Poems of Louis MacNeice* (London: Faber and Faber, 1966), p. 17. Subsequent page references to MacNeice's poems in the text are to this volume.

7 MacNeice, *Zoo*, pp. 85–6.

8 L. MacNeice, *The Strings Are False: An Unfinished Autobiography* (London: Faber and Faber: 1965), pp. 53–4.

9 MacNeice, 'The Notebooks and Papers of Gerard Manley Hopkins', in Heuser (ed.), *Selected Literary Criticism*, p. 80.

10 *Ibid.*, p. 81.

11 *Ibid.*

12 *Ibid.*, The terms in the square brackets are taken from the editor's translation of MacNeice's use of terms in Aristotle's Greek.

13 MacNeice, 'Subject in Modern Poetry', in Heuser (ed.), *Selected Literary Criticism*, p. 58.

14 L. MacNeice, 'John Keats', in *Fifteen Poets* (Oxford: Clarendon Press, 1941), p. 351.

15 *Ibid.*, p. 353.

16 *Ibid.*, p. 354.

17 *Ibid.*

18 MacNeice, *Strings Are False*, p. 220.

19 L. MacNeice, *The Poetry of W. B. Yeats* (London: Oxford University Press, 1941), p. viii.

20 L. MacNeice, 'To Hedli', *Collected Poems 1925–48* (London: Faber and Faber), p. 9.

21 MacNeice, 'John Keats', p. 354.

22 MacNeice, 'Autobiographical Sketch', in Heuser (ed.), *Selected Prose*, p. 72.

23 MacNeice, 'Poetry Today', in Heuser (ed.), *Selected Literary Criticism*, p. 39.

24 MacNeice, 'Statement of Beliefs', in Heuser (ed.), *Selected Prose*, p. 188.

25 See 'MacNeice's Irelands: MacNeice's Islands' in this volume.
26 MacNeice, 'Autobiographical Sketch', p. 71.
27 L. MacNeice, *Varieties of Parable* (Cambridge University Press, 1991), p. 30.
28 *Ibid.*, p. 31.
29 L. MacNeice, *The Dark Tower and Other Radio Scripts* (London: Faber and Faber, 147), p. 72.
30 MacNeice, 'Statement of Beliefs', p. 188.

CHAPTER 13

John Hewitt and memory: a reflection

In June 1972 in a periodical named *Alliance*, John Hewitt published his poem 'Neither an Elegy nor a Manifesto: for the people of my province and the rest of Ireland'.[1] It is an impassioned plea that the collective mind of province and country during a time of political violence should pay true respect to the individual victims of the troubles. In the poem the poet eschews the term 'remember' since he believes that in Ireland that term comes with a burden of partisanship, 'a cruel web / threaded from thorn across / a hedge of dead bramble, heavy/ with pathetic atomies'. It is associated too with discredited 'prayer', which for Hewitt in this poem is 'tarnished with stale breath'. Instead of acts of memory and prayer, Hewitt advises 'Bear in mind these dead'. In the final, eighth, stanza of the poem, the poet ponders the nature of a healthy patriotism (in stanza two he had to a degree indicted a patriotism which is stirred up by rhetorical drumbeats). He asserts:

> Patriotism has to do with keeping
> The country in good heart, the community
> Governed with justice and mercy,
> These will enlist loyalty and courage often,
> And sacrifice, sometimes even martyrdom.
> Bear these eventualities in mind also, they will concern you for ever:
> But, at this moment, bear in mind these dead. (p. 189)

The clear implication of this poem is that disregard for the individual deaths in the troubles, in all their particularity, in the name of some higher cause, such as patriotism or loyalty, will mitigate against this true form of patriotic feeling which involves justice and mercy.

Hewitt was always a poet who took for granted that bearing in mind the dead was part of a poet's duty. Although he asserted of himself 'I have no ghosts. / My dead are safely dead' (p. 42), a considerable portion of his poetry, if it is not haunted, is certainly aware of the dead and his responsibility to them and conscious of their presence in his imagination.

At a basic level the poet accepts a role as an obituarist, for fellow poets such as W. R. Rodgers (Hewitt composed two such poems for Rodgers) and for local painters and craftsmen. 'The Lagan in October: Remembering Frederick W. Hull (1967–1953)' is representative of that worthy vein in his work with its conscientious salute to a minor artist. Yet Hewitt's obiturarist's impulse is not only directed, it should be noted, towards those who have made some palpable artistic mark on the world but towards lesser folk who must also be afforded the respect of an appropriate poem on their passing. What he calls a 'little death' in a poem about a scarcely known Chinese poet killed in what was 'a vast campaign' (p. 44) is worthy of his poem, as is the work of a forgotten scholar, the subject of 'Pavanne for a Dead Professor', who had one brief moment of professional fulfilment when 'He smiled, in the street, / and scarcely limped at all' (p. 53).

If the prevalence of obituary verse in Hewitt's oeuvre may be attributed to a duty accepted and discharged by the poet as a responsible citizen, then there is also evidence that the poet was in fact imaginatively absorbed by death itself. He is notably the poet of the deathbed scene; one thinks of poems such as 'My Father's Death in Hospital', 'A Father's Death', 'On Choosing Some Verses for My Sister's Cremation', 'My Great Grandfather's Refusal' (a tribute to a man who stuck to ballads when the end came, refusing to sing the hymns of Zion) and 'Grandfather Robinson Dies in 1989'. The bleakest of these often grim poems is, I think, 'Northwest Passage: An Old Man Dying', with its awesome conclusion:

> The hulk's swamped. As the wheel whirls out of hand,
> awash the vessel drifts in mountainous seas,
> with tattered signals we've no skill to read. (p. 339)

As Hewitt's editor, Frank Ormsby remarks: 'Hewitt depicts the approach and arrival of death as piteous, clumsy, aimless, crude and lonely, and is not disposed to be comforted by visions of an afterlife.'[2] For Hewitt, death truly seems to be the end of things. His is a secular consciousness for which death is cruel in its defining finality. This is the burden of that heartfelt sequence 'October Sonnets' with its central poem 'I've seen no more than three loved persons die'. In its final stanza he confronts 'an instant singular event, / that sudden absence in the silent room' (p. 334) with awestruck awareness of death as an absolute.

That each person's death is his or her own is related in Hewitt's oeuvre to the way he bears in mind individual lives. If each death is 'an instant singular event', the poet is drawn over and over again to bring to mind those moments in life when people reveal themselves as most themselves, in their unique humanity. One might name this epiphanic recall, as people are summoned in his verse from the past in characteristic gestures, in postures, engaged in defining activities that expressed personality. In 'For Roberta In The Garden', the poet recalls his wife at work with a trowel, for a moment raising her eyes and resting. The poet comments, 'I wonder, when you pause, you do not sing, / for such a moment surely has its song' (p. 357). 'Calling on Peardar O'Donnell' is another such poetic epiphany, where a journey through a darkening, isolated landscape (objective correlative of O'Donnell's craggy, independent socialism) concludes in the following lines:

> But halfway up the drive we glimpsed the writer
> Still working in the garden with his wife;
> I shouted and he straightened up to answer,
> And in the gloom his fine head glimmered white. (p. 346)

A lifetime of committed toil in a cause, a career of lonely integrity, is caught in a moment of revelation in the twilight.

It is noteworthy that some of these poems of epiphanic recall are intimately personal to the poet, as, for example, when he imagines his wife's childhood in a poem like 'Clogh-oir, September, 1971', with its lines:

> Standing there, I saw the lonely child
> with the black tossing head, the dark brows,
> as intense and definite as now,
> as palpable, now musing by my side,
> close in a vivid murmuring congregation … (p. 178)

Yet we mark how this poem concludes. The loved one is seen 'among queens, heroes, bards, kneeling peasants, / immortally assembled, that child's face / known before time struck, known for ever / stuff of the fabric whereof I am made' (p. 178). The fact that for Hewitt each individual is unique in life and death does not occlude the social, the communal and the collective. Each person is himself or herself, each life precious, but in expressing their personalities in individual ways, men and women partake of humanity and its history. A wife recalled as a child taking her place in a congregation, is one image in a tapestry of representative figures. A woman, for example remembered from childhood in a single posture can be an almost mythic figure. Here is 'Mary Hagan, in Islandmagee, 1919', a seawoman who exists in the poet's memory in terms of a physical stance, 'knuckles on the gunwhale / the great boots crackling on the bladderwrack; / one with Grace Darling, one with Granuaile' (p. 179).

For Hewitt's imagination is dominated by a consciousness of the patterns life weaves through the ages. Humankind is a product of nature, of place and weather, of cultural formations that determine habits and mores, of change that can disrupt long-settled ways. For Hewitt, in whose poetry the structures of human social existence are an abiding theme, the family and ties of kinship are of central importance. His sense of the past is accordingly centred in familial acts of remembrance. And although he disavowed 'memory' when he wrote 'Neither an Elegy nor a Manifesto', familial memories are the focus of many of his poems. This, of course, climaxes in his autobiographical volume *Kites in Spring: A Belfast Boyhood* (1980), which gives us an affectionate, respectful mapping of a 'connection' (that Ulster term) of aunts and uncles, great-grandparents, grandparents, parents, a sister, cousins, a nexus of familial relationships that unfold lines of affiliation through time and space. The import of this lengthy sonnet sequence, with its marriages and births, quarrels and makings-up, departures and returns, is that family is crucial to the ways in which we remember the past (as a socialist of Marxist coloration Hewitt might have been expected to emphasise class as definitive in human affairs, but surprisingly he does not). It is an inheritance not only in the genetic sense (and early in the sequence the poet confesses how his fear of early death was occasioned by a history of such tragedy in his mother's immediate family), but of values, assumptions, social and political alignments. To one family member who with the poet's father 'crossed / to Liverpool to hear Keir Hardie speak' (p. 269), Hewitt attributes his own socialism. To another he attributes his adult pleasure in 'the curtained stage alight' (p. 270). Of another, a Darwinian, expelled for heresy as a Sunday School teacher, the poet records: 'So though I lost him early, I have held / close to that sceptic and enquiring look / at the old riddle of the universe' (p. 272). In this evocation of an Edwardian and Georgian Belfast, Hewitt particularly admires independence of mind. People who leave things on principle are to be honoured, those who do not bow to authority celebrated. He is glad that his father refused to have him baptised because of an overbearing Methodist minister although he employed him as a school teacher. A family member is recorded as having left his Orange lodge, his father is remembered advising him not to join the Freemasons. In consequence the poet avers: 'So, from then on, my path in life was clear; / unsworn, unbound for ever, I should go, / a free man, freely, to the infinite' (p. 302).

Kites in Spring, therefore, is predominantly a book of familial recollection, indicating how profoundly Hewitt felt his life was affected by genetic inheritance and factors of kinship. Composed in the main as a series of family portraits (reading it is like leafing through an album of sepia prints; the iterative sonnet form adds to this sense of dynastic arrangement), the volume does also expand its perspectives to the historical era in which the poet lived as a child. A family is seen to live its life through the generations as the Victorian age gives way to the modern and Irish history is affected by events in the wider world. The Great War comes with its family death. Scott dies in the Antarctic, the Titanic founders. The troubles erupt with street violence. The growing boy is introduced not only to family stories but to the history of his country, which accretively becomes through the work a constituent, along with family, of his memories. 'Orchard Country', for example, reveals indeed how intimately familial experience and Irish history are intertwined in Hewitt's imagination. In this poem he recalls how his grandfather's mind was 'an open door to our own history' with stories of how a great-grandmother had died of famine-fever in the 'Armagh orchard country' (p. 272).

In fact, for Hewitt it is through family that he makes his claim on identity as an Ulsterman of Planter stock. In 'Orchard Country', it is because a family name is 'hearth-rolled' that he can claim to belong. Salient, too, is bearing in mind the dead, as he asserts in 'Once Alien Here', where he claims he is 'because of all the buried men in Ulster clay... / as native in my thoughts as any here' (p. 21). The notion of the remembered dead endowing rights (and also responsibilities) recurs in his poetry. In 'Retreaded Rhymes', for example, he evokes the 'windblown grass upon the mounded dead' (p. 366). In 'Freehold', the stanza from which this line comes is repeated, and in the section of that work titled 'Townland of Peace' he comes on a 'church-topped mound where half the tombstones wear / my peoples' names' (p. 379), and later in 'Freehold' he makes his claim explicit. The memory of the dead is a kind of title deed.

> Three hundred years
> are long enough for these last wayfarers,
> our fathers, now compacted here
> of this bright soil, these peoples, this bright air.
> The limestone of these hills has sheathed our bones;
> our names and texts are cut upon the stones;
> the landscape and our thought so intermixed
> our wits are jangled when the soil is vexed ... (p. 384)

And it is a family memory of a particular death that not only allows Hewitt to claim his place as an 'Ulsterman of planter stock' on the island of Ireland (whatever political arrangements obtain), but makes him Irish.

In 'Orchard Country', as we noted, the poet's grandfather told of how 'his mother died / of famine-fever caught in the strangest way' (p. 272). Hewitt makes this sad occurrence the basis of his poem 'The Scar' (dedicated to the Belfast poet Padraic Fiacc), which recreates the moment of infection, when a starving man sick with cabin fever begged a piece of bread and passed on what proved to be a fatal illness. The poet comments: 'and that chance meeting, that brief confrontation, / conscribed me of the Irishry for ever'. He continues:

> Though much I cherish lies outside their vision,
> and much they prize I have no claim to share,
> yet in that women's death I found my nation;
> the old wound aches and shows its fellow scar. (p. 177)

One might wish to enter a caveat here, that for the planter poet inscription in the Irish nation is by the way of infection, contamination (a familiar colonial trope of the dangers involved in fraternisation with the native); however, the simple word 'accepted' in the line 'accepted in return the famine fever' suggests a more benign reading. Understanding that both the beggar and his benefactor shared the national catastrophe makes cultural and ideological differences secondary matters. Perhaps the poem can be read to imply that we all share the pain of what was atrocious in the island's history (in this poem the north of Ireland and 'the stricken west' are united by the fact of death).

This poem with its final image of the aching scar is a testament to the awesome persistence of memory, a point that Hewitt's own poetry certainly makes over and over again, especially in the way he keeps returning to memories of his father. In Hewitt's oeuvre humankind is a remembering creature, indeed our very humanity seems to be defined by that capacity. Remembering can be emotionally dangerous, yet this 'bearing in mind' involves moral demands on the poet; it is an obituary duty, a way in which we define who and what we are, a mode whereby the individual connects him- or herself to family, to community in its social and historical dimensions and to the nation. It is also, Hewitt's poetry gives us to understand, both a pleasure and a pain.

So many of Hewitt's best poems are in fact poems of memory, in the sense that they are couched in a deliberative past tense, that they make recollection seem his characteristic stance in life. This then, as a mode of consciousness, becomes associated in the reader's mind with one of the principal pleasures Hewitt's verse affords: that sense of the world being received into the steady accumulative structures of his conscientiously composed stanzas. The effect (though sometimes it must be admitted it can seem merely repetitious) is to suggest a reality, the past, made amenable to a sustained, reflective ordering that does not deny deep familial, communal, even national emotion. To remember past experience, to bear in mind the dead, in the world of Hewitt's poetry is to share in one of the mind's most creative activities, the recalling and ordering of experience as the past constantly makes its presence felt in the continuous present tense of our lives. That activity, as Hewitt makes it known to us in his poetry, is a curiously exhilarating one, remote from mere nostalgia or easy sentiment, different from regret or romantic longing for what has gone. Rather it makes memory seem a living principle of a mature sensibility, without which the present would be bereft of real meaning. Past and present, the moment of the poem and the experience it brings out of the past constitute a state of feeling that allows the reader to enjoy memory as something vital, crucial to a full humanity, a defining constituent of what we are as human beings. This is 'Et Tu in Arcadia Vixit', one of Hewitt's favourites among his poems. In this the very processes of memory seem dramatised: the mind's associative powers stitch together the decades, as the poem's complex syntax contrives to follow its temporal range. A Parisian moment in the past achieves Proustian talismanic powers in the permanent present tense of recollection. The effect is, as I say, exhilarating, in a quietly intense way. And we should note, the poet himself understands the significance of memory in his philosophy of life. What the senses give to us from observant attention are a bulwark against death itself. 'Nourish your heart', he advises in the poem of that name, 'through all the ports of sense', concluding

> See you miss nothing. Name and store
> and set in order all. Let nothing be
> a toy too small, a trophy overpast
> the weighing palm that reckons less or more;
> for all you know, or I know, these must last
> the slow attritions of eternity. (p. 219)

If Hewitt's poetry affords us the pleasure of sharing in his vital recollective activity, he does not balk at the ways in which memory can involve pain. For Hewitt is also a poet of grief and loss, in which recollection plays its complex part. I'm thinking of such poems as 'A Birthday Rhyme for Roberta', which describes a moment of autumnal beauty that a loved one he had hoped would accompany him into old age, can no longer share; or of ' My Father's Ghost', which asserts 'when I've since stood in some famous place, / I've always thought I'll tell him he must come'

(p. 209). 'A House Demolished' mourns the loss of his childhood home in Belfast and the effect of that loss on his dream-life: 'Walls, wood-work shattered, textures shredded, torn, / those haunted corners hoard my dreams no more' (p. 324). In the first of the 'October Sonnets' (the third was quoted earlier), the violent shock of the loss of a loved spouse, is movingly recounted: 'after our forty years so close enwrought / it seemed absurd that she'd be thrust aside / to leave me lonely to my crippled thought' (p. 333). The pain of this event is caught in 'For Jean', when he thinks of her 'riven' from him 'by a witless fate' and remembers how he and his wife spent forty years together creating a swathe of time 'none living shares' (p. 338). Yet Hewitt also knows that even grief passes, that memories fade, as he acknowledges in a stanza of his poem 'Grief', which concludes this reflection on a poet for whom memory constituted a mature way of being in the world:

> Yet though life signs its verdict
> on every breast and thigh
> it adds a kindly codicil
> that grief must also die. (p. 153)

NOTES

1 F. Ormsby (ed.), *The Collected Poems of John Hewitt* (Belfast: The Blackstaff Press, 1991), pp. 188–9. Subsequent page references in the text to Hewitt's poems are to this edition.
2 *Ibid.*, p. lxxi.

CHAPTER 14

Michael Longley and
the Irish poetic tradition

Michael Longley's forty-year career as a poet has represented a complex engagement (in which his awareness of English poetic modes has played a vital part) with the Irish poetic tradition. His work has in fact illuminated, extended and in crucial respects helped to redefine that tradition in quiet, subtle, unforced but intriguing ways.

To begin with, in his oeuvre lines of association with other Irish poets can be detected that have made his writing life a distinctive yet deeply rooted contribution to late twentieth-century Irish poetry. This essay will initially seek to trace those threads as they wind through Longley's poetry, his prose writings and the interviews he has given over the course of the years. It will then reflect on the way Longley has made English modes amenable to Irish experience in ways that extend the possibilities of the Irish poetic tradition.

A feature of Longley's earliest enthusiasms as a poet was an exuberant eclecticism. As he emerged as promising poet at Trinity College, Dublin, in the late 1950s and early 1960s, after a period of literary inhibition at his Belfast grammar school (Royal Belfast Academical Institution) valued Rugby and getting-on in the Belfast way of the period), he read voraciously. He took the English tradition and contemporary verse as a whole as his proper field of engagement. In this he was aided and abetted by a well-informed companion who took him 'with joy' on an exciting voyage of discovery, a wide-ranging, engagingly unscheduled, poetic grand tour. Derek Mahon had arrived at Trinity College, Dublin, a couple of years after Longley but surpassed his friend in critical and aesthetic self-confidence. These were heady days:

We inhaled with our untipped Sweet Afton cigarettes MacNeice, Crane, Dylan Thomas, Yeats, Larkin, Lawrence, Graves, Ted Hughes, Stevens, Cummings, Richard Wilbur, Robert Lowell, as well as Rimbaud, Baudelaire, Brecht, Rilke – higgledepiggledy, in any order. We scanned the journals and newspapers for poems written yesterday. When Larkin's 'The Whitsun Weddings' first appeared in *Encounter,* Mahon steered me past the documentary details, which as an aspiring lyricist I found irritating, to the poem's resonant, transcendental moments. He introduced me to George Herbert who thrilled me as though he were a brilliant contemporary published that very week by the Dolmen Press.[1]

The list of poets cited here is telling, for Longley's brilliant contemporaries (from the seventeenth century to the twentieth) include only two Irish poets, neither of whom was published in Dublin by Liam Miller's Dolmen Press. And the list is strikingly internationalist in scope. One gets an impression of an instinctive imaginative open-mindedness of the kind that has marked Longley's sensibility throughout his career. Yet here are significant exclusions. There is no mention of T. S. Eliot, nor of the Ezra Pound whom Longley's poetic predecessor at Trinity, Donald Davie (he lectured in English in the university in the 1950s), so admired. Nor of Austin Clarke, the learnedly obscure Irish poet whom Davie as critic had begun to sponsor during his time in Dublin. A certain disregard for high Modernism and willful experimentalism may perhaps be inferred. Nor is Patrick Kavanagh referenced, one of the 'brilliant contemporaries', although his *Collected Poems* would appear in 1964. At his death, however, both Longley and Mahon contributed to a memorial edition of *The Dublin Magazine* in the spring of 1968.

Longley had in fact encountered Yeats (one of the Irish poets mentioned) at school when he had requested as a third-form prize for English the Collected Yeats, published in 1950. Yeats was also included in the examination syllabus for the Northern Ireland Senior Certificate, in the set anthology *A Pageant of English Verse*. From Yeats it is possible that he derived his perennial sense that traditional poetic form is a poet's best resource; in Yeatsian terms that 'ancient salt is best packing'. And Longley's according poetry a kind of sacral numen in a secular world may also have its source in his early reading of Yeats. However, it was Louis MacNeice (whose wonderfully sensuous philosophic lyric 'Snow' was included among the modern offerings in *A Pageant of English Verse*) who was the major Irish influence on the neophyte poet, who would also name Geoffrey Hill's *Mercian Hymns,* Philip Larkin's *The Whitsun Weddings* and Ted Hughes's *Lupercal*[2] as key influences.

The publication in 1966 of E. R. Dodds's edition of *The Collected Poems of Louis MacNeice* was the occasion which allows us to see the young Longley engage critically with the recently dead, Belfast-born, elder poet (MacNeice died in the autumn of 1963), for he contributed a review article of the volume (entitled 'A Misrepresented Poet') to *The Dublin Magazine,* in the spring issue of 1967. This was a remarkably assured, insightful piece of critical writing from the hand of a twenty-seven-year-old. It displays a keen eye for the strengths and weaknesses of individual poems (this was the period of practical criticism, in which Longley had been instructed by Philip Hobsbaum in the group which met informally in the 1960s at Queen's University, Belfast) and for the high points of a career which had included, it must be admitted, rather extensive swathes of dull versifying.[3]

Longley noted immediately, among the juvenilia of the early pages of the volume, the formal and rhythmic assurance of 'Trains in the Distance'. He cites what he identifies as lines of an authority unusual for a poet in his early twenties:

> Trains came threading quietly through my dozing childhood,
> Gentle murmurs nosing through a summer quietude,
> Drawing in and out, in and out, their smoky ribbons,
> Parting now and then, and launching full-rigged galleons
> And scrolls of smoke that hung in a shifting epitaph.
> Then distantly the noise declined like a descending graph …[4]

Longley comments: 'The lines and their rhythms are bold and efficient, the rhyming is effortless, and the poet's senses are as alert to the physical minutiae of his environment as his intellect is to their significance. Indeed, this little poem exhibits what were to remain MacNeice's major strengths as a poet.'[5] He might perhaps have observed too of this poem, but did not, that MacNeice, like himself, is a master of the sentence, allowing it to weave down lines of verse to compose a poem that possesses a curious, block-like form on the page and in the mind (Longley elsewhere refers to Auden's notion of poems as 'oblongs and squares' and associates his own 'fascination with what can be achieved through syntax, the arrangement of a sentence' with his interest in Latin syntax.)[6]

Longley's essay on MacNeice is also notable for the way it accurately establishes the overall shape of MacNeice's career. He notes the early lyrical successes, the drab middle years, with the Second World War, rightly I believe, read as a particularly fruitful period of MacNeice's life.[7] He grants 'the ease and scope of *Autumn Journal*' ('one of the luckiest poems … in which everything somehow falls into place').[8] He responds to the revived lyric tones of the later books, of *Solstices* (1961) and the posthumously published *The Burning Perch* (1963), when MacNeice 'was working towards a new kind of music – hard, stark and adaptable'.[9] He acknowledges MacNeice's achievements as a love poet for as such he avoided his besetting weakness as a poet: 'that refusal to let his ideas settle to a depth, which in his lesser poems results in surfaces made brilliant in order to cover up imaginative inconsistencies, and in verbal ingenuities which distract from what is being said'.[10]

Since Harold Bloom's challenging book *The Anxiety of Influence*, we have become accustomed to the concept of poetic influence as an agonistic thing, compact of oedipal stress and straining ambition. Longley's relationship with MacNeice, by contrast, has been less a Bloomian attempt to supersede a precursor, than a generous, admiring, absorbent capacity, a negative capability if you like, to allow MacNeice's sensibility an extended though altered existence in his own poetic. A further reflection on MacNeice's poetry, which Longley published in 1971, suggests how his own work developed under the enabling influence of MacNeice as an example.

Longley in 1967 had recognised how MacNeice is often superficial, too worldly to be really wise, though he had exempted the love poetry from such strictures. By 1971 he had come to feel that when set against MacNeice's Ulster background, 'the dizzy word play and the riot of imagery', which for many English critics mars his work, can be read in quite different terms:

A proper consideration of his background, however, should help us to understand that all the gaudy paraphernalia of his poetry is finally a reply to darkness, to 'the fear of becoming stone'. His games are funeral games: the bright patterns he conjures from the external world and the pleasures of being alive are not fairy light and bauble but searchlight and icon.[11]

In a more measured, reflective way, Longley's own love poetry can be said to share something of this dialectic. For his love poems (such as, for example, 'On Mweelrea') are often elaborate conceits whose complex, elegantly detailed metaphors often carry rumours of war, of individual and mass slaughter (the Great War and Irish 'troubles' constitute Longley's primary historic horizons):

> September grew to shadows on Mweelrea
> Once the lambs had descended from the ridge
> With their fleeces dyed, tinges of sunset,
> Rowan berries, and the bracken rusting.
> Behind my eyelids I could just make out
> In a wash of blood and light and water
> Your body colouring the mountainside
> Like uncut poppies in the stubbly fields.[12]

For all the heavy-breathing, forced psycho-drama of Bloom's Freudian vision of influence, he is surely right, however, when he celebrates that moment of poetic power, of burgeoning authority, when a poet writes in a manner which makes the precursor seem the imitator (as when the Stevens of 'Notes Towards A Supreme Fiction' makes Keats seem to anticipate the

poetics of the American poet – he makes Keats sound Stevensish). At a
crucial moment in Longley's 1967 account of MacNeice, he alerts us to
how he performs a similar feat. He isolates a moment in MacNeice's verse
which in fact seems to anticipate some of his own poetic characteristics.
He categorises MacNeice's 'Mayfly' as 'a masterpiece' and cites four lines:

> Who make the mayflies dance, the lapwings lift their crests,
> The show will soon shut down, its gay-rags gone,
> But when this summer is over let us die together,
> I want always to be near your breasts. (p. 14)

Longley would later insist of the poem's conclusion that 'these two beautiful lines disclose the nucleus of his imagination'.[13] In fact such frank,
slightly plush eroticism with an intimation of decadent satiation is a
very unusual note, a Longleyan note indeed, in MacNeice's work. For
MacNeice's love poems are notable less for their consciousness of bodily
presence than for an intense awareness of time arrested in the passion of
the moment, with actual physicality rendered indirectly. 'Trilogy for X'
(written, as we know from Jon Stallworthy's biography of MacNeice, for
Nancy Sharp) is a telling instance:

> But now when winds are curling
> The trees do you come closer,
> Close as an eyelid fasten
> My body in darkness, darling;
> Switch the light off and let me
> Gather you up and gather
> The power of trains advancing
> Further, advancing further. (p. 88)

The phrase 'close as an eyelid fasten' is just the kind of surprising, yet
exact, Donne-like conceit we might expect to find in Longley's love
poetry. But where Longley would have elaborated upon it in an exploration of the sheer oddity of bodily experience, MacNeice shifts into a
more obviously literary trope, to distance the physicality of sexual intercourse, while allowing us to sense its rhythms and intensity. By contrast,
we may adduce Longley's 'The Linen Industry', whose final lines make us
hear the later poet in MacNeice's 'Mayfly':

> And be shy of your breasts in the presence of death,
> Say that you look more beautiful in linen
> Wearing white petticoats, the bow on your bodice
> A butterfly attending the embroidered flowers. (p. 119)

The metaphysical elaboration of this poem, rich in troping (an intimation of Herbert's rather than of Donne's poetics invests the whole with a religiose/erotic, emblematic quality), educates us to the way in which such a poem is both related to yet different from MacNeice's love poems, which are typically poems of sexual tension and bodily absence. Where MacNeice poises the moment of passion against an imagery of temporal movement, when 'the show will soon shut down, its gay-rags gone' ('Mayfly', p. 14), when 'the moving stair' will start up again ('Meeting Point', p. 167), Longley allows himself to settle into a protracted meditation in 'The Linen Industry' in which Eros and Thanatos are presiding deities at a celebration of the processes of bodily existence. For this is a poem of growth and decay, creativity and decline, hair, cloth, bone, the palpable presence of actual body and bed.

It is, nevertheless, the weighty physicality of 'The Linen Industry', its materialist awareness of things in themselves (flax, flowers, peaty water, grasses, stooks, skirts, in the first stanza alone), that alerts us to a further aspect of Longley's verse that establishes MacNeice as a precursor who has his Longleyan moments.

Longley remarks in his introduction to the *Louis MacNeice: Selected Poems* (1988): 'Like most true poets he relished making catalogues, whether of place-names ("West Meon, Tisted, Farnham, Woking, Weybridge") or film-stars ("Cagney, Lombard, Bing and Garbo") or things ("Cubical scent-bottles artificial legs arctic foxes and electric mops"). Seldom can the lyric have carried so much freight and remained airborne.'[14] Longley himself is a poet of catalogues, who has indeed made the list a principle of composition in some poems, with an exacting deliberation bred of a settled, materialist vision of the world. By contrast MacNeice's list-making seems an exuberant or appalled response to the 'drunkenness of things being various' ('Snow', p. 30) or to their weary torpor (note 'Flower Show' with its 'cream cheese, paper, glass, all manner of textile and plastic', p. 521).

Longley's fascination for lists increased over the years until he began to trust the list as a poem in itself. 'The Ice-Cream Man' and 'Trade Winds' in *Gorse Fires* (1991) and 'The Fishing Party' in *The Ghost Orchid* (1995) are the crucial instances. Such manifestations of a recurrent obsession also direct us to the way many of Longley's recent poems seem to take a list of objects as a kind of ur-text from which the poem has emerged. In 'The Dry Cleaners' (in *The Ghost Orchid*), for example, a list of named objects is brought into contiguity and relationship by grammar (three complex sentences) and the narrative occasion the poem summons into existence:

> That time I tagged along with my dad to the dry cleaners
> We bumped into Eurycleia whose afternoon-off it was
> And bought her tea and watched her smooth the table-
> Cloth and make her plate and doily concentric circles, then
> Pick up cake-crumbs with a moistened finger, since to us
> There was more to her than jugs and basins, hot water
> And cold bed-linen she tested against her cheek after
> The rainy trek from clothes-line to airing cupboard. (p. 221)

One notes here the predominately nominative quality of Longley's verse, with nouns held lovingly in such writing in a solution of exact grammar. This also contrasts significantly with MacNeice's poetry when in his late verse he too sometimes took lists as poetic ur-text. In MacNeice, however, such lists are verbs rather than nouns, as they record transient events rather than the secure givenness of material reality Longley values so much. For MacNeice sees the world characteristically in terms of motion and activity: 'Coffee leaps in a crystal knob / Chugs and glints while birds gossip' ('Country Week-End', p. 488). Longley's universe is a naming of things as they palpably are, as in the opening lines of 'Northern Lights' in *Gorse Fires*:

> When you woke me up and showed me through the window
> Curtains of silk, luminous smoke, ghost fires,
> A convergence of rays above the Black Mountain … (p. 182)

It is also a world of the naming of places (the Belfast place name of 'Northern Lights' is a typical instance). MacNeice could name places too in his poetry, as in 'The Strand' where he memorialised a father who 'So loved the western sea and no tree's green / Fulfilled him like these contours of Slievemore / Menaun and Croaghaun and the bogs between' (p. 226) in lines that have a direct echo in Longley's

> and all the stars are out
> Lighting up hill-tops, glens, headlands, vantage
> Points like Tonakeera and Allaran where the tide
> Turns into Killary, where the salmon from the sea … ('Campfires', p. 224)

Yet such use of Irish place names, common in Longley's work, is comparatively rare in MacNeice's poetry. He can, it is true, make his own music with the names of his adopted England: 'A smell of French bread in Charlotte Street, a rustle / Of leaves in Regent's Park …', (*Autumn Journal*, section V, p. 109), or 'We drove round Shropshire in a bijou car / – Bewdley, Cleobury, Mortimer, Ludlow ...' (*Autumn Journal*, section VIII, p. 115). However, it is Longley who can begin a poem in *The Ghost Orchid*, 'How does the solitary swan on Dooaghtry Lake' (p. 197), weighing a place name in his hand, like a magical talisman, in a distinctly Yeatsian fashion. For Yeats could famously begin a poem: 'He stood among a crowd in Drumahair ...' ('The Man Who Dreamed of Faeryland'). So it is Longley more than MacNeice who recalls Yeats to mind when he creates his English language music with an echo of Gaelic nomination, in such resonant lines as: 'From the townland of Carrigskeewaun, / From a page lit by the Milky Way' ('Remembering Carrigskeewaun', p. 170).

In his 1967 review essay of MacNeice's *Collected Poems*, Longley did not address at any length the matter of MacNeice's Irishness, beyond observing that 'his poetry is the direct reflection of an ironic Northern Irish personality'[15] and that he had a love–hate relationship with his native land. His 1971 observations on MacNeice, as we saw, took up that topic in a few telling sentences. He saw then how what can seem superficial to an English readership can, with knowledge of the poet's Irish background, allow MacNeice to be reckoned as 'a touchstone of what an Ulster poet might be'.[16] The implication is that context is a part of meaning, the tradition in which a poet works and the culture from which he derives in part determining how his work should be read and judged.

This instinctive early awareness of the ways in which interpretative communities bear on aesthetic experience is in fact a clue to a central aspect of Longley's career and to his recent work in particular. For Longley has been aware from quite early on that Ireland, its experience and imaginative traditions affect more general ways of apprehending the world when they are adopted, self-consciously or otherwise, by Irish poets and writers. In a 1972 symposium on 'The State of Poetry', published in England in *The Review*, he tackled the question of literary peripherality in interesting ways. Of a recent 'efflorescence of poetry in the provinces', he made the bold claim: 'most of the best contemporary Irish poetry is being written North of the Border' and asserted: 'the Irish psyche is being redefined in Ulster, and the poems are born – inevitably, one might say – out of a lively tension between the Irish and the English traditions'.[17] He wrote of 'a fruitful schizophrenia in someone trying to write poetry in Ireland' appreciative of the contemporary poetic vitality in the provinces of Britain. 'I ... am', he averred, 'proud to stand on the geographical and, possibly, the cultural edge of a vital tradition which can accommodate a few Irish accents.'[18]

Crucial to this thinking is the idea that lively tension between English and Irish traditions can help to redefine the Irish psyche – can bring something new to birth. It is akin to his view that MacNeice's poetry, apparently superficial in England, in Ulster can be vested with specific significance by a particular interpretative community. In Northern Ireland certain English traditions (in his contribution he endorses the then fashionable 'well-made poem') can take on new forms and alter Irish consciousness in significant ways.

In the light of this, it might be possible to ponder the shape and significance of Longley's career as an engagement not only with the Irish poetic tradition in the work of Yeats and MacNeice (both of course Irish poets whose work also extends the tradition of English language poetry as a whole), but as a semi-conscious programme in which a series of essentially English poetic modes and kinds have undergone a sea change in an Irish setting. One might list these as follows: the First and Second World War poem, the natural history poem, the well-made poem of Movement vintage, the classical poem (that is a poem employing classical allusion or with content derived from classical literature). A hasty reading of each of these kinds of work in the Longley canon might too readily assign them to the English tradition: the First and Second World War poems with their poetic respects paid to Isaac Rosenberg, Edward Thomas and Keith Douglas, the natural history poems with their roots in essentially English traditions of amateur botanising, the well-made poems, the product of the Movement's post-war reduction of imaginative horizons and empirical circumspection, the classical poems with their modern source in public- or grammar-school education, all might seem to fit comfortably within an English frame of reference. In Longley's work, however, these poetic kinds are carried over into Irish contexts (in effect they are 'translated'), thereby allowing them to find a new form of life in the context of an Irish poetic consciousness.

Longley's imaginative 'importation' of the classical poem is, perhaps, the most striking of his various acts of metamorphosis in which English poetic kinds are remade in an Irish context and can be considered as representative of his poetic acts of generic 'translation'. One must be careful here. For of course Ireland has no need whatsoever to import classical knowledge as a poetic resource from the neighbouring island.[19] Yet there is a distinct sense in Longley's early deployment in his verse of classical matter that the poems derive from the world of polite learning and gentlemanly education that made the study of the Classics in the Protestant Ireland in which the poet had his social formation seem a distinctly English kind of cultural activity. In 'Odyssey', 'Circe', 'Nausicaa' and 'Narcissus' in Longley's first volume, *No Continuing City* (1969), classical occasions and allusions served as imaginative stimuli for elegant, carefully constructed negotiations by a cerebral sensibility of the mythic possibilities of life in general. The tension in these poems between an urbane discourse and the awareness of a mythic dimension in experience does suggest, it is true, that Longley's classicism from the start was thematically driven, that it was no merely conventional literary trope. But the poems' generalised classical provenance remained their most obvious characteristic. It was his work in *Gorse Fires* and *The Ghost Orchid*, however, that suggested how classical occasion and Irish reality can be associated in ways that speak to a twentieth-century Irish preoccupation.

Since the turn of the twentieth century, in the work of Yeats and principally in the writings of James Joyce, Irish writers had been redefining a national relationship with the Greek and Latin origins of European civilisation. These have historically been compromised in Ireland in as much as classicism seemed so much a property of the conqueror, and of imperial Victorian England, with its colonial administrators governing an empire by means of the sword and a Latin tag. And the Church, with its Roman imperium mediated through the Latin tongue, added to the sense of a heavily entailed inheritance. Longley's work, as it 'translates' the classical poem for an Irish interpretative community, is therefore part of a process whereby the Greek and Roman legacy has been appropriated to modern Irish experience in fresh ways by twentieth-century poets and dramatists (Seamus Heaney, Tom Murphy, Brendan Kennelly and, before them, Austin Clarke spring to mind in this context). Longley's contribution has been to situate Homeric and Ovidian narratives in Irish contexts of locale and event in a strikingly intimate manner. In his versions of the old tales, familiar stories and events are renovated as they become grimly local, domesticated and yet nobly, poignantly strange once again in a fully realised material world (in 1985 Longley spoke of how in Homer, 'still a favourite poet – the sense of physical life ... comes out of that story beneath its mythological/historical overlay').[20] The ancient Greek world of the epic narratives and a fully Irish topography and nomination are brought together, therefore, with remarkable assurance in a poem such as the already quoted 'The Camp-Fires' in a way that enlarges our sense of what an Irish poem can be (note the magisterial control of parenthesis, as if in a brief Irish poem of place, a Homeric simile can unfold in all its spacious grandeur):

> All night crackling camp-fires boosted their morale
> As they dozed in no man's land and the killing fields.
> (There are balmy nights – not a breath, constellations
> Resplendent in the sky around a dazzling moon –
> When a clearance high in the atmosphere unveils
> The boundlessness of space, and all the stars are out
> Lighting up hill-tops, glens, headlands, vantage
> Points like Tonakeera and Allaran where the tide
> Turns into Killary, where salmon run from the sea,
> Where the shepherd smiles on his luminous townland.
> That many camp-fires sparkled in front of Ilium
> Between the river and the ships, a thousand fires,
> Round each one fifty men relaxing in the fire-light.)
> Shuffling next to the chariots, munching shiny oats
> And barley, their horses waited for the sunrise. (p. 224)

NOTES

1 M. Longley, *Tuppenny Stung: Autobiographical Chapters* (Belfast: Lagan Press, 1994), pp. 36–7.

2 'Michael Longley', in 'The State of Poetry: A Symposium', *The Review,* Nos. 29–30 (Spring/Summer 1972), 47.

3 Longley published his selection of MacNeice's verse in 1988. It is a much more generous, celebratory volume than W. H. Auden's somewhat grudging selection of 1964.

4 Cited in Longley, 'A Misrepresented Poet', *The Dublin Magazine,* 6, 1 (Spring 1967), 69. Page references to MacNeice's poems in the text refer to E. R. Dodds (ed.), *The Collected Poems of Louis MacNeice* (London: Faber and Faber, 1966).

5 Longley, 'A Misrepresented Poet', 69.

6 See Robert Johnstone, 'The Longley Tapes', *The Honest Ulsterman,* No. 78 (Summer 1985), 20 and 15.

7 See 'Louis MacNeice and the Second World War' in this volume.

8 Longley 'A Misrepresented Poet', 72–3.

9 *Ibid.*, p. 74.

10 *Ibid.*, pp. 69–70.

11 M. Longley, 'Poetry', in M. Longley (ed.), *Causeway: The Arts in Ulster* (Belfast: The Arts Council, Dublin, in association with Gill and Macmillan, 1971), p. 97.

12 M. Longley, *Collected Poems* (London: Cape Poetry, 2006), p. 142. Subsequent page references to Longley's poems in the text are to this volume.

13 Longley, 'Introduction', in *Louis MacNeice: Selected Poems* (London: Faber and Faber, 1988), p. xxii.

14 *Ibid.*, pp. xvii–xviii.
15 Longley, 'A Misrepresented Poet', 68.
16 Longley, 'Poetry', p. 97.
17 Longley, 'The State of Poetry', p. 47.
18 *Ibid.*, p. 48.
19 See W. B. Stanford, *Ireland and the Classical Tradition* (Dublin: Allen Figgis and Co. Ltd, 1976; Totowa, NJ: Rowman and Littlefield, 1977). Stanford was one of Longley's teachers in Trinity College, Dublin, where he read Classics.
20 Johnstone. 'The Longley Tapes', 16.

CHAPTER 15

Seamus Heaney: the witnessing eye
and the speaking tongue

From the start Seamus Heaney has seemed oddly guilty about being a poet at all. Indeed, one of his earliest widely admired poems, 'Digging', scarcely disguised its embarrassment at the inadequacy of a poetic career in comparison with Heaney's father's more obviously useful skills. The association in that poem, the first in *Death of a Naturalist* (1966) and therefore standing at the head of Heaney's oeuvre, of the pen with gun seems a rather desperate stratagem to invest the poet's art with something of the male authority of the father's spade and the ancestral achievement it consolidates. 'Real men don't write poems' is the emotional undercurrent of the piece. So it is not until 'Funeral Rites' in *North*, as the poet steps in to accept a communal role at the funeral of 'dead relations', that he can assert, 'I shouldered a kind of manhood.'[1] The implication is that it is only in such an act of social involvement that the poet can begin to feel truly adequate as a man.

This sense of the questionable worth of a poetic career, which in its simplest form may involve a doubt as to whether the writing of lyric poems is any work for a man, frequently finds expression in Heaney's poetry and criticism as an interrogation of the ethical efficacy of the poetic act itself. For Heaney has always been a poet anxious to do the world some good, troubled by his art's apparent incapacity to make things happen. He has known from the beginning that the peculiar power of poetry is to offer a kind of liberating music, a lyric occasion which can seem free of all moral motions, secure in its own self-delight. Indeed, in *Death of a Naturalist*, one of the charms of the apprentice poet's work is how often he accedes to his ardent conviction that the lyric note is the true one. Poems such as 'In Small Townlands', 'The Folk Singers' and 'The Play Way' celebrate the moment of artistic licence, the moment caught in 'Saint Francis and The Birds' when the saint preached love to the birds and they

> Danced on the wing, for sheer joy played
> And sang, like images took flight.

> Which was the best poem Francis made.
> His argument true, his tone light.[2]

Poetry in this book is a kind of incantatory magic for which music is the obvious metaphor but which has analogies with the diviner's craft, as in *Door into the Dark*, it bears comparison with the alchemical powers of the thatcher ('Thatcher') or the priestly energies of the blacksmith ('The Forge'), who at the altar of his anvil 'expends himself in shape and music'.[3] It is in 'The Given Note' in *Door into the Dark* that Heaney managed his most devil-may-care early declaration of faith in the art to which he was serving a somewhat earnest apprenticeship. The poem invokes as a type of the true artist a Blasket Island fiddler who has heard spirit music in the Atlantic winds, which sets him apart from the more pedestrian musicians who cannot follow his bewitched strains. He has the courage of his gift and for a moment the poet is at one with him in his solitary indifference to conventional expectation:

> For he had gone alone into the island
> And brought back the whole thing.
> The house throbbed like his full violin.
> So whether he calls it spirit music
> Or not, I don't care. He took it
> Out of wind off mid-Atlantic.
> Still he maintains, from nowhere ...
> It comes off the bow gravely,
> Rephrases itself into the air. (p. 46)

Heaney, insufficiently secure in his sense of himself as poet when in 1969 the Northern crisis erupted, could scarcely have been expected to maintain in the face of such exigencies so insouciant, so debonaire an indifference to everything but his art. And in 'Land' (included in *Wintering Out* in 1972), he reckoned with the painful entanglements which would be involved if he listened as an artist to the sounds of an island loud in comfortless noises.

> I expect to pick up a small drumming
> and must not be surprised
> in bursting air
> to find myself snared, swinging
> an ear-ring of sharp wire.[4]

From *Wintering Out* onwards those entanglements are everywhere: the work is heavy with duty, weighted with 'responsible *tristia*' (*North*, p. 73) as the poet seeks to discover whether the lyric gift can consort with communal disaster. Throughout, a tone of meditative resolution, a note of grave ethical piety, contains the lyric impulse as if to force a wanton to some kind of fidelity, to contain music in a civic consciousness.

Heaney, one senses, knew that poetry would never settle for containment, but his own familial, communal and national loyalties were so deeply engrained and his ethical impulses as artist so undeniable that he sought an aesthetic which could allow poetry its efficacious role in the Ireland of 'neighbourly murder' (*North*, p.16). He did so in terms of a theory of poetry as emblem. It was in his Royal Society of Literature lecture of 1974, 'Feeling into Words', that Heaney outlined this personally enabling theory. There he spoke of the moment, the summer of 1969, in Belfast when 'the problems of poetry moved from simply being a matter of achieving the satisfactory verbal icon to being a search for images and symbols adequate to our predicament'.[5] In other words, the aesthetic impulse must reckon with the ethical and social demands of a grievous historical crisis. For Heaney, this dilemma presented itself in a conflict of beauty, the poet's most natural concern, with the rage of political and sectarian violence. He writes, quoting a Shakespeare sonnet, "'How with this rage shall beauty hold a plea?' And my answer is by offering 'befitting emblems of adversity'".[6] From this aesthetic, expressed in allusion to Yeats's "Meditations in Time of Civil War', emerged in the 1970s those powerful, brooding poems 'The Tollund Man', 'The Grauballe Man', 'Punishment', 'Funeral Rites' and 'The Strand at Lough Beg', which attended to atrocity through a strangely supplicatory art, as if ritual enactments of one kind or another, drawing on mythology, might salve the public wound. But alongside such poems of dreamlike iconographic originality went others which sought to hold to a freer poetic faith, which hunted an endorsement of the poetic act itself. Heaney's poems of visionary iconography, where he seeks an almost Yeatsian phantasmagoria, are compromised, therefore, by a tone of reiterative admonition, as if the poet wishes to trust the song but lacks that final assurance of the unselfconscious singer. 'Lie down', he has the longship's swimming tongue say to him in 'North', the title poem of the 1975 collection,

> in the word-hoard, burrow
> the coil and gleam
> of your furrowed brain.
> Compose in darkness.
> Expect aurora borealis
> in the long foray but no cascade of light. (p. 20)

In Heaney's poetry of that difficult decade, there are suggestions of guilty fear that he has betrayed his art to the gross conditions of a squalid conflict, and, conversely, that he has stood idly by as others have suffered, his only contribution the telling of a species of poetic rosary beads. It is in his 1984 volume, *Station Island*, and particularly in the title sequence, that his guilt feelings about his artistic career and his poetic role surface clearly as matter for poetry. In 'Station Island', set on a pilgrimage island in Lough Derg in County Donegal, the poet confronts those guilt-feelings as a series of ghosts from his own and Ireland's literary past. They address him with an authority of tone and conviction that his poetry had latterly tended to lack. They proffer a comprehensive indictment, as if the poet hoped for exoneration of a Kierkegaardian kind, as he brings to mind that gloomy Dane who once recorded that our greatest comfort is in knowing that before God we are always in the wrong. The poet Aiden Carl Mathews has thoroughly, if not quite comprehensively, summarised the case of Heaney against Heaney:

He pleads guilty to having left home; he pleads guilty to having exercised his gifts with something not unlike single-mindedness at a time when murder and mayhem have blocked the sewers of his home and hinterland; he pleads guilty to not having felt deeply enough about it all, as if deep feelings weren't, in every sense, a bloody liability in such a situation; he pleads guilty to having devoted a great part of his life to, well, himself and his loved-ones ... he pleads guilty to having become a laureate and luminary by writing poems about events which have walked filth, misery, and strickenness into the living-room carpets of a legion of families afflicted by louts with kalashnikovs; and in a strange sad way he pleads guilty to the very fact that he exists.[7]

What Mathews does not include in this litany of self-accusation is the fact that on top of all this Heaney accuses himself, in the scornful accents of James Joyce, of betraying his art to the ethical demands of a decent but inadequate humanism and concern for his people:

> You lose more of yourself than you redeem
> doing the decent thing. Keep at a tangent.
> When they make the circle wide, it's time to swim
> out on your own and fill the element
> with signatures of your own frequency ...[8]

Like the fiddler in 'The Given Note' one supposes. But how is this to be done? The answer to that question has been the matter of Heaney's poetic and critical reflections in *The Haw Lantern* (1987) and *The Government of the Tongue* (1988).

Station Island was dominated by self-accusation. In *The Haw Lantern*, Heaney reckons with the accusatory eye of a public in whose gaze he has lived much of his adult life. So in 'Alphabets', with which the book begins, he is caught in the public eye as he lectures on literature and poetry; 'From the Frontier of Writing' transposes the experience of the military checkpoint to the television interview:

> The guns on tripods;
> the sergeant with his on-off mike repeating
> data about you, waiting for the squeak
> of clearance; the marksman training down
> out of the sun upon you like a hawk ...[9]

and the title poem itself imagines a scrutiny at once completely local and completely knowing:

> so you end up scrutinized from behind the haw
> he holds up at eye-level on its twig,
> and you flinch before its bonded pith and stone,
> its blood-prick that you wish would test and clear you,
> its pecked-at ripeness that scans you, then moves on. (p. 7)

The trope is that of the haw lantern as Diogenes seeking the just man, his departure in that final line a judgement. Elsewhere the volume is absorbed by occasions of judgement, attentive to the moment of verdict, as if the poet yearns for some release from the stresses of public trial. In 'Two Quick Notes', the pain of self-accusation is remembered, certainly, as a peculiarly active form of suffering beside which the more public sort must seem less demanding. But it is wearisome none the less. So there is a strong sense in this volume that the poet has had quite enough of certain kinds of public examination which he must persistently undergo, and which are peculiarly impertinent since in *Station Island* he has conducted his own exacting self-scrutinies. There are accordingly frequent occasions in *The Haw Lantern* when Heaney conceives a moment of transformation, of release into a freer form of imaginative life, as in the concluding lines of 'From the Frontier of Writing':

> And suddenly you're through, arraigned yet freed,
> as if you'd passed from behind a waterfall
> on the black current of a tarmac road
> past armour-plated vehicles, out between
> the posted soldiers flowing and receding
> like tree shadows into the polished windscreen. (p. 6)

In 'A Ship of Death', this mysterious process of artistic liberation, whereby a poet escapes imposed public duties, judgement, is imagined in a version of the ship burial of Scyld Scefing from *Beowulf*. The strong ruler, founder of a dynasty, like Cuchulain comforted, laid aside 'when his time came' the burden of kingship for a magical journey without known landfall. He goes forth like a child with a kind of innocence: 'No man can tell, / no wise man in the hall or weathered veteran / knows for certain who salvaged that load' (p. 20).

All this accusation and desire for exoneration and release in *The Haw Lantern* gives a resonant ambiguity to the book's centrepiece, the sequence 'Clearances'. And the accusatory context alerts us to the various implications of the title. For a clearance is not only an act of clearing land for future productive use: the term also suggests the clearance afforded by the jury's favourable verdict, acquittal, vindication, the clearing of a debt. And, linking the sequence to 'A Ship of Death', a clearance can also be a document certifying that a ship has satisfied all demands of the custom house and has received permission to sail. That the second poem of the sequence establishes an accusatory metaphor as a controlling presence in the work further links 'Clearances' to the rest of the book. The sequence explores the poet's relationship with his recently dead mother, re-entering his first world, in which his early lyric impulse had its source, with a delicacy and tact that poignantly suggest the possibility of new beginnings even amidst the sense of loss. The poet therefore seems to imply that a highly self-conscious, literary return to a world once taken wholly for granted, to the world indeed which energised his earliest and more naive work as a poet, can allow him to escape the accusatory eye and to write by contrast the poetry of the witnessing eye. It is no accident, therefore, that the first poem in 'Clearances', the same one as remembers a stony and tribal judgement ('the first stone / Aimed at a great-grandmother's turncoat brow', p. 25) realises itself in terms of a painterly metaphor. Life is remembered as art. No experience in maturity comes to the mind unmediated:

> Call her 'The Convert.' 'The Exogamous Bride.'
> Anyhow, it is a genre piece
> Inherited on my mother's side
> And mine to dispose with now she's gone. (p. 25)

The consciousness of the artist's freedom is in the word 'dispose', but it is the visual constituents of a painter's world that he is free to dispose as he wishes, or indeed, in the more customary usage, to set aside. The eye is the instrument of vision. So, in what must be a key metaphor for the volume, in 'A Daylight Art' the poet's pen becomes a 'nib's eye', associated with a fisherman's rod:

> *Practise the art,* which art until that moment
> he always took to mean philosophy.

> Happy the man, therefore, with a natural gift
> for practising the right one from the start –
> poetry, say, or fishing; whose nights are dreamless;
> whose deep-sunk panoramas rise and pass
> like daylight through the rod's eye or the nib's eye. (p. 9)

This is an arterial moment in Heaney's oeuvre, taking us back through 'Casualty' in *Field Day*, with its murdered fisherman, to 'A Lough Neagh Sequence' in *Door Into The Dark* and to 'Digging' in *Death of a Naturalist*, where the pen was gun was spade. Now the pen observes and disposes a visual world where once it sank into the bog in guilty emulation of the ancestors or momentarily threatened violence. Poems such as 'The Old Team', 'A Postcard from Iceland' and 'A Shooting Script' in *The Haw Lantern* accordingly make play variously with the tropes of photography and documentary film, self-consciously signalling their artfulness with reference to visual occasions. 'The Spoonbait' knowingly begins, 'So a new similitude is given us / As we say' (p. 21), introducing an elaborate conceit 'Glimpsed once and imagined for a lifetime' (p. 21). The world is, as it were, made the object of a purely visual attention. It is held in the rapt observation of a poet rediscovering in 'The Disappearing Island' the vitality of sight upon release from a dark imprisonment:

> The land sustaining us seemed to hold firm
> Only when we embraced it *in extremis*.
> All that I believe that happened there was vision. (p. 50)

However, the witnessing eye of vision turned, as in 'Clearances', on the primal world must register more than simple delight (Yeats's phrase 'the delighted eye' from 'In Memory of Major Robert Gregory' readily springs to mind as one reads the book). It must take account of the implications of a true witnessing, a bearing witness to the intractable aspects of experience which are unamenable to any simple artistic disposition. For he who sees is a witness and must bear testimony. This Heaney seeks to do in the political parables he has included in the book. By indirection, obliqueness, the artfulness of the allegorical mode, he offers not a painter's disposition but a deposition; he makes a statement. Some of these parable poems of imaginary but recognisable places ('From the Republic of Conscience', 'From the Canton of Expectation', 'Parable Island') seem a little forced to this reader, at their weakest moments collapsing into banality. It is as if Heaney had sought to learn from such poets as Milosz and Mandelstam, Herbert and Holub (whose work occupies him in his collection of critical essays *The Government of the Tongue*), but, crucially and indeed fortunately in other respects than the artistic, had lacked the sense of actual, immediate pressure which finds release in their work, as urgent and risky parable. The air of a literary exercise (as in 'From the Republic of Conscience') is fatal to the mode. For the truly convincing political parable must bear the stark imprint of necessity.

But one of these poems in *The Haw Lantern* escapes such strictures. 'The Mud Vision' is an allegory, wholly convincing in its strangeness, of a disrupted people experiencing a moment of authenticating vision. And it is a vision of themselves 'vouchsafed' in 'original clay' ('Clay is the word', Kavanagh asserted, to launch *The Great Hunger*). The moment of course passes, but not before it has charged the future with a sense of cultural possibility. The truly witnessing eye opens without apologetic self-regard or self-accusation. The poet is ready to accept the public's gaze. For he once again possesses the lyric faith. Not the ardent freedom of youthful exuberance discovering the lyric potential of the given and familiar, but something hard-won which takes the duty of the witnessing eye for granted, which does not avert its face from 'the beggar at the gate'. And in such writing, guilt is transcended in an art which, wholly responsible to its own form and the language of its expression, can rest easy in a kind of chastened delight, knowing its own untrammelled possibility. As the poet himself expressed it:

The achievement of a poem, after all, is an experience of release. In that liberated moment, when the lyric discovers its buoyant completion and the timeless formal pleasure comes to fullness and exhaustion, something occurs which is equidistant from self-justification and self-obliteration. A plane is – fleetingly – established where the poet is intensified in his being and freed from his predicaments. The tongue, governed for so long in the social sphere by considerations of tact and fidelity, by nice obeisances to one's origins within the minority or the majority, this tongue is suddenly ungoverned. It gains access to a condition that is unconstrained and, while not being practically effective, is not necessarily inefficacious.[10]

For Heaney such an achievement, this movement from the eye to the tongue, does not represent an evasion of the necessity to witness, but the most authoritative kind of testimony. For 'In this dispensation, the tongue (representing a poet's personal gift of utterance and the common resources of the language itself) has been granted the right to govern. The poetic art is credited with an authority of its own.'[11] It is in the 'Clearances' poems in *The Haw Lantern* and in the controlled envisioning of 'The Mud Vision' that we sense what such writing might be like, as Heaney speaks with unfettered freedom in the language which he has for so long courted with the brooding guilt of the ethical dialectician, anxious about the efficacy of the lyric act. At last the kind of assured utterance which in 'Station Island' he seemed only to be able to allow to voices of admonition and accusation, to admonitory ghosts and sibylline voices of rebuke, gets direct, ample expression, in verse of full-throated ease, an earnest of what we could hope for from this most gifted of poets in his maturity:

> Those nights when we stood in an umber dew and smelled
> Mould in the verbena, or woke to a light
> Furrow-breath on the pillow, when the talk
> Was all about who had seen it and our fear
> Was touched with a secret pride, only ouselves
> Could be adequate then to our lives. When the rainbow
> Curved flood-brown and ran like a water's back
> So that drivers on the hard shoulder switched off to watch,
> We wished it away, and yet presumed it a test
> That would prove us beyond expectation. (p. 49)

NOTES

1 S. Heaney, *North* (London: Faber and Faber, 1975), p. 15. Subsequent page references to poems from this volume are given in the text.
2 S. Heaney, *Death of a Naturalist* (London: Faber and Faber, 1966), p. 53.
3 S. Heaney, *Door Into The Dark* (London: Faber and Faber, 1969), p. 19. Subsequent page references to poems from this volume are given in the text.
4 S. Heaney, *Wintering Out* (London: Faber and Faber, 1972), p. 22.
5 Seamus Heaney, 'Feeling into Words', in *Preoccupations: Selected Prose 1968–1978* (London: Faber and Faber, 1980), p. 56.
6 *Ibid.*, p. 57.
7 Aidan Carl Mathews, review of *Station Island* and *Sweeney Astray*, *Poetry Ireland Review*, No. 14 (Autumn 1985), 83.
8 S. Heaney, *Station Island* (London: Faber and Faber, 1984), pp. 93–4.
9 S. Heaney, *The Haw Lantern* (London: Faber and Faber, 1987), p. 6. Subsequent page references to poems from this volume are given in the text.
10 S. Heaney, 'The Interesting Case of Nero, Chekhov's Cognac and a Knocker', in *The Government of the Tongue* (London: Faber and Faber, 1988), p. xxii.
11 *Ibid.*, p. 92.

CHAPTER 16

Derek Mahon: the poet and painting

Light plays a crucial part in the imaginative world of Derek Mahon's poetry. He is in fact a markedly visual poet, one who attends patiently, even contemplatively, to the look of things and especially to the way light falls on them. The opening stanza of 'A Postcard from Berlin' is entirely typical of a poet whose impressions of the world are refracted through an eye caught by the glimmer of light on water, the flash of sunlight through cloud, the bright glitter of the sea, the glistening of moonlight on rainwater:

> We know the cities by their stones
> Where Ararat flood-water shines
> And violets have struggled through
> The bloody dust. Skies are the blue
> Of postcard skies, and the leaves green
> In that quaint corner of Berlin.
> Wool-gatheringly, the clouds migrate:
> No checkpoint checks their tenuous flight.[1]

Mahon seems fascinated by the idea of a landscape lit as if by some creative light that purifies everyday experience. So Aran in 'Thinking of Inis Oir in Cambridge, Mass.' is for him

> A dream of limestone in sea-light
> Where gulls have placed their perfect prints.
> Reflection in that final sky
> Shames vision into simple sight;
> Into pure sense, experience. (p. 25)

And in 'Aran' the island is 'unearthly still in its white weather' (p. 31). He is moved too by the moment when light breaks in darkness, when shadow suddenly releases its hold on the mind. Dawn is his prime time, particularly in the washed light after the storm at sea, as in 'The Sea in Winter', when a northern coast awakens to a transfigured world:

> But morning scatters down the strand
> relics of last night's gale-force wind;

> far out, the Atlantic faintly breaks
> sea-weed exhales among the rocks … (p. 114)

'Bright' is a key word in a poetry that responds to the play of light on surfaces, to the way a scene is transformed by the breaking of darkness, by spectacular moments of vision, as in 'An Image from Beckett':

> In that instant
> There was a sea, far off,
> As bright as lettuce,
> A northern landscape
> And a huddle
> Of houses along the shore. (p. 34)

Mahon is attentive also to the act of seeing. There is a visual self-consciousness in much of his poetry, as if he is intent on watching himself and others watching the world through eyes that know light is a kind of artist which composes landscapes and cityscapes, still-life interiors, as it falls on sea and shore, on street and table. His is a poetry of visual epiphanies, of 'light music' as he calls it in a sequence of haiku-like poems he first published in 1977 and to which he has subsequently added and subtracted entries. Poem after poem in his work directs us to the effects of light in a poetic that insists that (as he has it in 'A Lighthouse in Maine') 'The north light / That strikes its frame / Houses is not / The light of heaven / But that of this world' (p. 142). The poet, and the light he so celebrates, together remind us in Mahon's work that consciousness, whatever else it is, is a visual construct, an ordering of the random stuff of the world's reality where light and the eye conspire to suggest a formal synthesis in an otherwise chaotic experience. Accordingly the poet asks in 'Everything Is Going to Be All Right':

> How should I not be glad to contemplate
> the clouds clearing beyond the dormer window
> and a high tide reflected on the ceiling? (p. 111)

He recognises in this markedly self-reflexive meditation that the poems 'flow from the hand unbidden / and the hidden source is the watchful heart' (p. 111). But they do so only as the heart is 'watchful', receptive to moments such as this when light composes a world of visually arresting relationships ('a high tide reflected on the ceiling', p. 111) which the poet is privileged to contemplate, as he might a skyscape glimpsed through a painted window in an artist's canvas.

'Midsummer', the first of the 'Surrey Poems' collected in *Poems 1962–1978*, reveals how self-consciously painterly an eye Mahon brings to the act of verbal description in his work:

> Today the longest day and the people have gone.
> The sun concentrates on the kitchen garden
> with the bright intensity of June.
> The birds we heard singing at dawn
> are dozing among the leaves
> while a faint soap waits its turn
> in a blue sky, strange to the afternoon –
> one eye on the pasture where the cows roam
> and one on the thin line between land
> and sea, where the quietest waves
> will break there when the people have gone home. (p. 73)

The poem it is true does contain aural references but the primary impression is visual. The concentration of the sun on a kitchen garden focuses our attention too. We are aware of 'bright intensity', a 'faint soap … in a blue sky', and of the moon's eyes[2] in the poem and the poet's eyes cast on a pastoral scene. We see also the waves poised timelessly as they await the moment when they will break and time will begin again. The 'thin line between land / and sea' serves as a visual and conceptual metaphor for midsummer's timeless moment of painterly stasis.

That so visually aware a poet as Mahon should have been attracted as an artist to the work of painters does not therefore surprise. Moved as he is by light and its effects, conscious as he is of seeing as a mode of ordering ordinary reality, art and painting plays a more important role in Mahon's oeuvre than simply offering occasional subject matter (and fairly frequent passing allusion).

In the introduction to his translation of selected poems by the French poet Philippe Jaccottet, Mahon reflected on the relationship between painting and the poet whose work he had translated. His remarks confirm that for Mahon the relationship between poetry and painting is complex but central:

Consider Bonnard's *Snow Garden* (1900), where the dusk is inflamed by a red blaze from the setting sun. Garden, snow and light combine in a fierce synthesis such as Jaccottet himself often achieves. Jean Grenier, in *La Galerie des Arts* (no. 41, February 1967), says of Bonnard that 'he had a child-like vision which transforms the quotidian into the marvellous, the scene needn't be unusual or impressive: on the contrary, it's the most familiar things which exercise the strongest hold upon his attention'. Nabokov, in *The Real Life of Sebastian Knight*, says of

Clare Bishop that 'she possessed that real sense of beauty which has less to do with art than with the constant readiness to discern the halo round a frying pan or the likeness between a weeping willow and a Skye terrier'. They might have been speaking of Jaccottet.³

Indeed, they might have been speaking of Mahon's own poetry, which so frequently attends to luminous moments as in a Bonnard canvas. For Mahon too is absorbed by the way light falls on the visible world to invest it with numinous presence and an impression of inherent relationships.

Mahon has written several poems specifically about painters: 'A Portrait of the Artist', first collected as 'Van Gogh Among Miners' in *Night-Crossing* (1968) (subsequently also published under the title 'Van Gogh in the Borinage'), 'The Forger' also first collected in *Night-Crossing* and a reflection on the career as painter of the Modernist master Wyndam Lewis in 'A Kensington Notebook', first collected in *Antarctica* (1985). The first two of these are very much about the artist's love affair with light and belief in its transfiguring powers.

In 'A Portrait of the Artist' (dedicated to the Northern Irish painter Colin Middleton), Mahon has Van Gogh as an obsessive devotee of light in a dark country, one who glimpses not truth but vision in the ordinary world of objects:

> light
> Refracted in a glass of beer
> As if through a church window,
> Or a basin ringed with coal-dust
> After the ritual evening bath. (p. 20)

He has him declare a desire to go south and paint what he has seen:

> A meteor of golden light
> On chairs, faces and old boots,
> Setting fierce fire to the eyes
> Of sun-flowers and fishing boats,
> Each one a miner in disguise. (p. 20)

Light is now the only spark from heaven ('meteor') which does nevertheless make radiantly beautiful even the grim world of the Borinage. For such things as chairs, faces and old boots in a Van Gogh canvas are as mysteriously significant as the sunflower and fishing boats of his more exuberant period. Appropriately, the forger of the poem of that title is brother to Van Gogh in his love for light ('The thing I meant was love', p. 18) since his speciality is fake Vermeers, the artist who above all paints light as if it were itself composing the scene before its viewers' eyes. The forger, like Van Gogh before him, dreams of a world transformed by light as he suffers in a bleak zone of being:

> And I too have wandered
> In the dark streets of Holland,
> With hunger at my belly
> When the mists rolled in from the sea;
> And I too have suffered
> Obscurity and derision,
> And sheltered in my heart of hearts
> A light to transform the world. (pp. 18–19)[4]

Mahon is fascinated in his poems on specific pictures (or groups of pictures) by the way light seems to bear witness to moments of perfection, where the visible world becomes a static wonder. In his famous meditation on Pieter de Hooch's canvas 'The Courtyard of a House in Delft' (Mahon's title is 'Courtyards in Delft') and on paintings in a similar vein by that artist, we see 'Oblique light on the trite, on brick and tile – / Immaculate masonry' (p. 120). We are in a world of 'trim composure', 'chaste / Perfection', a reality 'As vividly mnemonic as the sunlit / Railings that front the house opposite' (p.120). So although the emotional temper of the poem is predicated on a comparison between the still perfection of art and the untidy squalor and political ambiguity of the real world, the poem cannot help rising to a celebration of the ordinary represented in terms of a Dutch still life of the seventeenth century:

> I lived there as a boy and know the coal
> Glittering in its shed, late-afternoon
> Lambency informing the deal table,
> The ceiling cradled in a radiant spoon. (p. 120)

This is certainly to put a halo round a frying pan.

In the equally remarkable poem based on Edvard Munch's 'The Girls on the Pier', there is the same concentration on the moment of stillness caught for ever by the painter. The road in the picture (and one presumes that Mahon has a specific version of this repeated image in Munch's portfolio in mind, for he dates his poem 1900):

> stops to find
> The girls content to gaze
> At the unplumbed, reflective lake,
> Their plangent conversational quack
> Expressive of calm days
> And peace of mind. (p. 173)

And the poem ends with the girls remembered in a long-lost past as they 'gazed at a still pond' (p. 175). Caught as they are in a picture which arrests our gaze, their world is as timeless as the reflective lake is unplumbed, although they are named 'Grave daughters / Of time' (p. 173) by the poet who knows what horrors may await them outside the dimensions of art. To invoke these he depends on 'The Scream', another of Munch's well-known images (indeed the 'ghastly sun' which 'watches in pale dismay', lighting and composing the scene in the poem is as much the summer light in the other picture as it is the source of fading light in 'Girls on the Bridge'): 'A mile from where you chatter / Somebody screams' (p. 174).

Mahon responds with such reverence to moments like that recorded in Munch's painting, when the world achieves a momentary, significant stasis, because his own imagination, as we have observed, is profoundly attracted to such epiphanic, luminous occasions in life itself. So many of the most memorable moments in his verse record instances of light's transfigurations. Yet the poet knows they may simply be tricks of light whether they occur randomly in the life of the world or as the product of artistic craft in a painting. Accordingly, it is in his poems on paintings that he confronts in a direct way an issue that troubles him throughout his work – that is, whether the composed achievement of art may be an illusory misrepresentation of the real for all its beauty.

Mahon expresses this aesthetic doubt most explicitly in his 'Rage for Order', first collected in *Lives*. There he deprecated with self-conscious irony the futility of art in a world of urban warfare with its burnt buses and broken glass. Against this the poet can only proffer, in a metaphor which combines light with observation, 'the fitful glare of his high window'. Poetry is 'an eddy of semantic scruples / in an unstructurable sea.'[5]

Mahon's poetry as a whole is pervasively alert to the conditions of the unstructurable sea of contemporary history. His predominant tone is that of an elegist for a vanishing civility, a pessimist of the present moment. So instants of visual luminosity in his poetry are almost invariably accompanied by signs of social degradation and political desuetude, which humiliate the pretensions of all art forms. A poem like the marvellous 'The Sea in Winter' can advise:

> A fine view may console the heart
> with analogues for one kind of art –
> chaste winter-gardens of the sea
> glimmering to infinity ... (p. 116)

But it does so in '*un beau pays mal habité*' (p. 114), where

> The shouts
> of souls in torment round the town
> at closing time make as much sense
> and carry as much significance
> as these lines carefully set down.
> All farts in a biscuit tin, in truth –
> faint cries, sententious or uncouth. (p. 116)

Mahon's poems on paintings are striking occasions in his work when the claims of art itself are tested. The still moment of youth poised on the brink of time in 'Girls on the Bridge', for example, is set against a vision of modernity as nightmare that calls into question the innocence of that moment of arrested time which the painting and the poet capture. In fact the evocations of a domestic interior which Mahon discerns in it are more suggestive of the images of a Dutch Golden Age canvas than of the expressionist angst of Munch's universe: 'beds, / Lamplight and crisp linen' (p. 173). Indeed Mahon treats the picture as a rare moment of idyll in Munch's customarily anguished work, the more to emphasise the horrors of the present. In the context of 'the arctic dark' we now inhabit 'Under the arc-lights of / A mineral heaven' (p. 174), the painting serves therefore as a version of pastoral.

In 'Courtyards in Delft', the calm immanence of a moment from puritan domestic life, of a kind passingly evoked in the Munch poem, is set against an awareness of all that is missing in the painting. Such composure can be achieved in life and art only by excluding music, eroticism, lust, politics and the imperial adventurism which was the source of that wealth which made Dutch society so stable and secure but which in the late twentieth century became the cause of 'fire / And sword upon parched veldt and fields of rain-swept gorse' (p.121). What makes 'Courtyards in Delft' so moving a poem is the fine balance of its emotional weighting. The poet both censures a reality of limited possibilities – implicit provincial rectitude, underlying colonialism – and is moved by the values immanent in the scene portrayed in the canvas. In 'the thing made', as the poet notes with a well-judged apposition: 'Nothing is random, nothing goes to waste: / We miss the dirty dog, the fiery gin' (p. 120).

'Courtyards in Delft' has appeared in two versions.[6] It was first collected in the volume of the same name (1981). It then appeared as the opening poem in *The Hunt by Night* in 1982. This added a fifth stanza which expanded on the colonial implications of the final lines of the fourth stanza and concluded with an invocation of the forces of disorder which might overturn a world which for all its frugal decencies is a source of evil:

> If only, now, the Maenads, as of right,
> Came smashing crockery, with fire and sword,
> We could sleep easier in our beds at night.[7]

In *Selected Poems* (1991), this stanza is once again excluded by the poet. The fifth stanza had upset, one senses, the sustained ambiguity of the poem's affective response to the painting, compact of irritation and nostalgia, censure and reluctant admiration. It was that which in its original version had made it so gravely thoughtful an entry in Mahon's perennial, meditative investigation of the relationship between art and life. Neither art nor life had been granted priority.

For in Mahon's sense of things, a fine painting through its effects of light, shade and colour is a paradigm of the way in which all art can affect perception of the world, even if the world customarily is refractory and chaotic. As aesthetician Mahon is instinctively sceptical of high-flown claims for the aesthetic itself, yet he is at the same time markedly loath to abandon the possibility that the truths of art are truths indeed. 'The Studio' (first collected in *Lives* as 'Edvard Munch') is accordingly a kind of manifesto. Focusing on a Munch canvas, the poet acknowledges the pressure of the world on the aesthetic moment to which the painting bears witness in its tormented fashion, but does not permit it the final say. One might expect the objects in the studio to disintegrate in a wild disorder, in chaos,

> But it
> Never happens like that. Instead
> There is this quivering silence
> In which, day by day, the play
> Of light and shadow (shadow mostly)
> Repeats itself, though never exactly. (p. 30)

The picture remains intact, its centripetal energies resisting the centrifugal tug of a world outside the canvas which could destroy it. Such is art's and poetry's claim on us, the poem implies. It provides, in Robert Frost's phrase from 'The Figure a Poem Makes', 'a momentary stay against confusion'.[8]

In Mahon's world it is human suffering and violence that offer the most disturbing challenges to the aesthetic. The girls in 'Girls on the Bridge' could occupy a pastoral zone of feeling since they 'knew no pain' (p. 175).

By contrast, ours is manifestly a world of anguish. It is colonial 'ire / And sword'⁹ which rebukes the 'modest but adequate' (p. 120) mode of life represented in 'Courtyards in Delft'. In 'The Studio', the simple bulb in the ceiling is 'honed / By death to a worm of pain' (p. 30), reminding us of the suffering that must threaten the quivering silence of the painting. If that became definitive, everything in the painting would 'abruptly / Roar into the floor' (p. 30). Mahon's poetry as a whole is permeated by its sense of apocalypse and disaster, which was the fate of countless millions in the twentieth century. At moments he seems to write after some absolute catastrophe, from a kind of post-history in which the light that fitfully redeemed the past has finally been extinguished. It is no accident in the imaginative universe of this writer that his most famous and perhaps his finest poem, 'A Disused Shed in Co. Wexford', should end with an apostrophe – 'You with your light meter and relaxed itinerary' (p. 63) – as if to address a technologist of light in a world where technologies of death have put out all illumination.

Two of Mahon's poems about pictures are occasions when aesthetics and violence are directly juxtaposed, since the pictures (themselves so wonderfully composed) provoke reflections on man's inhumanity to man and beast. About suffering they were never wrong, the old masters, one is minded to comment, reading Mahon's 'The Hunt by Night' and 'St Eustace' as stops on his personal tour of the Musée des Beaux Arts. Both these poems employ the elegant stanza form which is also to be observed at work in 'Girls on the Bridge', where each stanza seems to encapsulate its vision within a consciously limited canvas. The effect is of a series of miniatures, skilfully wrought, aesthetically satisfying. Yet the matter with which they have to do is the brutality of the hunt and the horrors of death by execution.

In Mahon's poetic study of Uccello's 'The Hunt by Night', the picture itself is reckoned a demonstration of how art aestheticises reality. What in the dark past of the 'neolithic bush' was a thing of 'foetid / Bestial howls' has become in the imagination of the painter a 'pageantry' made irresistibly desirable in a stylised deployment of light and shade, of oddly exquisite colour and sensory effects:

> The mild herbaceous air
> Is lemon-blue,
> The glade aglow
> With pleasant mysteries,
> Diuretic depots, pungent prey
> And midnight hints at break of day

Where, among sombre trees,
The slim dogs go ... (p. 176)[10]

Yet Mahon knows this is a version of a reality which has its actual origins in the predatory instincts of the species that no aesthetics can wholly disguise. So the poem, for all its own artifice, remains sceptical of the painterly *sprezzatura* of an Uccello, in which the hunt ('our hunt by night / So very tense / So long pursued', p. 177) can seem 'some elaborate / Spectacle put on for fun' (p. 177). Art and reality vie in the poem for primacy. That neither is victor gives to the poem that tone of charged, meditative tension which is one of Mahon's most compelling poetic registers.

'St Eustace' also involves the hunt, in Pisanello's version of the conversion of the saint who will himself as a martyr be 'Braised in his own fat for his contumacy / And vision' (p. 144). The vision of St Eustace, in a poem about a light which can change a man's destiny, is no mere aesthetic moment of immanence or luminous possibility. It is 'His nemesis'. Art and reality finally conjoin in painting and poem, no longer separable, to leave only a terminal pathos (perhaps Mahon's quintessential poetic note) in the face of illumination and suffering. St Eustace, the hunter, converted to the Christian faith, who refuses to offer a sacrifice to the gods of Rome, in his dying is briefly: 'One with the hind, the hare /And the ring-dove' (p. 144).

NOTES

1 D. Mahon, *Selected Poems* (London: Viking; Oldcastle, County Meath, Ireland: Gallery, in association with Oxford University Press, 1991), p. 149. Subsequent page references to Mahon's poems in the text (unless stated otherwise) refer to this volume.

2 That Mahon intends the moon by the image of 'faint soap' is indicated not only by the context but by the poem entitled 'Dawn Moon' in the sequence entitled 'Light Music', which begins 'A slip of soap in the sky' (p. 68).

3 D. Mahon, 'Introduction', in *Selected Poems: Philippe Jaccottet* (Harmondsworth: Penguin Books, 1988), p. 13.

4 In *Night-Crossing*, for 'wondered' Mahon originally gave 'wandered'.

5 D. Mahon, *Poems 1962–1978* (Oxford University Press, 1979), p. 44. In the version collected in *Lives*, which was arranged differently on the page, 'scruples' read 'scruple'.

6 For an excellent analysis of Mahon's many poetic revisions, see P. Denman, 'Know the One? Insolent Ontology and Mahon's Revisions', *Irish University Review*, 24, 1 (Spring/Summer, 1994), 17–37.

7 D. Mahon, 'Courtyards in Delft', in *The Hunt by Night* (London: Oxford University Press, 1982), p. 10.

8 Robert Frost, 'The Figure a Poem Makes', in *The Complete Poems of Robert Frost* (London: Jonathan Cape, 1967), p. 18. It is perhaps worth noting that Frost associates this experience, which a good poems provides, with 'clarification', a visual term.

9 In its first collected form this simply read 'war'.

10 In its first collected form in *Courtyards in Delft* (1981), the phrase 'diuretic depots' read 'sylvan excitements'. The change was made in *The Hunt by Night* (1982) and was probably intended to offer a more complex sense perception with its implied reference to excrement.

CHAPTER 17

Telling tales: Kennelly's Cromwell *and Muldoon's* 'The More a Man Has the More a Man Wants'

Brendan Kennelly's *Cromwell* appeared to variously astonished and celebratory reviews in Dublin in 1983. Since then, despite its republication in England in 1987, it has attracted surprisingly little critical attention. Perhaps there was something overwhelming about its obsessional tones, its urgent formal repetitions, its piling of horror on horror, its Blakean raid on the palace of wisdom by the road of excess, which has not allowed it to appeal to the critical intelligence with its taste for allusive uncertainties, irony, structural niceties and the aesthetic frisson. The poem therefore has enjoyed to date a curious kind of critical half-life, reckoned the work in which Kennelly achieved a breakhrough from being a poet of minor lyric successes (in itself a misreading of his earlier work) to being a poet with something altogether more significant to say, and simultaneously as a work which does not require sustained analysis or exacting attention. It is absorbed into critical comprehension as a work of shock effects, video nasty sensationalism, scarifyingly explicit violence and bold, rhetorical drama. Seamus Heaney in nominating *Cromwell* as one of his books of 1983 in the Dublin-published *Sunday Tribune* newspaper encapsulated this general critical consensus when he spoke of 'a sense of an outbreak'. An outbreak is certainly hard to pin down, is critically difficult to contain and tends to lack apologists and sponsors. And the unsettling kind of authority which this work exercises in those places in which Irish poetry gets talked about did not, it seems, compel the editors (Derek Mahon and Peter Fallon) of *The Penguin Book of Contemporary Irish Poetry,* published in 1990, to represent Kennelly's work by any selection from what many readers have assumed to be his most important work to date.

So the work has been easy to celebrate and then ignore as another bold attempt to dramatise the savage complications of our past. Certainly the choice of so loaded a figure as Cromwell as subject matter did tend to suggest that the Irish experience was its primary preoccupation. What has not been considered, therefore, is the degree to which in this work

Kennelly's preoccupation is not simply with Irish history as an arena of conflict, struggle, colonial suppressions and rebellions and terrifying violence, all made graphically if sometimes unsubtly present in the text, but with the psychological springs of evil and the sources of hate-filled action in the human heart. In *Cromwell*, Kennelly offers the insights of the psychologist and not those of the historian or social philosopher. His object of attention in this remarkable work is the human condition itself, the imagination, ego and will to power and to satisfaction of appetite, which make of Man, angel and beast, statesman and demon, survivor and victim.

Oliver Cromwell is of course the most fully realised presence in the poem. He is such since he is the only inhabitant of this house of dreams, phantoms, this echo-chamber of voices, cries, curses and black comic asides, to possess a developed sense of his own personhood. Indeed, it is his self-confident grasp on his own sense of self and mission which makes him so frightening an entity in this poem of monstrous shapes, chimeras and nightmare visitants.

We first encounter Cromwell as 'the butcher' invited into Buffún's room in a sonorous prose preface entitled 'Measures'. So we are introduced to the two central personages of the work, the Lord Protector himself and a representative Irish figure, Michael Patrick Gusty Mary Buffún with whom the imaginary Cromwell will conduct a bizarre relationship throughout the poem. But it is not as butcher that Oliver (so referred to throughout much of the poem in grimly comic intimacy) first enters the poetic text, but as an English child in his native countryside, mythologised into a primal English locale in the individual poem's title (for *Cromwell* is in fact a sequence of two hundred and fifty-four named poems), 'Oak'. Here the child is father of a God-obsessed man. But in this poem his psyche seems possessed of some animistic local deity of the oak and a 'firm green land / Looking over black marshes with willows and alders'.[1] This god is an English god, a pagan god of locale and region who could be transformed in the mind of a Cromwell into a national deity for whom it would be appropriate to 'Live and die'.

> Drunken Barnabee, staggering all roads,
> Making Latin rhymes through satyr eyes
> Sang of an oak-tree
> On a hill behind Godmanchester. (p. 17)

It is Cromwell's fate in this poem to be a man so persuaded of the truth of his own vision that he lacks all self-doubt. From such assurance, from such secure egotism, comes an authoritarian urge to command and a disregard for the ambiguities of language and experience which confuse less executive minds. In an extended, unpublished reflection, which Kennelly wrote on his own poem during its composition, the poet considered the Cromwell who so absorbed him in this work. There he admitted that Cromwell 'was a great man, whatever that means' and continued:

I think it means he was strong enough to bend circumstances to his will, to turn his own attitudes to God into God's intentions for him, to establish himself as a master ... and therefore to see the world as his servant ... there are other examples of English history, some serious, some extremely unserious at work in the poem, but Cromwell is the chief one, the focus, the paradigm. The paradigm of what? Well to start with the paradigm of power; of an egotism hard to understand and impossible to measure; of a compulsive need to possess and control; of an unquestionable sense of the unquestionable value of his own being as a model for erring humanity, even as he took care to remain humble before his God; of a truly passionate sense of mission and purpose; of discipline, sincerity, honesty, devotion to duty and powerful military philosophy; of that vision of violence which transforms murder and massacre into moral necessities; of the scrupulous need to see domination of others as just and resistance by others as criminal; and above all, perhaps, of the unshakeable conviction that Oliver, like the England he loved and fought for, was always right.[2]

This is the Cromwell he brings before us in the work in those passages where the butcher speaks in the accents of command and imperious certainty. One senses at such moments that Kennelly the artist, the dramatist, is not without respect, even admiration for the Cromwell whom he permits to speak with a fierce, controlled eloquence, a voice of thunder:

> What could I do with individuals
> Whose word was worthless as the barking of dogs?
> I addressed the black ravening coil
> Of blusterers at Drogheda and elsewhere:
> 'In this hand the laws of earth and heaven:
> In this, my sword. Obey and live. Refuse and die.'
> They refused. They died. These letters are fire,
> The honest chronicle of my desire,
> Rough, shaggy as the Numidian lion,
> A style like crags, unkempt, pouring, no lie. (p. 24)

And as artist, one suspects the poem is in awe of one whose style is so distinctively the man, for whom language and action, word and deed are conjoined in some immediate exercise of power:

> I speak plainly. I have no words, no wit.
> I love England. I love the very thought of it.

> I would lay open the danger
> Where in my conscience I know we stand.
> If you do not see what is obvious here
> We shall sink, our house will fall about our ears.
> I tell you plainly what is dangerous.
> I see what threatens us.
> I see what is.
> Sluggish men will not acknowledge this,
> Preferring the happiness of lies.
> I see what is. I speak what is.
> These are things – not words. (p. 65)

But the poet also knows that the English language in Ireland, which Cromwell employs with such unself-conscious rhetorical certainty (a 'man for whom a word is a deed come true' (p. 71), is a weapon in the hands of a butcher. For as Kennelly asserts in his own reflection on the poem: 'above all violence is the *speech* of England, the truest language of the men and women who never cease prattling about rationality and restraint, dignity and discipline'.³ His language is the medium of an artist who trades in terror:

> Write this down in the blank page of your mind.
> Cromwell is my friend as England is my friend,
> And will be, if I obey, to the end of time. (p. 54)

So Kennelly would wish to understand how such a paradigm of power could come into being, how such a psychology is created and sustained. Accordingly, the figure of Cromwell is subjected to a series of black comic indignities and is cast in improbable roles the greater to highlight all those aspects of his personality which may account for his greatness but which are less than great in themselves. He is the bluff, complacent Englishman enjoying a little fishing on a Kerry estate, the man whose passionate mission disguises the economic interests of his comfortably landed class; he is the self-important fool who never realises what a ludicrous figure he cuts even when at his most terrifying or when covered in shite ('the bowels of Christ') in William Street, Listowel. He is the conventionally condescending voice of a presumed civility which turns a blind eye on the consequences of its own prejudice; he is coarsely amused by crude practical jokes; and above all he is incapable of empathy with the victims whose lives he has blighted. In these character traits lie the origins of his consistently hortatory treatment of Buffún, the representative of the nation whose life and history he has permanently affected and whose psyche is dominated by a relationship with a man and a country it never sought.

Buffún in *Cromwell* is everything that Oliver is not. Where Cromwell is self-assured, Buffún lacks any certainty of selfhood at all; where Oliver has a language which he unthinkingly exploits as a weapon of oppression, Buffún languishes in the shadow of an English which he knows is not his own; where Cromwell thinks and acts Buffún dreams, chatters, wheedles, pleads, rages and despairs. Above all he lacks a voice where Cromwell speaks with the voice of authority. In Kennelly's view he's 'the poem's persona'[4] but one who 'lives in contradiction':

> Buffún is, if anything, a haunted conglomeration of voices, history's echo-chamber ... some sort of a man with many voices; not merely a man who speaks but one who is spoken through, a human wound through which history's blood seeps, congeals and then re-works itself into a new fluency. A bit of a nightmare, in fact. In fiction too.[5]

Buffún certainly is fluent. Indeed, part of the immediate impact of this work, its instant readability, comes from the way Kennelly has given Buffún a persuasively knowing command of a suavely sardonic demotic which he employs with fertile, bravura self-disgust. He is the inventive, casual, cynical voice of an Irish everyman as victim, survivor, hero, villain, the voice of contradiction, of the colonised mind. In Buffún we are given an object lesson in the psychology of oppression, of victimage:

> One moment I was nothing to the crowd
> The next so helplessly a part of it
> I had lost what I had come to regard
> As myself. I was drowning in a river of hate
> I was a grub half-way down a sparrow's throat
> I was the look Judas threw at the tree
> I was fingers fit to handle a pound-note
> I was a voice and a sickness of voices
> I was a hunger-striker wrapped in a Union Jack
> In the rain on a slippery roof in the city
> I was crying out to be judged I was
> the crime I was the hangman the rope
> I was a prisoner longing for love and pity. (p. 29)

Buffún's psychology in this poem seems determined by his fraught relationship with Cromwell. His world is defined by Cromwellian edict and his life consists in responding to its constraints and conditions. But what makes Cromwell what he is, this monster of an egotism 'hard to understand and impossible to measure'? To suggest answers, Kennelly peoples his poem with a series of archetypical presences, figures from myth, history and folklore which embody insights into the psychic

energies at work in the force that is Cromwell and in the reactive stratagems of Buffún. We meet the Giant, the Belly, the Hand, Mum, Ed
Spenser, King Billy, Balder, Big Island and Little Island, the Golden
Man. They populate the poem in imagistic, collage-like fashion, implying
states of consciousness, impulses, appetites, attitudes of mind and heart,
obsessions, desires, collective fantasies and whimsical mischiefs that find
expression in the exercise of power and the commission of atrocity. The
Golden Man, for example, is the human impulse to seek a transcend-
ant resolution of the pains of human consciousness. Kennelly in fact
based this figure on 'the state of clear' in J. Ron Hubbard's Scientological
schema.[6] Buffún finds in him the answer to his sense of emptiness. He is
the false antidote to Cromwell's fatal poison:

> Icy water intimidates my heart.
> Whenever I see the golden man, I am.
> I'm water now. Must go again I think, (p. 32)

But he is also that idealist aspiration which makes Cromwell the monster he is; he is the fatuous antithesis of the appetitive savagery of the
Belly which craves satisfaction; the Hand which must meddle; the sexual
drive which seeks the womb and Mum and which, in disappointed rage
at being cast into the uncaring world, gets off on rapine and blood lust, or
on dreams of the Dark (because blind) Rosaleen:

> A soldier has a feeling for his gun
> And likes to use it. I recall a town
> Where my army went on the rampage.
> I had them laughing. They had a ball,
> Splitting the woman. Well, Buffún, they were men.
> I sat astride a stallion, a little off-stage.
> He was a noble brute, throbbing. We saw it all. (p. 45)

> There's a laugh somewhere.
> Rosaleen thumbs out her eyes.
> 'Here are specimens of the best native diamonds.
> Wear them, please …' (p. 90)

Cromwell is therefore an attempt to read not only Irish history but
historical reality as a product of that crazed, confused, driven creature
Man himself, who seems always in thrall to the most terrible imagining
in the poem, the Old Murderer who takes perverse pleasure in carrying
the mark of Cain:

> Yes, I throttled words in many a throat
> And was the blood boiling in their eyes

When they stared into the face of silence.
I've witnessed this for centuries. (p. 39)

If *Cromwell* is a reading of human psychology, it is also an experience of dream and nightmare states. Some of its power derives indeed from its capacity to suggest a dance of language 'among the shapes of death' (p. 135), and from the dramatic energy by which the poet outfaces both the dark and the terrible things which haunt it. Kennelly has always been interested in altered states of consciousness, in those moments when out of the pits of unconscious memory and fear, emotions come in predatory forms to affright the insomniac poet. 'Dream of a Black Fox', for example, in the volume of that name published in 1968, was one such avatar of darkness. *Cromwell* seems such a waking dream writ large, the entire work possessing a visionary intensity as of sleeplessness or hallucination. The violence we witness through the poet's mesmerised attention has a random, fictive quality as if image provoked image in some bizarre and uncontrollable cinematic sequence. The work's vision of life is extremist, an unrelenting engagement with psychic conditions which find expression in spectacular effects. Its primary mood is awe-struck, as if trapped in some dark trance where reality unfolds itself in monstrous metaphor. It insists that only the transfigured imagination of the poet as prophet is adequate to the true horrors of human experience, to a world that has given us Cromwell, Buffún, the Giant and the rest of them and the daily atrocities which assail us in news broadcast and television image.

Altered states of consciousness are central too in Paul Muldoon's poem 'The More a Man Has the More a Man Wants', that other long poem of the 1980s which sought to engage unsparingly with, if not to comprehend, the violence at the heart of human experience, which daily Irish life in the period inescapably forced on the attention. They are of course very different works of art, *Cromwell* and Muldoon's poem (published in his volume *Quoof*, also 1983). Where Kennelly's tone, particularly in the opening and closing passages, is almost orphic in its commitment to the contents of vision, Muldoon's work is a coolly ironic, often chillingly understated, even mischievous trip through a kaleidoscopic mental terrain. And where Kennelly's poem employs almost throughout a rough sonnet form with a direct energy which allows it to contain readily recognisable multitudes, Muldoon uses an attentuated, even anorexic, sonnet through forty-nine unnamed poems to carry a heavy weight of sly allusion with sprightly insouciance. But what these works share is a sense that the violence of human affairs cannot be rendered in a literature which does not take account of the worlds of dreams and hallucination, of fictive protean image. And Muldoon's poem in its ostensibly casual fashion is as extreme a statement as Kennelly's more obviously obsessional creation. Both works share the capacity to unnerve, to take things as far as they will go, allowing the reader no unearned consolation. In as much as both poems can be read as responses to the contemporary violence of Ireland, they share a bleak uncompromising eschewal of cheap grace, of too easy ameliorative hope. The one is a poem of night thoughts, the other a work of chemically heightened daylight vision. But they share a radical, iconoclastic impulse to tell it as it is, to tell tales not normally reported on in the conservative schools of Irish verse.

Kennelly's *Cromwell* confronted 'the terrible incestuous angers of Ireland' (p. 124) in the historical dimension and read there a psychology of the human condition. In 'The More a Man Has', Muldoon engages with the present moment and uncovers there the traces of historical experience, mediated through the tropes of language and literature. In so doing, he is less a psychologist at work than experimental clinician who employs chemical resources to isolate and reassemble the constituents of consciousness at the behest of an apparently whimsical curiosity. Therapy is not on the agenda, though might be a surprising side effect. The sequence (like the volume *Quoof* in which it appears, Muldoon's fourth full collection and the one in which his understated gnomic method came fully into its own) is intrigued by the mind-altering effects of drugs, violence and travel, and the world it summons to perception is one where disassociated experience is rendered with aleatory unconcern for logic, coherence and narrative consistency. And the dominant tonal register, shockingly precise, hushed, elegant, iconoclastic in its deadpan ironies, is, finally, more bleakly pessimistic than Kennelly's urgent report from hell. The surfaces of everyday life in the consumer society (product names, road signs, contemporary argot) are juxtaposed with folklore, myth, literary allusion and quotation, descriptions of atrocity, to constitute a mode of consciousness that might be compared to computer overload. At any given moment the reader is aware of multiple levels of description, evocation and allusion, as if to deny that perception is ever capable of being organised in stabilising narratives. So Irish reality, part of larger realities, of which the contemporary violence in Northern Ireland was a part, cannot be comprehended simply as historical, or as indeed psychological narrative or merely as narrative event. It is all of these and perhaps something else entirely, to which altered states of consciousness may or may not give us access. Above all it is incapable of categorisation. 'Anything', stated Muldoon in an interview published in 1981, 'that swims into your world picture is *in* your world picture. That's why I'm very much against expressing a categorical view of the world.'[7]

In 'The More a Man Has', Muldoon militates against his work arriving at any such categorical world-view by a number of strategies. The poem offers a pseudo-narrative that constantly arouses and then disappoints the reader's expectation of plot development and resolution. It exploits the concept of metamorphosis with mischievous unconcern for the reader's bemused condition. And it juxtaposes world-views through its allusive linguistic textures as if reality can be re-imagined through clever shifts in register, like changing channels on a television set.

The narrative content of this tantalisingly inscrutable poem involves, it would appear, a bizarre thriller-like exchange between the poem's protagonist, one Gallogly, who is some kind of mercenary engaged in subversive activity in the North of Ireland and an Amerindian who may be a self-accusing alter-ego of the protagonist. Muldoon himself suggests that:

In the *aisling* or 'dream-vision' which forms the middle section of the poem Gallogly muses on his own mercenary past. He has made an abortive trip to the United States to buy arms, in the course of which he imagines himself to have killed a girl. That for him is the root cause of his present plight, the reason for him being pursued by an avenging Indian.[8]

An improbable enough scenario in this outline screenplay. In the poem itself it is impossible to follow its film noir plot-line, which takes us from the orchards of Armagh to New York and North of Boston (the title of a famous collection by the poet Robert Frost) in a sequence of cinematic images so skilfully set in motion and narrated with such assurance that we are carried along in mingled disbelief and expectation. What does unify the action line is not the consistency of event (with beginning, middle and end) but the impression that this bizarre pseudo-narrative is in some mysterious way a guide to the spiritual dereliction of our violent and violence-obsessed world. Muldoon has of course been much influenced as a poet by his Northern Irish predecessor, Louis MacNeice,[9] the MacNeice who wrote on parable in *Varieties of Parable* and whose late work is distinguished by such brilliant, thumbnail nightmare poems as 'The Taxis' and 'After the Crash'. These brief narratives of apparent allegorical significance achieve what MacNeice himself termed 'double-level poetry',[10] in which both levels defy analysis, leaving only a numbed sense that dark conceits have touched on dark truths. 'The More a Man Has the More a Man Wants'[11] is a MacNeice parable for the big screen; its narrative content is what baits the hook. It offers meaning as it traps the attention in a stream of images which act to disrupt categorical thought, to subvert the idea that such a world as that with which the poem engages could admit of narrative resolution, the consolations of closure.

Narrative consistency is also subverted in the poem by the poet's gleeful preoccupation with metamorphosis, that principle which would deny all categories in a free play of difference, of shifting identities. Indeed metamorphosis, invoked by allusion to Ovid, allows Muldoon to make his Gallogly a shape-changing inhabitant of a modern trickster cycle based on the mythology and folklore of native American tribes. In the poem he appears as Gollogly, Golightly, Ingoldsby, English, and in multiple zoological shapes. He also makes an appearance as the Green Knight from *Gawain* and as Sweeney from Celtic legend. And he leaps back to life after both barrels of a shotgun have blasted him to kingdom come, as in an animated cartoon:

> Running on the spot
> with all the minor aplomb
> of a trick-cyclist.
> So thin, side-on, you could spit
> through him.
> His six foot of pump water
> bent double
> in agony or laughter.
> Keeping down-wind of everything. (p. 4)

The effect on the reader of this protean extravagance is hard to measure. The whole thing is done with such card-sharper legerdemain that a kind of perplexed admiration is an initial response. But the changes in shape, context, locale are in sum so bewildering that they induce a disorientated acquiescence in whatever authorial invention cares to offer. That this is sometimes a conceitful extremism, the imaginative and moral equivalent of the horrors the work is addressing, is surely what Muldoon has been preparing us for in this poem, which does not shrink from the most terrible of metamorphoses:

> Once the local councillor straps
> himself into the safety belt
> of his Citroën
> and skids up the ramp
> from the municipal car park

> he upsets the delicate balance
> of a mercury-tilt
> boobytrap.
> Once they collect his smithereens
> he doesn't quite add up.
> They're shy of foot, and a calf
> which stems
> from his left shoe like a severely
> pruned-back shrub. (p. 53)

The work's manifold transformations, its hallucinogenic elisions and shifts of context and perspective, make such exacting similitudes as the grimly horticultural conceit in this stanza, just part of a variegated set of world-views, none of which can claim priority in a reality so incapable of categorical comprehension.

World-views are of course affairs of language, just as in this stanza the unnerving effects of the writing depend on the way in which atrocity is invoked through a rhetoric of civility ('councillor', 'municipal', 'safety', 'delicate balance', 'shy'). Languages and their relationship with ways of seeing the world are accordingly preoccupations in this work, which seeks to show how reality exceeds all possible descriptions of it. Muldoon himself drew attention to the centrality of language in the work when he wrote:

In 'The More a Man Has the More a Man Wants' I hoped to purge myself of the very public vocabulary it employs, the kennings of the hourly news bulletins. In so far as it's about anything, the poem is about the use, or abuse, of the English language in Ireland. Indeed, one form of the name of the central character is 'English', though it may also be instructive to remind oneself that 'Gallogly' is itself a corruption of a Gaelic name meaning 'foreign young warrior' – a mercenary.[12]

The intense allusiveness of the text heightens a reader's sense that language as style, as mode of consciousness, is part of Muldoon's purpose in 'The More a Man Has'. This is most obvious in the parody of Heaneyesque pastoralism of the Ulster countryside, and of the linguistic ponderings of that poet's volume *Wintering Out* ('Toome' is a probable target):

> Gallogly lies down in the sheugh
> to munch
> through a Beauty of
> Bath. He repeats himself, *Bath*,
> under his garlic-breath.
> *Sheugh*, he says. *Sheugh*.
> He is finding that first 'sh'

increasingly difficult to manage.
Sh-leeps. (p. 49)

Such nativist broodings are immediately preceded in the poem by the
graphic images of terrorist murder. Accordingly, in their cosmopolitan
('garlic-breath') artfulness they seem somehow implicated in a general
atrociousness. And in the *aisling* section of the poem, a sacral motif in the
nationalist tradition is mediated in the language of sixties hippy hedon-
ism. This section of the poem, which echoes the language and style, the
sensual/culinary excess, of a cult text, Richard Farina's *Been Down So
Long It Looks Like Up To Me*[13] (a title that must have appealed to the poet
of this curiously entitled poem), highlights the drugged, self-indulgent
eroticism of the language in which nationalist feeling has often found
expression in Ireland:

> A weekend trip to the mountains
> North of Boston
> with Alice, Alice A.
> And her paprika hair,
> the ignition key
> to her family's Winnebago camper,
> her quim
> biting the leg off her.
> In the oyster bar
> of Grand Central Station
> she gobbles a dozen Chesapeakes –
> 'Oh, I'm not particular as to size' –
> and, with a flourish of tabasco,
> turns to gobble him. (p. 51)

But these are only two examples of the allusive complexity of a text
which involves the reader in recognising quotations from Shakespeare's
tenth sonnet, from Huxley's *The Doors of Perception*, Thoreau's *Walden*
and picking up references to Indian (and Eskimo) folklore, to Castaneda
the anthropologist of Shamanism, to *Mangas Jones* as the title of a radical
sixties magazine as well as the name of an Apache Native American,
to Knut Hamsen, to Robert Louis Stevenson, to Picasso's *Guernica*, to
Hopper's pictures of suburban America, to *Alice in Wonderland*, to Alice
B. Toklas and Gertrude Stein and to the punning and playful poems and
stories of that master of disguise the Reverend Richard Harris Barham,
the author of *The Ingoldsby Legends*. The dutiful reader who sets him- or
herself the task of unlayering this poetic palimpsest is sent on as improbable and wide-ranging a scholarly trip as the spaced-out Gallogly takes

in the course of the poem. And to what purpose? Some allusions seem to add to the linguistic theme. For example, allusions to Thoreau's idyllic and romantic idealism, when set against the America of arms-dealing and revolutionary ideology betrayed, echo the literary escapism of their Irish equivalents. But others seem almost perversely obscure and add only to the dreamlike disassociation of the work, its unsettling capacity to shift linguistic registers from urban demotic and throwaway commentary to subtle wit and elaborate conceit. The guile and panache with which the work handles allusion often seems merely an extension of linguistic bravura in a text which takes us verbally from 'quim', 'blethering', 'dickering' to 'perruque', 'petits fours', 'Velveteen' by way of those curiously familiar signifiers of modernity's distress, 'Armalites', 'Kalashnikovs', 'Mogadon', 'Valium', 'Balaclavas', 'Durex', 'Coca Cola', 'Cortex', 'Esso' and 'Mobil'. World-views fade in and out of focus as the language and the allusive target come in and out of our sights. We get glimpses of possible order and pattern in the work only to find them running into the interpretative sands just as the plot denied closure. The poem seems therefore to exist irresolvably between two aesthetic possibilities: it is either a piece of wonderfully playful nonsense (a deadly enough kind of thing given its violent subject) or it has the power of parable or double-level writing. Crucially, the allusions to Robert Frost (that other master with MacNeice of surreptitiously double-level writing) and to his poem 'For Once, Then, Something' raise the possibilities that some kind of truth may be made available in the altered states of consciousness to which this work attends, or conversely they may not. Frost's poem, which Muldoon has warned us is one his avenging Indian has 'a lot of time for',[14] offers a moment of hermeneutic ambiguity as the poet peers into a semi-opaque well:

> *Once*, when trying with chin against a well-curb,
> I discerned, as I thought, beyond the picture,
> Through the picture, a something white, uncertain,
> Something more of the depths – and then lost it.
> One drop fell from a fern, and lo, a ripple.
> Water came to rebuke the too clear water.
> Shook whatever it was lay there at bottom,
> Blurred it, blotted it out. What was that whiteness?
> Truth? A pebble of quartz? For once, then, something.[15]

We know that Mangas Jones, coming through customs at Aldergrove Airport (the one that serves Belfast) at the start of the poem, declares 'A pebble of quartz?' (p. 40). We know too that the bombed victim of the poet's final sonnet, who dies with the words 'Moose – Indian' on his lips, clutches 'a luminous stone no bigger than a ...' (p. 64; the poem is in a literary version of an Ulster dialect) and the mind must read, if we follow the allusive thread, 'a pebble of quartz. Or truth?' 'Huh', to quote the poem's conclusive enigmatic word. And finally, we know that for Muldoon 'It's pretty well established ... that the world has an order. There is an order among things which has got to do with more than our ordering of them, our perception of them.'[16] So perhaps 'The More a Man Has the More a Man Wants' is for once, then, something, a momentary glimpse from a chemically disordered consciousness of that absolute reality, or just a stone gripped by a dying hand, no more meaningful than the jingle which gives the poem its conundrum of a title:

> *The more a man has the more a man wants,*
> *the same I don't think true.*
> *For I never met a man with one black eye*
> *who ever wanted two.*
> *Never throw a brick at a drowning man*
> *when you're near to a grocer's store.*
> *Just throw him a cake of Sunlight soap*
> *let him wash himself ashore* (p. 61)

NOTES

1 B. Kennelly, *Cromwell* (Newcastle upon Tyne: Bloodaxe Books Ltd, 1987), p. 17. Henceforth, page references to this edition are given in the text.
2 Orthograph notebook kindly made available to me by the poet.
3 *Ibid.*
4 *Ibid.*
5 *Ibid.*
6 In conversation Brendan Kennelly informed me that he was for many years in unsolicited receipt of Hubbard's writings, courtesy of the Church of Scientology. On these he based the figure of the Golden Man, as a personification of the 'state of clear'.
7 Paul Muldoon in interview with John Haffenden, in J. Haffenden (ed.), *Viewpoints: Poets in Conversation with John Haffenden* (London and Boston: Faber and Faber, 1981), pp. 141–2.
8 P. Muldoon, 'Paul Muldoon Writes', *The Poetry Society Bulletin*, 118 (Autumn 1983), 1.
9 Muldoon signalled his regard for the work of Louis MacNeice by including a substantial selection of his work in his notably exclusive anthology *The Faber Book of Contemporary Irish Poetry* (1980). See also Muldoon's poems 'History', in *Why Brownlee Left* (1980), and 'Louis' in the sequence '7 Middagh Street', in *Meeting the British* (1987).
10 L. MacNeice, *Varieties of Parable* (Cambridge University Press, 1965), p. 8.

11 P. Muldoon, *Quoof* (London and Boston: Faber and Faber, 1983). Henceforth page references to this edition are given in the text.

12 Muldoon, 'Paul Muldoon Writes', 1. The use of the word 'kennings' is interesting here, perhaps indicating the poet's sense that such broadcasting indulges in stock phrases, as in Old English poetic diction (to which the term normally refers). He may mean that they are a kind of public verse. However, Dillon Johnston in his *Irish Poetry After Joyce* (1985) misreads (or corrects) 'kennings' as 'keenings'. In so tantalising a poem, the crux seems part of the more general conundrum that it poses.

13 J. P. Waters makes this pleasing identification in his acute, very useful unpublished Trinity College, Dublin, Master of Philosophy thesis 'The Complexities of Being Here: Representative and Narrative Strategy in the Poetry of Paul Muldoon' (Dublin, 1987), to which I am happy to acknowledge my indebtedness. I am also indebted to students of the Master in Philosophy course in Anglo-Irish literature in Trinity College, Dublin, who in seminars have instructed me in the reading of this poem and have tracked down various allusions.

14 Muldoon, 'Paul Muldoon Writes', 1.

15 R. Frost, *Complete Poems* (London: Jonathan Cape, 1967), pp. 252–3.

16 Haffenden (ed.), *Viewpoints*, p.141.

CHAPTER 18

Redeeming the time: John McGahern and John Banville

Joyce stands behind us like the ghost of the father.
(John Banville)

Part of the legacy of James Joyce to subsequent Irish writers is the inexorable realism of his vision. In *Dubliners*, *A Portrait of the Artist as a Young Man* and *Ulysses*, there are passages of exacting social and psychological observation – Lenehan and Corley on the streets of Dublin seeking their human prey, Stephen appalled at adult passions released at a family Christmas meal, Bloom cooking kidneys at 7 Eccles Street – which supply object lessons for subsequent Irish writers as to the revelatory powers of fictional realism, its capacity to suggest the density and complexity of human consciousness in its material contexts. Joyce's realism, it is important to stress, is more than a matter of technique (his own work goes well beyond the limits of realist art); it is a matter of world-view. A materialism of a fundamental and unshakeable kind allows him to submit human subjectivity throughout his oeuvre to a searching but almost always compassionate inspection: nineteenth-century conceptions of character no longer obtrude their moral and complacently humanistic perspectives.

It was not until the 1960s that Irish writers began to lay full claim to the inheritance of Joycean realism. Until then the harsh facts of Irish censorship had deformed the development of modern Irish fiction. This meant that even those writers like Seán O'Faoláin, Frank O'Connor, Kate O'Brien and Mary Lavin, who had sought to chronicle in their work the emergence of the new social order in a fiction which drew on the realist tradition, found themselves inhibited by the prevailing puritanical ethos or cut off from their natural audience by legal interdiction. Ireland was accordingly denied the kind of Joycean anatomising which might have subjected its early development to an astringent fictional analysis. What did in fact occur was a retreat from the Joycean inclusiveness of insight (where self and society were reckoned to be intimately related) to an often sentimental concentration on the privacies of selfhood. Thus, in the Irish short story of the period – the form in which Irish realism found its limited expression in the thirties and forties – the reader encounters an anachronistic foregrounding of subjectivity in a fictional world that takes wholly for granted a kind of romantic humanism of feeling only sustainable in disregard of the writing of Freud or indeed of Joyce himself.

The uncompromising realism of John McGahern's literary method in the four novels considered in this essay allowed him to address subjects which had remained taboo in the Irish novel since Joyce.[1] Eroticism, sexual abuse, masturbation, sadism, abortion and homosexuality are some of the experiences which his novels confront. And they do so with an exacting honesty, an unabashed determination to speak of human truths. Indeed, the publication of McGahern's second novel, *The Dark* (1965), and the public controversy it aroused, made the work something of a watershed in Irish literary history.[2]

On first reading, however, McGahern's novels do not impress one as being works of unalloyed realism. One is initially struck by the intense subjectivity of his fiction. For each of his novels has a protagonist whose private world of feeling is explored with an obsessiveness which reminds us of the traditional Irish short story (and McGahern has in fact excelled in the shorter form).[3] Indeed, a McGahern novel can sometimes seem like a short story writ large, the familiar sensitive protagonists of that genre at last being allowed to enjoy and suffer the very experiences which were denied to the young men of, for example, Frank O'Connor's frustrated world. Young Mahoney in *The Dark* is assailed by feelings of loathing for the sadistic father who made his childhood a nightmare and by the guilt which youthful sexuality gives rise to in an overpoweringly Catholic environment. And the two young men who constitute the protagonists of *The Leavetaking* and *The Pornographer* are both initiates of bodily pleasure and erotic intensity, about which they ruminate in passages of subjective poeticism and metaphysical solemnity. Only Elizabeth Reegan in McGahern's first novel, *The Barracks*, the terminally ill wife of a rural police sergeant, escapes from the dominant mood of heightened subjectivity to be observed from the wider perspectives of a more comprehensive realism.

For all the obsessive subjectivity of McGahern's work, each of his novels also signals that the author is attending to social and historical fact in the manner of the realist writer as social commentator. What happens to his various characters is governed not only by the weather of feeling but by the social climate as it is affected by historical change. Sergeant Reegan in *The Barracks* is a disillusioned revolutionary, a former member of an

IRA flying column who had fought in hopes of a new order but finds it betrayed by the burgeoning bureaucracy represented by his immediate superior, Superintendent Quirke, whom he hates with self-destructive ferocity. Reegan's bitterness in the novel, his furious attempt, as his wife dies before his eyes, to augment his meagre income with illicit extra work, are accounted for in socio-historical terms, as the product of post-revolutionary despair.

The Dark also signals that it is attending to a particular moment in a country's social development. The perennial conflict between father and son in Irish fiction is given added poignancy in this powerful portrayal of generational strife by the fact that a scholarship is available for young Mahoney, offering an educational escape from the abject, grinding poverty of a small farm in the west of Ireland. No such opportunity had offered fulfilment to his father, despite his own evident gifts as a pupil in the local school. And in a telling conversation between young Mahoney and his clerical cousin, who had hoped to recruit him for the priesthood, McGahern alerts us to the fact that the novel itself is poised at a moment of fundamental change in Irish life. 'Did you ever', asks Father Ryan, 'hear of the word *bourgeoisie?*...Most of us in Ireland will soon be that, fear of the poor-house is gone, even the life your father brought you up on won't last hardly twenty years more.'[4] With *The Leavetaking* and *The Pornographer* we are introduced to the new Irish society where country-bred young men find employment in a Dublin which affords them every chance of sexual libertinism as their society adjusts, in a confused and often clumsy fashion, to the instant pleasures of the consumer society.

It is not, however, attentiveness to social fact that primarily distinguishes McGahern as a realist, as a successor to the Joyce of *Dubliners*. Rather, it is his keen awareness of the processes of human psychology which marks him out as a writer for whom realism is more than a readily available tool for the exploration of his protagonists' worlds of feeling. He employs realism as an instrument of clinical investigation, and what interests McGahern as a psychological realist is the family romance.

In each of his novels McGahern insistently, even obsessively, examines the effects of family feeling on the course of individual lives. A recurrent preoccupation is the Oedipal love of son for mother, together with the appalling psychological effects of early bereavement on the developing emotional life of a child. In fact, all his novels are concerned with premature death and bereavement. So, despite the self-consciousness and brooding subjectivity of McGahern's heroes, the reader is impressed by how little they are in control of the contents of their minds or the course of their lives. They are driven by instincts and needs, desires and compulsions which have their sources in the childhood home and in the shocks of adult experience. Most significantly, a man's love for a woman is reckoned a version of a boy's love for his mother. And the search for and loss of love can be a pathological matter, a kind of sickness. Indeed, a recurrent figure in McGahern's novels and short stories is the lovesick and abandoned lover.[5] Both the pornographer and the publisher he writes for in the novel of that name have been unsuccessful in love, and their commercial exploitation of sex seems a consequence of their self-protective cynicism as disappointed sensitives. In *The Leavetaking* the hero, as a love affair ends, associates the moment of abandonment with the death of his mother in childhood, as he is overwhelmed by a sickness of desire bordering on insanity. McGahern also senses that women are as afflicted by the tortures of unrequited love as the men in his fictional world. The woman who falls in love with the pornographer and bears his child is one such victim; another is Elizabeth Reegan in *The Barracks*, who has a destructive love affair with a self-hating nihilist whose death sends her back to the security and frustration of marriage to an unsympathetic man in the depressed heart of rural Ireland. In *The Leavetaking*, indeed, McGahern attempts to account for the adult emotional problems experienced by a young woman as a consequence of an unhappy relationship with her father. The American woman whom the hero marries in a registry office (precipitating his dismissal from a Dublin teaching post in a version of the author's own experience) is the daughter of a quite monstrous egotist who seeks to possess his daughter with all the greed he brings to his daily consumption of food and drink. In the first edition of this novel, McGahern seems to be making her experience some kind of equivalent of that endured by his motherless hero (both have had unhappy affairs), though in the rewritten edition the role of the father is not so emphatic – as if the author realised his psychologising was a little too schematic to be wholly convincing.

Religion is a force which also determines the lives of McGahern's characters. His books are pervaded by religious imagery, ritual and feeling. There is guilt in the very air his characters breathe, and religiosity of tone is a characteristic of his self-obsessed heroes even when they lack orthodox faith. Some of the most unconvincing moments in McGahern's work are when these glum introspectives ponder the imponderable; and it is not clear how the author intends us to read such self-regarding poeticism – as diseased subjectivity or something more significant? One suspects that McGahern at such moments is not in full control of the constituents of his vision, for the controlling import of his work is resolutely realistic, and these passages of metaphysical elevation obtrude uneasily in the context of his determining method. For McGahern, despite the Catholicism of his characters and the frequent religiosities of tone in his work, is a writer much closer in spirit to the materialism of a Joyce than he is to the metaphysics of a Mauriac or a Graham Greene.

This underlying materialism in McGahern's work is suggested by his deployment of imagery. The world of his fiction is fixed in a universe which contains not only mood and emotion but implacable physical reality. Even so inward a novel as *The Leavetaking* begins with imagistic reference to a world which exists before and after human experience: 'I watch a gull's shadow float among feet on the concrete as I walk in a day of my life with a bell, its brass tongue in my hand, and think after all that the first constant was water.'[6] And the novel ends with evocations of that primal sea, framing the novel's action with a sense of a determining materiality. Throughout McGahern's work we are reminded that life is lived in rooms, houses, places, and that consciousness shares a universe with objects, machines, natural phenomena. In both *The Barracks* and *The Pornographer*, emotional suffering coexists with sounds from a sawmill. In *The Dark*, the frightened and abused children of that book's sad family seek comfort in a lavatory: 'There they all rushed hours as these to sit in the comforting darkness and reek of Jeyes Fluid to weep and grope their way in hatred and self-pity back to some sort of calm' (p. 10). At times McGahern almost insists on a reductive perspective on human existence. When, for example, the hero's aunt is removed from her death-bed in *The Pornographer*, he notes that 'there was a brown stain in the centre of the snow-white undersheet where she had lain'.[7] Throughout there is a sense, as Elizabeth Reegan has it in *The Barracks*, of the 'starkness of individual minutes passing among accidental doors and windows and chairs and flowers and trees, cigarette-smoke or the light growing brilliant and fading, losing their pain …'[8]

In such a world what hope or alleviation of suffering does McGahern afford his tormented characters? Almost none; they remain as fixed in their destinies as the various victims of Joycean paralysis in *Dubliners*. Only in rare moments are they permitted intimations of the mystery of their lives which, however grim they may be, achieve thereby the dignity of the ineffable. It is such moments as these that redeem from complete pessimism McGahern's grim vision of human conflict and disillusionment.

James Joyce's legacy to Irish writers was not only an object lesson in the analytical powers of realism. The texts of this Modernist master created for the Irish writer, as they did for writers of fiction everywhere, a consciousness of the fictionality of writing itself. The self-reflexive quality of the major Modernist texts found compelling fictional expression in sections of *Ulysses* and of *Finnegans Wake*. Henceforth, the canon of classical realism could no longer be taken for granted, and writing itself, in the prose work of Beckett, in the French *nouveau roman*, in the work of John Fowles, in that of Nabokov, was accordingly subjected to a subversive, increasingly radical investigation, in which the threads of expression were made visible in the very fabric of the literary weave. For such texts advertised their textuality, insisting on the sheer inventiveness of all fictional occasions. It is as a writer working within the context of such post-modernist experiment that the work of John Banville must initially be assessed.[9]

Banville's first two full-length works of fiction were uncompromising experiments in what Seamus Deane has dubbed 'technical narcissism'.[10] In fact Banville himself has admitted of his first novel, *Nightspawn* (1971), that it was 'a kind of betrayal, of the reader's faith in the writer's good faith, and also it is a betrayal of, if you like, the novelist's guild and its secret signs and stratagems. It is an inside-out novel, it wears its skeleton and its nerves on the outside.'[11] The work purports to be a thriller about political espionage in contemporary Greece. As such it allows the author cruelly to disappoint any reader who comes to it in expectation of that satisfying resolution of the complex plot which is characteristic of the genre. For instead of clarification (which is the assumed fictional trajectory of even the most convoluted plot in a conventional thriller), the plot of *Nightspawn* becomes more and more involved, reveals itself as a mere contrivance upon which are hung the epistemological and emotional problems of narration itself. The novel's narrator, Ben White, fails in two respects. As a self-loathing introspective he fails to resolve his emotional difficulties, and as narrator of the novel he fails adequately to realise in fiction the world of action in which these difficulties occur. Yet there are stylistic consolations. Firstly, there is the pleasure of parody – not only of the thriller genre itself, but of the parasitical delights of rewriting the masters, the first paragraph being a parody of Dostoevsky's *Notes from Underground*.[12] Secondly, there are those moments when writing itself seems to compose an alternative reality to the dismal conditions of its originating matter. There are passages of compellingly composed metaphorical writing in the book that suggest the transformative powers of the literary art which the narrator seeks to achieve as writer of the text. These metafictional moments, haunting in their own right, are highly significant in directing us to Banville's primary obsession as a writer: the relationship between fiction and the world it ostensibly takes as its subject. *Nightspawn* clearly values writing beyond any of its occasions; it is a young man's bravura celebration of self-consciousness. *Birchwood* (1973), Banville's second novel, is less sure of the efficacy of the artfulness that can make a book like *Nightspawn* seem a self-indulgence.

Birchwood signals its literary provenance from the outset. A Big House novel, it subverts the Irish genre with wicked panache, subjecting a venerable Irish fictional tradition, notable for exaggeration, to a zestful fictional overkill. The narrator, Gabriel Godkin, the inheritor of Birchwood, the Godkin family seat, recounts a tale of dynastic disintegration. The tale is ostensibly set in the time of the Great Famine, but anachronistic details (the family has a telephone, bicycles have been invented) make this an improbable historical reconstruction of the past. Events have a distinctly literary quality in this most bookish of works. One character is dispatched by way of spontaneous combustion, in a display of fictional pyrotechnics that summons to mind the grotesquerie of the world of Dickens's *Bleak House*. The characters are all stock types, as if recruited from central casting to play recognisable parts in a *reductio ad absurdum* of a generic fiction: 'the dark, angry father; the long-suffering mother; ghastly grandparents; the artistic son; the wild son; the strange aunt; it has them all'.[13]

Birchwood also has conventional elements drawn from other modes of writing. The plot of the book involves the unravelling of a mystery about parentage, siblings, twins and inheritance in the manner of a Gothic romance, and the text makes much of symbolic clues in masquerading as a work of mystery and imagination. The hero embarks on a quest for a sister whom he comes to believe must exist as his alter ego, a quest which takes him on an unlikely series of adventures with a travelling circus whose impresario is a never-appearing genius by the name of Prospero. The weight of significance which the text is apparently asked to bear becomes almost a matter for baroque comedy, even as it suavely relishes its own mannered mastery of the various modes it assays. The pleasures of this text are conspiratorial recognition and a strangely compulsive awareness of the odd vitality of the conventional. The reader's attention is undeniably retained even as he is warned by the narrator himself, '*be* assured that I am inventing'.[14] Part of what compels the reader's attention, of course, is the sheer extravagance of the writing, its contrived rhythmic intensities, its metaphoric polish. But the work as a whole seems more measured and thematically serious than Banville's earlier writings. The existential unease of its narrator and protagonist, Gabriel Godkin, seems more than a mere literary device appropriate to this particular work. His brooding on historical ambiguity and on the obliquity of memory in time seem matters of real consequence, darkening the entire work. His discomfort as artist at his imperfect recall for an essentially irrecoverable set of experiences sounds an almost tragic note in the novel, hinting at the author's own awareness of the limits of the powers of art in a brutal, ineluctable world.

Accordingly, the dialectic in the book between the powers of imagination and the cruel facts of time and history must be reckoned more than a further trope exploited for the purposes of a factitious literary Romanticism. It is the stuff of authorial concern. This is a book of views (of interiors, landscapes, vistas) in which a contemplative intelligence is constantly struck by the mysterious otherness of the world in itself in passages of speculative lyricism. Banville's narrator addresses the paradoxical condition of art itself, apparently free to create as it wills in its own dimension, but in actuality only a dream of consciousness, which at last must bow to the unsayable, knowing the world to be everything that is the case:

Spring has come again, St Brigid's day, right on time. The harmony of the seasons mocks me. I spend hours watching the sky, the lake, the enormous sea. This world. I feel that if I could understand it I might then begin to understand the creatures who inhabit it. But I do not understand it. I find the world always odd, but odder still, I suppose, is the fact that I find it so, for what are the eternal verities by which I measure these temporal aberrations? Intimations abound, but they are felt only, and words fail to transfix them. Anyway, some secrets are not to be disclosed under pain of who knows what retribution, and whereof I cannot speak, thereof I must be silent. (p. 171)

The protagonists of Banville's next two novels are also sky-watchers. *Doctor Copernicus* (1976) and *Kepler* (1981) compose the first half of a tetralogy on scientific subjects, a tetralogy completed by *The Newton Letter: An Interlude* (1982) and *Mephisto* (1986). It is in this remarkable quartet that Banville most fully explores his obsessional theme as a writer – the relationship between fictionality and the world that gives rise to it.

In the first two novels, Banville exploits the historical novel to address his theme. That chosen form may reflect some disillusionment with the metafictional ostentation of his earlier work: in 1977 he confessed that his attitude to such artistic fabulation had 'altered from at first a high enthusiasm, to, lately, a deep suspicion'.[15] The sense of fabulation remains, however, for these two books are only ostensibly historical fictions. Their true provenance is the novel of ideas, where metafictional experiment is made to serve thematic purposes. Banville chooses to write about Copernicus and Kepler because their intellectual biographies – especially as mediated in one of his primary sources, Arthur Koestler's *The Sleepwalkers* – allow him to deal in a recognisably human context with the central problem of the relationship of thought to the objects of thought.[16]

Banville's Copernicus is a life-denying recluse whose dedication to truth involves him in terrible failure. In this work the controversies of late Medieval and early Renaissance cosmology are made the stuff of a meditation on imaginative exploit itself. For the work of a great scientist (and the same is true of Banville's Kepler) is reckoned to be as much the work of fundamental imagining as is the work of the artist. (This perspective on intellectual history seems influenced by Thomas H. Kuhn's concept of the paradigm shift in the structure of scientific revolutions.)[17] Copernicus constructs his model of the universe in the belief that he is *explaining* phenomena.

In this respect Banville's Copernicus is portrayed as a modern hero of thought in a way which somewhat disregards historical accuracy. For it seems probable that although Copernicus did think his system bore a real relationship to what actually exists (and was not just a mathematical tool useful for prediction, in the way some of his contemporaries were prepared to view any cosmological system), his was a deeply conservative mind, concerned to *save* the phenomena rather than explain them.[18] So, when Banville presents Copernicus as being arrogantly disdainful of a teacher who strenuously sought to save the phenomena – 'that is, to devise a theory grounded firmly in the old reactionary dogmas that yet would account for the observed motions of the planets'[19] – we are again in the world of invention.

Other aspects of the work suggest the fictional activity of the implied author as historian. Section 3 of the book, tellingly entitled 'Magister Ludi', contains obvious parodies of the eighteenth-century epistolary novel, and of Joycean realism (the latter is a parody of parodies, for Copernicus's mistress is introduced to us in the simpering clichés of the 'Nausicaa' chapter of *Ulysses*). Throughout we are made aware of the circularity of the fiction; as images and patterns recur, we note what Rudiger Imhof has described as its 'ring-like compositional pattern'.[20] This associates the work of the artist himself with the scientist whose obsessional activity is bound up with the circulation of the spheres. Both seek a kind of perfection which, more true than the quotidian world of change, might redeem the time. But the emotional import of Banville's version of the Copernican endeavour (and by implication the writer's own) is that such imaginative and rational aspiration is a dangerous kind of crying

for the moon. In contrast to Copernicus's Faustian contract with per-
fected order, Banville offers the astronomer's brother Andreas, a rogue
who dies terribly from syphilis. Andreas is employed in the novel to offer
a poetic vision (drawing on Wallace Stevens's 'Notes Towards a Supreme
Fiction') of *'redemptive* despair' (p. 239), a humanistic acceptance of the
tragic ambiguity of life itself.

The significance of Andreas's perspective on his sibling's doomed quest
for perfect order is reaffirmed and developed in the subsequent works
in the tetralogy. In *Kepler*, a work of almost dizzying formal complexity (the geometric and Pythagorean obsessions of the scientist's thought
are the basis of the novelist's structural design),[21] Banville makes his hero
one who learns that, despite his revolutionary method and his elegant
solutions to celestial problems, he has truly learnt very little about the
mystery of being. At the last he remembers what he was told by a Jewish
lensgrinder whom he met on his travels, and affirms a stoic humanism,
touched with mysticism: 'What was it the Jew said? Everything is told us,
but nothing explained. Yes. We must take it all on trust. That's the secret.
How simple! He smiled. It was not a mere book that was thrown away,
but the foundation of a life's work. It seemed not to matter.'[22] Kepler's first
book had been a work of the purest fiction in which he had mistakenly
placed the five perfect Platonic solids in the five intervals between the six
known planets. His subsequent work laid the basis for scientific method
and Newtonian mechanics. In Banville's sense of things, both achievements partake of an aesthetic formality: they are expressions of a rage for
order which may or may not afford ontological consolation or certainty.

In *The Newton Letter: An Interlude* (1982), Banville questions the very
possibility of the historical imagining which has ostensibly engaged him
in the first two parts of his tetralogy. A biographer of Isaac Newton during the course of an unsatisfactory love affair comes in his own work and
life to just such an impasse as apparently terminated the scientific career of
his subject. Banville has his anonymous academic quote from an imaginary second letter from Newton to the philosopher John Locke in which
he confesses to essentially epistemological despair. A crippling inability
to trust his own experience and his own perceptions about history gradually overwhelm the narrator in this hallucinatory book, until he finally
abandons his project. While in the country house where he had settled to
complete his biography, he fails hopelessly to read aright the social and
emotional realities of the human situation which there confronts him. He
must learn a humility before the facts which his literary ambition would
have him interpret all too readily. Past and present for this frustrated

suitor of the muse of history are alike redolent of ambiguity: 'So much is unsayable: all the important things. I spent a summer in the country, I slept with one woman and thought I was in love with another; I dreamed up a horrid drama, and failed to see the commonplace tragedy that was playing itself out in real life.'[23]

Banville concludes his tetralogy by immersing a final protagonist in the suffering and pain of a tragedy more horrific than that so uncomprehendingly observed by the narrator of *The Newton Letter*. In *Mephisto*, Gabriel Swan, a mathematician of genius, is corrupted by the Faustian hubris of his personal quest for order. Through dreadful pain (he is hideously burned in an explosion) he, like all the heroes of the tetralogy, must learn the lessons of ineluctable facts, however he might wish to avoid them:

I woke up one morning and found I could no longer add together two and two. Something had given way, the ice had shattered. Things crowded in, the mere things themselves. One drop of water plus one drop of water will not make two drops, but one. Two oranges and two apples do not make four of some new synthesis, but remain stubbornly themselves.[24]

The text is markedly allusive (even more so than is customary in the work of this formidably well-read author), but the effect is strangely disconcerting. Throughout, nomenclature, image and symbol all suggest a novel structured with mathematical precision (the second part is a near mirror-image of the first); the reader is overwhelmed by a sense of informational overload. The mind reflects on analogies, correlations, attempting to complete symbolic patterns, only to encounter frustration.[25] New material is always complicating the picture. The work embodies, therefore, its own theme as the impulse to discern symbolic order is constantly defeated by the changing conditions of a literary artefact attentive to chance as well as choice, the random as well as the ordered. Here a highly self-conscious text advertises its own inadequacy.

It is not, however, only chance and disorder that challenge the possibility of symbolic pattern in *Mephisto*. The novel is pervaded by a sense of evil, made actual in the figure of a seedy familiar, a cut-price Mephistophiles who does the dirt on life whenever he can. In a subsequent novel, *The Book of Evidence* (1989), Banville further explores the nature of evil, placing at the centre of a work a problem which has always concerned him. Indeed, what gave his humanistic vision its peculiar strength in the tetralogy was that in establishing a philosophy of redemptive despair, of almost mystical acceptance of the given, even as he celebrated the heroic tragedy of the creative imagination in its interpretative endeavour, he never averted his gaze from the general savagery and cruelty of life. This disciple of Wallace Stevens and Rilke is no poet of cheap grace or of the unearned sublime.[26] Rather, the compacted poetic prose, the intently constructed paragraphs of his fiction, draw on a mordant, often chillingly precise awareness of the abject condition of much life and of many corrupted things.[27] And so, *The Book of Evidence* confronts the psychopathology of almost motiveless violence in a novel where a casual act of irresponsibility initiates a sequence of meaningless events, climaxing in the hideous murder of a young woman. The narrator from his prison cell as he awaits sentence recounts a tale of dreadful inattention for all that he has achieved academic distinction in, of all things, probability theory. This is a book of ghastly improbabilities which have their origin in the criminally inattentive, self-regarding persona of the narrator himself. The novel has its Gothic aspects, as so much of Banville's work has; it compels attention with its curious combination of psychological thriller and the burlesque. A literary tour de force, a novel of self-reflexive strategies, a fiction that knowingly addresses the condition of the fictional, it is a characteristic Banville performance of exuberant artfulness and high art. But it is also characteristic of this wonderfully talented writer in its insistence on the moral demands of the given, which require supremely difficult acts of imagining to give them their due. And it is that obsessive preoccupation with the given, with the facts of the case, which makes both Banville and McGahern, so different in many ways, worthy inheritors of the materialist envisioning of their Irish master, Joyce himself.

NOTES

1 The novels of John McGahern (b. 1934) considered in this essay are *The Barracks* (1963), *The Dark* (1965), *The Leavetaking* (1974; revised 1984) and *The Pornographer* (1979).

2 See M. Adams, *Censorship: The Irish Experience* (Dublin: Sceptre Books, 1968) p. 253. McGahern was dismissed from his job as a primary schoolteacher in a Dublin school following the publication of *The Dark*. See also O. Sheehy Skeffington, 'McGahern Affair', *Censorship*, 2 (Spring 1966), 27–30.

3 McGahern's three collections of short stories are *Nightlines* (1970), *Getting Through* (1978) and *High Ground and Other Stories* (1985).

4 J. McGahern, *The Dark* (London: Faber and Faber, 1965), pp. 99–100. Hereafter, page references will be given in the text.

5 See, in particular, 'My Love, My Umbrella' in *Nightlines* and 'Parachutes' in *High Ground and Other Stories*.

6 J. McGahern, *The Leavetaking* (London: Faber and Faber, 1974), p. 9.

7 *The Pornographer* (London and Boston: Faber and Faber, 1979), p. 238.

8 *The Barracks* (London: Faber and Faber, 1963), p. 59. Hereafter, page references will be given in the text.

9 The novels of John Banville (b. 1945) considered in this essay are *Nightspawn* (1971), *Birchwood* (1973), *Doctor Copernicus* (1976), *Kepler* (1981), *The Newton Letter: An Interlude* (1982), *Mephisto* (1986) and *The Book of Evidence* (1989).

10 S. Deane, '"Be Assured I am Inventing": The Fiction of John Banville', in P. Rafriodi and M. Harmon (eds.), *The Irish Novel in Our Time* (Lille: Publications de l'Université de Lille, 1975–6), p. 229.

11 Quoted by R. Imhof in 'An Interview with John Banville', *Irish University Review: John Banville Special Issue*, 11, 1 (Spring 1981), 6. This issue contains much valuable information on Banville and a checklist of his work (including his short stories).

12 See Imhof, 'An Interview', 9. See also Rudiger Imhof, 'John Banville's Supreme Fiction', *Irish University Review*, 11, 1 (Spring 1981), 61.

13 J. Banville, quoted in 'Novelists on the Novel: Ronan Sheehan Talks to John Banville and Francis Stuart', *The Crane Bag*, 3, 1 (1979), 83.

14 John Banville, *Birchwood* (London: Secker & Warburg, 1973), p. 13. Hereafter, page references will be given in the text.

15 Quoted by F. C. Molloy, 'The Search for Truth: The Fiction of John Banville', *Irish University Review*, 11, 1 (Spring 1981), 29.

16 In the Acknowledgements to *Doctor Copernicus*, Banville cites as 'the two works on which I have mainly drawn', T. S. Kuhn's *The Copernican Revolution* (1957) and A. Koestler's *The Sleepwalkers: A History of Man's Changing Vision of the Universe* (1959).

17 See T. S. Kuhn, *The Structure of Scientific Revolutions* (Chicago: University of Chicago Press, 1970).

18 I was helped in my understanding of the background to Banville's scientific novels by discussion with my wife Suzanne Brown and by the Open University text, C. A. Russell (ed.), *The 'Conflict Thesis' and Cosmology*, (Milton Keynes: Open University Press, 1974). See especially the chapter by R. Hooykaas, 'The Impact of the Copernican Transformation', pp. 55–85. See also Koestler, *The Sleepwalkers*.

19 John Banville, *Doctor Copernicus* (London: Seeker & Warburg, 1976), p. 29. Hereafter, page references will be given in the text.

20 Imhof, 'John Banville's Supreme Fiction', 73.

21 In 'John Banville's Supreme Fiction', Imhof demonstrates that *Kepler*'s structure is based on certain scientific and musical analogues.

22 John Banville, *Kepler* (London: Seeker & Warburg, 1981), p. 191. Hereafter, page references will be given in the text.

23 John Banville, *The Newton Letter: An Interlude* (London: Seeker & Warburg, 1982), p. 79. Hereafter, page references will be given in the text.

24 John Banville, *Mephisto* (London: Seeker & Warburg), p. 233.

25 Rudiger Imhof has provided a detailed study of the intellectual background to the novel in 'Swan's Way, or Goethe, Einstein, Banville: the Eternal Recurrence', *Études Irlandaises*, 12 (December 1987), 113–29. I find the debts

to earlier writers in this novel less coherently worked out than Imhof suggests: I think the author exploits them to suggest symbolic possibilities rather
than to compose a *roman à thèse*.

26 J. Banville, 'A Talk', *Irish University Review*, 11, 1 (Spring 1981), 13–17; Banville
    cites both Stevens and Rilke in relation to his own artistic aspirations.

27 Some of Banville's manuscripts and notebooks are now owned by Trinity
    College, Dublin, Library. These show what a remarkably deliberate art-
    ist Banville is. A paragraph in his work, for example, can be worked and
    reworked around a set of key words until it achieves that polished, almost
    marmoreal assurance which characterises his style.

CHAPTER 19

'Have we a context?': transition, self and society in the theatre of Brian Friel

Brian Friel's drama has always attended to precise social moments in the history of the Irish people, and his imagination has repeatedly been drawn to those phases in Irish social experience that can be reckoned as transitional. His earliest success achieved in *Philadelphia, Here I Come!* (first performed at the Gaiety Theatre, Dublin, in 1964) accordingly took as its ostensible subject Irish emigration as social fate, at the very moment when altering economic conditions and communications were to make the act of departure from the native place altogether less absolute and definitive than they had traditionally been. Ten years later, Gar O'Donnell would have had the chance of university in Galway, Dublin or Coleraine (to which many Donegal students flocked in the 1970s), and twenty years later he would have lobbied for a Green Card and spent his summers in Ireland reckoning Boston to Shannon a comparatively inexpensive, short flight. *The Loves of Cass McGuire* (first performed in New York at the Helen Hayes Theatre in 1966) also caught a poignant moment of transition in Irish/Irish American relations, focusing at just that point in social history when an economically resurgent country, with its eyes on membership of the European Community, was beginning to recover from its infatuation with all things American (that infatuation reaching hysterical proportions during John Kennedy's all too brief presidency and a kind of orgasmic intensity during his visit to the land of his forebears in 1962). Poor Cass McGuire, vulgar, ebullient, every bit the returned Yank in 1966, finds her family well able to do without the money she has faithfully dispatched to them during her impoverished years in New York. They had never really needed it, her brother informs her in a cruel kindness which lets her (and a whole generation of Irish American exiles) know that they do not really need *her* either.

It was in 1970, however, that Friel himself made clear that he thought of himself as a socially conscious artist in a transitional society, drawing explicit attention to what had only been implicit in his earlier work, even if the dramatic power of his early successes came rather more from their ability to explore emotional ramifications of social fact than from their analytic presentation of a social dimension. In that year Friel expressed the ambition 'to write a play that would capture the peculiar spiritual, and indeed material, flux that this country is in at the moment. This has got to be done, for me anyway, and I think it has got to be done at a local, parochial level, and hopefully this will have meaning for other people in other countries.'[1]

Within two years, grim events across the Donegal border with County Derry and Northern Ireland gave him ample opportunity to dramatise a society in flux by focusing on the inhabitants of a particular district, the Bogside in Derry city, as its inhabitants were caught up in the waves of a violent political crisis. *The Freedom of the City* (first produced in the Abbey Theatre in 1973) represents Friel's most explicitly social drama of that troubled decade, as it addresses the dilemma of the citizen when he or she is confronted by the manipulative power of the state to mould a disintegrating reality to its own purposes. That play is Friel's most damning indictment of contemporary society. In it we see the actual lives of three victims of violent political repression denied any social significance by a state which must define them as legitimate targets of its claim to exercise control in a society undergoing revolutionary transition. But its stark theme does in fact alert us to a dominant feature of his work as a whole – that is the inability of his characters to express themselves as social beings in any context other than the family or the local community. In *The Freedom of the City*, we see indeed the local, distinctive identities of three Derry citizens, who as such might be expected to enjoy the rights of civic space, denied any mode of self-expression in a political system which finally takes their lives, reputation and very individuality. 'I must', the judge at the play's end announces as he gives the state's judgement on its own actions, 'accept the evidence of eye-witnesses and various technical witnesses that the three deceased were armed when they emerged from the Guildhall, and that two of them at least – Hegarty and the woman Docherty – used their arms. Consequently, it was impossible to effect an arrest operation.'[2] But *The Freedom of the City* is only the most graphic statement of a problem with which Friel has grappled throughout his career. For a sense of the dislocation between public definitions of the self, of personhood, of citizenship, and the actual life of the affections is something which is present in almost all of his work, though at its most explicit in Friel's dramatic stratagem of Private Gar and Public Gar in

Philadelphia. It is very much a concern, for example, of *Living Quarters* (first produced in the Abbey Theatre in 1977).

In *Living Quarters*, a career soldier in the Irish army who has won distinction serving with a United Nations' peace-keeping force cannot resolve the ambiguities involved in his role as public hero and private participant in familial discomfiture. He has just been presented with a celebratory parchment by the people of Ballybeg, the Donegal village near which he has been stationed for many years; this public moment draws from him the rueful observation: 'Yes, I suppose the intention was good. But being addressed by the people of Ballybeg – "You are our most illustrious citizen" sort of stuff – my God they don't know me and we don't know them' (p. 234). There is a sad irony in his sufferings as the middle-aged man whose young wife has had an affair with his son while he was away on the one piece of active service his career has demanded. And for the Irish public, which in the 1960s had gained in confidence as economic growth replaced the stagnation of the previous four decades (taking especial pride in the 1970s in the dutiful exercise of its peace-keeping responsibilities in the Middle East), the sufferings of Commandant Frank Butler were a troubling reminder of the defeated quality of so much Irish life, even in a decade which seemed to see Ireland escaping from the impotent isolation of its recent past. That the hero of such a mission as that undertaken by the commandant is seen in this play to be deeply flawed as a man and who, incapable of resolving his emotional and familial crises, chooses suicide is peculiarly shocking. For it highlights (suicide being rarely admitted as a cause of death in Ireland) the disjunction between the public and the private in contemporary Irish experience in an immediate way. There is even the suggestion in the play that the quality of Irish civic life, the role it offers its army officers, for example (who must await promotion from one year to the next in some provincial town or village), works its poison on the private and familial worlds:

Walking over here from the camp, d'you know what I was thinking: what has a lifetime in the army done to me? Wondering have I carried over into this life the too rigid military discipline that – that the domestic life must have been bruised, damaged, by the stern attitudes that are necessary ... (p. 194)

So Friel's theatre in its social dimension is a theatre of societal transformations, of transitions. But it is also a theatre in which the individual characters are beset by manifold difficulties when they seek to define themselves as anything other than members of a family or of a markedly local community. The society in which they live, move and have their being affords little or no civic space for such self-expression, and at moments of transition this becomes strikingly evident. For transition itself confronts the familial and local worlds of Friel's characters (in which they seek such meaning as seems available to them) with fundamental challenges. George O'Brien has written of Friel's theatre: 'It speaks on behalf of its characters' inner lives rather than for their social existence',[3] accurately highlighting the essentially subjective concerns of Friel's dramaturgy. But the fact that almost all his characters must perforce ground their sense of personal meaning in the emotional life in its familial and local contexts is an aspect of their social existence to which Friel's writings consistently bear a pained and poignant witness. They can do no other, Friel's work implies, since the public life of a transitional Ireland, its institutions, professions, self-definitions, social modes, offer them nothing commensurate with their capacity to demand fulfilment and a sense of personal and collective significance.

Two of Friel's most remarkable plays exhibit how perennially Friel has been concerned as a dramatist with the problematic I have outlined in these terms. *Aristocrats* (first performed in the Abbey Theatre in 1979) and *Translations* (first performed in Deny by the Field Day Theatre Company in 1980) both in their different ways addressed the crisis of transition and suggested how profoundly that involved, for the individual, problems of public, societal definition.

Aristocrats was a Chekhovian elegy, lyrical and redolent of pathos, for the life of a Catholic family which has long inhabited a Big House near Friel's quintessential Donegal village, Ballybeg. A dynasty that has served both the British and Irish state in meeting and doling out 'unequal laws unto a savage race' in a spirit of Victorian duty, the O'Donnells are reaching a point of terminal decline. The old judge is senile following a stroke, and the house and all that it stands for can no longer exist in the new Ireland of slot-machine empires, entrepreneurial greengrocers who supply the tourist hotels and political violence across the border. The family has returned for the marriage of one of the daughters of the house to the widowed greengrocer many years her senior who is scarcely a suitable match for the depressive, sensitive, musically gifted young woman who can see no other future for herself in the diminished, unfulfilled world she has inherited. Through the action of the play, which sees the death and burial of the old judge (a funeral is the focus of the family reunion rather than the anticipated wedding, in a nice dramatic irony), we slowly learn of the family's history and of the lives of the dispersed children of a marriage which imprisoned a vibrant young woman of the theatre in the living death of respectability until she took her own life. None of the children has been able to make any sort of life in Ireland. Casimir, the son of the house, is the repository of family traditions and mythology. It is he who remembers, misremembers, invents its significant social past as a centre of aristocratic Catholic influence in the district and an island of literary and intellectual cultivation in a sea of rude peasant life. His imagination is drawn to a fiction in which his family represented the epitome of Catholic Victorian and Edwardian civilisation (Gerard Manley Hopkins rested on one of their armchairs and read from *The Wreck of the Deutschland*, Chesterton and Belloc were family friends, the O'Donnells arranged John McCormack's papal knighthood). But Casimir, the nostalgic celebrant of all this imaginary tradition (his evocations of past familial occasions are an anachronistic mélange which he scarcely troubles to authenticate in his instinctively mythological animadversions on the past), is a failed lawyer who has married a German woman and now works in a food-processing factory in his wife's country where she works as a cashier in a bowling alley. The O'Donnells have become a little German family, and Casimir cannot even converse with his own German-speaking children. He is adrift between the fictional social existence of the family's past and its actual life in a new European consumer and leisure society, without satisfactory public meaning. He has, in a bemused transition, forsaken a dying dynasty for the nuclear family and consequently spends much of the play on the long-distance telephone trying to communicate across unbridgeable cultural and social gulfs.

The women of the house in their various ways embody the dynastic crisis and the improbability of a social role for themselves in the Ireland of the later twentieth century. Judith is a martyr to her father's illness, and her illegitimate child (the fruit of an affair with a Dutch reporter who had no doubt covered the siege of the Bogside in which she had participated) is in an institution, unacceptable to the one man, an owner of mobile homes for tourists, who might wish to marry her. Claire has had her belief in herself as a musician crushed by her overweening father in just the way he crushed the life of her mother, and Alice, who married a village boy, is an alcoholic who keeps her probation officer husband on permanent duty. Her husband Eamon is perhaps the most interesting character in the play, and he asks the most pertinent question in this drama of the transitional crisis and failed social possibility. One of the new Irish, a young man of humble birth who has married into a good family and embarked on a promising career as a diplomat, he has thrown it all away because of an injudicious involvement with the republican cause in Northern Ireland (which would scarcely have pleased his superiors in the Department of Foreign Affairs in the 1970s during the Coalition Government led by Liam Cosgrove, when Northern Policy was being articulated by Conor Cruise O'Brien). He now works in London at a job he does not really enjoy. It is he who, as the play ends and we know the house will have to be sold, expresses the hope that it may in some way be saved. His wife Alice, by contrast, feels a sense of release. She acknowledges that the death of the house is harder for Eamon than for herself because she recognises that he has always been regretfully in love with her sister Judith (to whom he first unsuccessfully proposed):

ALICE: You and Judith always fight.
EAMON: No we don't. When did you discover that?
ALICE: I've always known it. And I think it's because you love her; and that's the same thing. No, it's even more disturbing for you. And that's why I'm not unhappy that this is all over – because love is possible only in certain contexts. And now this is finished, you may become less unhappy in time. (p 324)

'Have we', asks Eamon in reply, 'a context?' in a question which goes to the heart of the play. Do any of the O'Donnells and those associated with them have a context where they can experience the meaningful social existence without which love cannot blossom into an innovative and creative life. Love in the oppressive atmosphere of Ballybeg House, cut off from the life which surrounds it, has bred suicide, madness, neurosis, alcoholism, confusion and loneliness. As the world changes, the audience wonders if anything can really change for these hurt human beings who desperately need 'a context'.

Translations is a play of contexts too and dramatises a moment when social transition presses acutely on the individual who seeks a mode of social existence that has substance in public and private reality. Friel himself has supplied a succinct summary of the play's contents:

Translations is set in a hedge-school in Ballybeg, County Donegal. The year is 1833. The British army is engaged in mapping the whole of Ireland, a process which involves the renaming of every place name in the country. It is a time of great upheaval for the people of Ballybeg: their hedge-school is to be replaced by one of the new national schools; there is a recurring potato blight; they have to acquire a new language (English); and because their townland is being renamed, everything that was familiar is becoming strange.[4]

And in this journal, which he kept while he was working on the play, Friel identified the social and cultural significance of the historical matter which preoccupied him in his work:

In Ballybeg, at the point when the play begins, the cultural climate is a dying climate – no longer quickened by its past, about to be plunged almost overnight into an alien future. The victims in this situation are the transitional generation. The old can retreat into and find immunity in the past. The young acquire some facility with the new cultural implements. The in-between ages become lost, wandering around in a strange land. Strays.[5]

Owen, the play's principal character, is most fully the victim of this transitional state of affairs. It is he who has left Ballybeg and its tribal, communal satisfactions for Dublin and a life of commerce, which has made him a man of some substance. Just the sort of person, with the local knowledge to boot, that the imperial power would happily recruit to aid it in its progressive and yet colonially inspired mission, the mapping of the country and the changing of place names from Irish to English. But it is Owen's mistake, as he comes to recognise, to believe that he can negotiate with impunity between the two contexts which constitute his social experience, Ballybeg and the new order which is asserting its authority in cartography, a system of national schooling and in taxation. By the end of the play he knows he cannot. He is left without any context in which he could live with integrity other than that offered by the armed rebellion of the Donnelly twins, whose menacing shadow hangs over the entire play. So the play's primary concern is alienation from the modes of social existence which are possible in a society enduring transition under the impetus of colonial government. The theme of language explored here, with its disjunctions, in a period of fundamental change, between a linguistic contour and social fact, is, I would argue, subsidiary to the dominant theme which preoccupies Friel in this as in so much of his work. Disjunction between an Irish-language consciousness and a social reality being recreated from English-language moulds is just another reason proffered by Friel as to why it is impossible in Ireland to achieve a creative and fulfilling relationship between public and private experience. So emigration (represented here in the person of Maire, who wants to learn English so that she can seek work in America), cultural nostalgia of a frozen and self-delusive kind (represented here by Jimmy Jack the polymath classicist), complacent accommodation (represented by Hugh who would take a job at the national school if he could get it) and internal exile (the innocent Manus, suspected of complicity in the murder of the English soldier Yolland, flees to an Irish outback) are all hopelessly inadequate social and imaginative contexts within which to confront the realities of an Ireland shaped and controlled by the experience of colonialism. Such an Ireland leaves no room, allows no real civic space for its

Owens, its Manuses, its Maires. At the end only three possibilities remain apparent: the acquiescence of Hugh ('Take care, Owen. To remember everything is a form of madness', p. 445); emigration; or making contact with the mountainy men.

Such a reading, of course, does some damage to the play as a theatrical experience. For it is the peculiar power of the best moments in the play to suggest the privacies of the human heart, even as it dramatises a complex socio-cultural situation. One thinks of the dual language love scene between Maire and Yolland, as touching as anything in Irish drama since Christy Mahon met Pegeen Mike; Maire reciting in wonderment the magical names of an England she knows only in the person of the murdered Yolland; Hugh remembering his unheroic role in 1798. When writing the play, Friel advised himself to avoid the too obviously political and public issues which the situation in Ballybeg in 1833 inevitably raises. 'The play', he reflected, 'must concern itself only with the exploration of the dark and private places of individual souls.'[6] But the play as written and performed shows those private places as determined by the prevailing conditions of public life and consequently as places where pain, loss, a sense of betrayal prevail, and where the right to privacy itself, most immediately expressed in the right to one's own name and mother tongue, is publicly denied. In focusing most obviously on the language question in *Translations*, Friel wrote a play for contemporary Ireland which would inevitably touch on a pressure point in a society that still reckons itself in transition between a Gaelic order in which the Irish language determined reality and an English language context which, although it affords economic opportunity, is somehow felt to be out of step with the needs of the Irish spirit. That fact, together with the dramatic power of some of its most affecting scenes in which individual, private feeling is tenderly revealed on stage, I believe distracted audiences from the more searching critique Friel was offering of late twentieth-century Ireland. The work was neither a lament for a vanished civilisation (a kind of *aisling* as Edna Longley posited[7]) nor an historical investigation of the roots of our distress (the anachronisms which critics have noted and the self-conscious modernity of the dialogue, all semiotics and ethnography, signal that), but a fiction in which is inscribed the social and cultural dilemma of living in a society that offers no ready means for the individual to negotiate between the private life of feeling and the public life of action, in which even language, which might supply a negotiatory instrument, is implicated in the social problematic. The Ireland of *Translations* was therefore an Ireland in which it was impossible to imagine any satisfactory social reality emerging from the processes of change which the play dramatised. It was at its most reflective moments marked by a bleak pessimism that the Irish context could be anything other than disabling and destructive to its confused inhabitants. All it could offer by way of hope was Hugh's resigned commitment to continue his wrestling with words and meanings as an alternative to his son's determination ('I know where I live') to cast in his lot with the forces of rebellion which must resist the coloniser's theodolytes as well as his bayonets:

But don't expect too much. I will provide you with the available words and the available grammar. But will that help you to interpret between privacies? I have no idea. But it's all we have. I have no idea at all. (p. 446)

Friel's *Dancing at Lughnasa* (first performed in the Abbey Theatre in 1990) was once again a major play of social transition. But this time the sense of contextual inadequacy, which so dominated his work in the seventies and eighties, was replaced, in a striking shift in Friel's career, by a vision of Irish life that suggests there are residual energies in its culture which can enhance individual and collective experience. It is perhaps the most warmly celebratory of any of this dramatist's works and represents a moment in his imaginative development when he reckons the Irish context not wholly without spiritual resources in which the individual can discover personal and collective meaning.

The time is August 1936 in the home of the Mundy family, two miles outside the village of Ballybeg. Five sisters (the youngest twenty-six, the oldest forty) live together in the family home, along with the seven-year-old child of Chris, the youngest sister, and their brother Jack who has recently returned from a missionary parish in Uganda, his health apparently broken and his mind in disarray. There is only one wage-earner in the household, the pious, strait-laced oldest sister Kate. Maggie, at thirty-eight, is the housekeeper, Agnes, thirty-five, and the simple-minded Rose, all naivety and sexual innocence at thirty-two, supplement the family income by knitting gloves at home. Chris, mother to the illegitimate Michael (who as a young man narrates the action of the play as a personal memory), has given birth to the son of a devil-may-care Welsh travelling salesman (one possessed of an English accent) and adventurer who visits Ballybeg very occasionally. Change is in the air. The family has fun with the new wireless on which the dance music of the 1930s (subject in the Ireland of that time to much ecclesiastical censure) supplies a steady diet of syncopated frivolity (interrupted only when the valves overheat or the batteries give out). More threateningly, old ways of life seem at risk. A new arcade is opening in the town, no doubt disturbing local shopkeepers, and a new factory has started up making machine gloves, thus undercutting the cottage industry in which our two sisters are engaged. A war in Spain will also take Chris's ne'er-do-well lover off in quest of excitement. There is almost a hint, indeed, in the precision of the historical detail in *Dancing at Lughnasa* that Friel is humorously poking a little sly fun at those who noted the anachronisms of *Translations*. This most definitely is 1930s rural Ireland. But it is also of course Ireland in 1990, since the country still reckons itself essentially rural and judges traditional modes of life to be at risk from the forces of economic growth and rapid social change. Much of contemporary Ireland is Ballybeg writ large.

At the end of the play, we learn of the many disasters which overtake the Mundy family and we realise that the vibrant, colourful, exuberant, comic two days we have, imaginatively, spent in their company are only the nostalgic memories of the narrator who has composed the past into a personal myth of individual fulfilment and content. It is the constituents of this myth that are the most challenging aspects of the play, for they amount to a way of thinking about modern Ireland as a context, which excitingly augments Friel's analysis of Ireland as a colonised society in his earlier play *Translations*.

The play is set at harvest time during the feast of Lugh, the pagan god of the sun worshipped by the ancient Celts. There are rumours of strange rites, involving fire and dance in the hills, at which a local boy has been terribly burnt. As we get to know the brave-spirited bunch of women who confront a life of hardship and economic insecurity with wit and dignity in their simple home, we realise that there stirs within them a love of life and an unexpressed sexual energy which makes them unconscious pagans even as they accede to the pieties of conventional religion and the rule of the parish priest. Father Jack, the repatriated missionary, is the character whom Friel employs to articulate the vision of Ireland's pagan vitality in this work. He has, it transpires, gone native in Africa. He found there the ceremonial of native religion, its efficient polygamy and communal ritual all too easy of synthesis with his own life-enhancing version of Catholicism and has accordingly been forceably retired by his Church. The suspicion that attends his return inevitably falls on the family as a whole and Kate will, as summer ends, lose her job as a teacher in the parochially controlled local school because of her brother's heterodoxy. But for a moment Jack's vision of African life and the exuberant vitality of the five women of the house seem to provide a way of thinking about Ireland which sets it apart from the developed world and hints at a shared experience with the colonised societies of the developing world where indigenous religion has not been completely overlaid by alien concepts. In a poignant fancy, the women ask Jack if he could find them husbands in Africa. He replies that they would have to live polygamously there, sharing the same man. They are less than appalled by such a prospect, frustrated as they are by the manless parish of Ballybeg. And Chris, who in the course of the play 'marries' her son's father in a dance of perfect communion (which 'marriage' saves her from depressive illness when he leaves for Spain), is in fact sharing Gerry with a wife and child in Wales. Or so Michael the narrator discovers after the death of his father. A bigamous relationship in Ireland seems as oddly workable as the polygamy of Africa. Sexual and familial needs in traditional societies, it is implied, are not to be contained within the conventional bounds of orthodox monogamy, whatever the clergy and the anti-divorce vote in a referendum in 1986 may say (*Dancing At Lughnasa* is among other things a powerful post-referenda statement).

It is in the extraordinary dance scene in Act I of *Dancing At Lughnasa* that the pagan energies of Ballybeg are allowed their freest expression. Marconi's magical invention, which brings the strains of an Irish dance tune over the ether to a cottage kitchen, presides like some lord of misrule over an increasingly uncontrolled outbreak of uninhibited celebration and carnivalesque exuberance. In the Abbey performance, this was a moment of unambiguous joy for actors and audience alike, the communal female world of the Mundy family raised to ecstatic self-forgetfulness. The text in fact suggests a more complex occasion and indicates that Friel's aligning of Irish life with Third World experience in this work is not merely sentimental evasion of the crisis of Ireland's transitional condition for some pastoralism of the primitive. The pagan notes, to which the Mundy family are made individually and collectively subject, beat out, Friel indicates in his stage directions, a tune with dark as well as liberating implications. Maggie is first to fall under their hypnotic power: 'her head is cocked to the beat, to the music. She is breathing deeply, rapidly. Now her features become animated by a look of defiance, of aggression; a crude mask of happiness.' For ten seconds she dances alone 'a white-faced, frantic dervish'. All the sisters but Kate, horrified that Chris tosses Jack's surplice over her head, then join her in a wheeling dance that Friel indicates should be 'almost unrecognisable' and 'grotesque'. Suddenly Kate is overwhelmed, the tart piety of her persona abandoned for some more authentic expression of her essential nature:

Kate dances alone, totally concentrated, totally private; a movement that is simultaneously controlled and frantic; a weave of complex steps that takes her quickly round the kitchen, past her sisters, out to the garden, round the summer seat, back to the kitchen; a pattern of action that is out of character and at the same time ominous of some deep and true emotion.

And Friel advises of the dance as it reaches a crescendo of noise and violence:

With this too loud music, this pounding beat, this shouting – calling – singing, this parodic reel, there is a sense of order being consciously subverted, of the women consciously and crudely caricaturing themselves, indeed of near-hysteria being induced.[8]

Their dance is the dance of the misplaced, of proud, gifted, bravely energetic women whose lives are misshapen by an Irish society that will, as it changes, destroy the life they have struggled to achieve. A key word in the play is ceremony. It is the word Father Jack struggles to remember (his mind failing) as he recalls the efficacy of an African sacrificial ritual. Michael invokes the 'marriage' of Chris and Gerry as a 'ceremony' and in Act II Father Jack offers a vision of the ceremonial richness of tribal life and the 'magnificent ceremonies' of the Ryangans in Uganda: 'And the interesting thing is that it grows naturally into a secular celebration; so that almost imperceptibly the religious ceremony ends and the community celebration takes over.'[9] But the dance in the first act, so like and yet unlike the tribal dancing Father Jack recalls from his Ugandan days, indicates that Friel does not believe Irish life can readily be transposed to the ceremonial innocence of some Third World context. Nevertheless the play, with its highlighting of the pagan aspects of the Irish tradition, suggests a context within which it may be possible to read the colonial experience of the country in a more benign light than Friel's work had hitherto deemed possible. Ballybeg – with its feasts of Lughnasa, the mask-like designs a child paints on a toy kite, the vibrant and yet dangerous call of its music, the instinctive animism of its feeling for the material world which makes of a wireless a whimsical presiding deity and a gramophone (Gerry thinks he will make a killing selling them in Ireland) appropriately named a Minerva (Minerva was an Italian goddess of handicrafts) – functions here as a vision of some alternative to the world of apparently inevitable dislocation and familial disruption represented by the economic and social changes that destroy the Mundy household as summer ends. It hints at residual springs of Irish energy and personality which, if tapped, might allow self and society to flow more readily together, carried along as they must be in the changeful waters of a post-imperial history.

NOTES

1 B. Friel, *Selected Plays* (London: Faber and Faber, 1984), p. 168. Subsequent page references to Friel's plays in the text (unless stated otherwise) are to this volume.
2 Quoted in G. O'Brien, *Brien Friel* (Dublin: Gill and Macmillan, 1989), p. 126.
3 *Ibid.*, p. 125.
4 B. Friel, 'Extracts from a Sporadic Diary', in T. P. Coogan (ed.), *Ireland and the Arts*, special issue of *Literary Review* (London: Namara Press, n.d.), pp. 56–7.
5 *Ibid.*, p. 59
6 *Ibid.*, p. 60.
7 E. Longley, *Poetry in the Wars* (Newcastle upon Tyne: Bloodaxe Books, 1986), pp. 190–1.
8 B. Friel, *Dancing at Lughnasa* (London: Faber and Faber, 1990), pp. 21–2.
9 *Ibid.*, p. 48.

CHAPTER 20

Hubert Butler and nationalism

One of the most poignant, yet unsettling, of Hubert Butler's essays is his short evocation of the social ambiance of Riga Strand in 1930 which stands at the head of his second Lilliput collection, *The Children of Drancy* (1988). A text of the Great War's aftermath, it reminds one of the atmospherics of the opening section of T. S. Eliot's *The Waste Land,* published eight years earlier, with a cosmopolitan caste of Eastern Europeans cast up on a shore where history had so recently been at its terrible full tide. Eliot's poem had been moodily attentive to the *déraciné* voices of those left behind as the waters of empire subsided, following the cataclysm of 1914–18. Butler, in 'Riga Strand in 1930', brings more of a realist's eye to social anomalies to be observed in the young and fragile Latvian republic that had carved out a temporary space and peace for itself after the deluge. For, Butler remarks (intrigued by a social mix lost on departing Russian officers and merchants frustrated by 'the petty officialdom of a young nation, proud of its new independence and snatching at all opportunities of asserting it'[1]):

All the same Riga Strand must have a fascination for more leisured visitors, who have time to be interested in the past and the future of the small republics which rose from the ruins of the Russian Empire. It is the holiday ground not only for the Letts but for all the newly liberated peoples of the Baltic. There one may meet Estonians and Finns, Lithuanians and Poles, bathing side by side with Germans, Russians and Swedes, who were once their masters.[2]

For all the sane good spirits of Butler's prose reflection, as compared with Eliot's neurotic nostalgias, 'Riga Strand in 1930' does in fact share a precise preoccupation with Eliot's early verse: the role of the Jews in European culture. It is difficult not to read this early essay (unpublished, as far as I know, until its inclusion in *The Children of Drancy*) in the light of Butler's subsequent writings, especially the searching and heartbreaking 'The Children of Drancy' (first published in 1968) with its exacting appreciation of the numbing scale of genocidal atrocity. In so doing

252

we may, I think, risk misreading what is being said in 'Riga Strand' and therefore miss especially how this essay relates to his analysis of nationalism, which remained consistent throughout Butler's career. It is necessary to analyse what Butler had to say of the Jews in this early piece.

Most of the essay expresses a genial visitor's relish for a certain down-at-heel social levelling in the new, insecure Latvian republic where he finds himself; a slightly discordant note sounds, however, when Butler remarks:

the fashionable specialists have no prodigal Caucasian Princes to diet in the sanitoria, they have to haggle with Jewesses about mud-baths and superfluous fat. The disinherited have come into their own, the Jews have descended like locusts on Riga Strand … for them it has the fascination of a forbidden land.[3]

Perhaps that egregious simile ('descended like locusts') is a moment of free indirect style, in which we can take amused pleasure at the discomfiture of a fashionable and prejudiced medical specialist. However, the extended set of gloomier reflections with which the essay concludes suggests that it is Butler himself who reckons the Jews of Eastern Europe a people of a diasporic consciousness, among whom certain forms of separatist self-definition could take hold. The nature of Jewish identity and self-awareness is raised in a passage which must be quoted at length:

As the evening grows colder the strand empties and a group of boys come out of the pinewoods where they have been collecting sticks, and build a bonfire on the shore. The rest of the sand sinks back into the night and they are islanded in the firelight. As the flames burn higher it is easier to see their keen, Jewish faces. They have not yet lost the colours of the Mediterranean, though it may be many generations since their ancestors travelled up from Palestine to the shores of the Baltic. The leaders are a woman with loose black hair and a Messianic youth of seventeen. Are they making speeches or telling stories? The eyes of twenty boys are fixed, black and burning in the firelight, on the woman as she cries passionately to them in Yiddish. Three or four boys reply to her and they sing strange, unhomely Eastern tunes. Only a few yards away are the cafés and sanitoria but in the darkness the sand seems to stretch away interminably and the Jewish scouts seem to be the only creatures alive on the shore, a nomad tribe, camping in the desert. They are of the same race, the same families perhaps, as the predatory blondes in the beach costumes, but the spirit that fills them now is alien from Riga or from Europe. Persecution has hardened them and given them strength to survive war and revolution and even to profit from them and direct them. Perhaps it is they who will decide the future of Riga Strand.[4]

In the lurid light of the flames that were to engulf European Jewry a short decade later, it is possible to read this passage with its images of fire, sanitoria and 'predatory blondes', with its reference to persecution, war and revolution, as mysteriously prescient of the awful fate that awaited young people such as these glimpsed at evening in the Latvian pinewoods. Yet as a document of 1930, Butler's 'Riga Strand in 1930' was, arguably, evoking Jews in the kinds of terms which shortly thereafter would make them vulnerable. (Perhaps that is why Butler, with his finely tuned moral antennae, did not publish this piece at the time). They are in their perse-cution-forged hardness 'alien' in spirit from contemporary Europe; and the passage dramatises their presence in Riga as that of a displaced desert people far from their Mediterranean home: 'a nomad tribe camping in the desert'. Their songs are 'strange, unhomely Eastern tunes'; we can not be sure if they are 'telling stories' or 'making speeches', but they may be about to 'profit by ... and direct events'. Even a sojourn of generations in northern Europe, and familial ties to those among whom they live, do not mean they have been assimilated.

Why did Butler write in this way in 1930, even if he chose not to publish what he had written? The question forces itself on us, even if pos-ing it might seem otiose given the moral certitude and sheer personal courage of the writer's later activities as antagonist of Nazi anti-Semitism in Vienna in 1938–9 and the alert sensitivity of his writings to its gross, particular abominations. For the mature Butler unambiguously believed that 'Hitler had brought into the world misery such as no man had pre-viously believed possible'[5] and had lived his life in that implacable con-viction. So what was he really thinking of when he wrote of the Jews on Riga Strand in the way he did in 1930? Answering that takes us, I believe, to his analysis of nationalism, which he presented in its most explicit form in an essay of *circa* 1936, 'Fichte and the Rise of Racialism in Germany'. In that posthumously published essay, the nature of Jewish identity was once again raised, this time as part of a complex argument in cultural his-tory and in relation to a general theory.

'Fichte and the Rise of Racialism in Germany' was first published in *In the Land of Nod* in 1996. It would in fact have been, had it been published in the mid-1930s when it was written, a contribution *avant la lettre* to the study of nationalism that has gone on apace in the academic world since the 1970s. This, of course, received added impetus from the re-emergence of the nationalistic politics Butler understood so intimately in Central and Eastern Europe, following the disintegration of the Communist world after 1989.

Butler's 1930s reflections on the subject of nationalism began with a distinction, now familiar enough in the literature, between two forms of the phenomenon: 'till recently it has been to nobody's interest to draw distinctions between patriotism and nationalism, for the two sentiments, deriving indefinably from land and people, seemed to be two complementary aspects of the same emotion'.[6] He then immediately complicates the matter by identifying a third category of analysis, one which is not a matter of land and people but of 'loyalty and devotion to common traditions, history, social and political institutions'.[7] This latter category is fundamentally different, Butler suggests, from the other two, being dependent on individuals rather than collectivities and on 'thought' rather than 'instinct'. As such it is fragile and easily overwhelmed by the other 'two more primitive sentiments'.[8] It is the 'more primitive' forms of the phenomenon that interest Butler in this essay, and in particular 'the attainment or recovery of solidarity through racial sentiment'.[9]

Like subsequent theorists of nationalism (the Ernest Gellner of *Nations and Nationalism* immediately springs to mind), Butler in this essay does not presume that racial feeling or indeed any kind of nationalism is a given of the human condition. It emerges as a consequence of circumstance. As such racial sentiment 'seems always to have represented a transitional and regressive phase in the history of peoples, a disorganised period when a settled equilibrium has been disturbed'.[10] In ancient times primitive man both in hunter-gatherer and settled communities had no need of racial sentiment. In such conditions

It is clear that the community is a spiritual rather than a material fact, and its preservation or destruction does not depend primarily on aggression or blood kinship or other physical factors. It is only when the spiritual continuity of the tribe is fatally interrupted that these assume importance.[11]

In the ancient world, however, droughts, floods, pressure from other tribes, often uprooted a community and set it wandering, making it prey to feelings of 'racial solidarity', until the group once again became settled and 'under the influence of property, sentiment attach[ed] itself to the country and its institutions, not to race'.[12] In fact, its members became civic nationalists and abandoned ethnic nationalism, in the terms recent theorists of nationalisms have frequently deployed. Yet in such peoples, 'the habits and feeling of nomadic life lie there still in germ, and at a threat the people'[13] will regress to racial solidarity. Among modern nations, Butler then declares, the Germans were the first to experience and to justify such a regression, following their defeat by Napoleon's forces. At that moment (and throughout the essay an implicit analogy is being drawn with the Germany of the 1930s, reacting against the defeat of 1918), they were already 'dispersed and divided'[14] and under the pressure of conquest, all too likely to adopt racialism as a unifying force. In that, for all his 'reputation for solid domesticity and love of material security', the German, like 'the homeless Jew', has remained a 'racialist'.[15] For neither Jew nor German has had the good fortune of the Irish, whose material and historical circumstances have to a large extent kept them free of 'any idea of racial solidarity'.[16] The Germans and the Jews, so the argument of this essay runs, as peoples share more than they can conceive. In a terrible irony, Butler observes of German depredations on Jewry in the 1930s: 'German racialism has exterminated its most capable interpreters.'[17] And the modern Germans have succumbed to 'a homeless ravening passion hungering for eternal triumphs and universal empire'.[18]

So the Jews of Riga Strand are nomads in whom a spirit of racial nationalism could burgeon, as it had done among the Germans of Fichte's day and in Butler's own. In the context of Butler's thinking about nationalism in the 1930s, therefore, they are by no means to be seen as exhibiting an essential Jewishness that is to be deprecated. Rather they remind one what dispersal and a nomadic experience can do to a people. It can foment a latent racialism, which can flare up under stress and persecution.

In 'Fichte and the Rise of Racialism in Germany', Butler identifies the French, the Swiss and the Irish as peoples in whom patriotism ('which kindles a binding sentiment for their native land'[19]), rather than racialism, has predominated. In the Irish case, this was in part because the Anglo-Irish, who invented Irish patriotism in their 'idealization of a country rather than a race',[20] did not mingle easily with the mass of the Irish population. Yet they managed to impose some of their patriotic values along with their language on the people. And as property owners they developed, too, 'an intimacy with the unchanging earth which its too easily detachable cultivators found it more difficult to entertain'.[21] The second part of that rather surprising sentence indicates that Butler was aware, for all his faith in Irish patriotism, that the modern Irish could fall victims of racialism too. For they also were a 'scattered ... people'.[22] ('Too easily detachable cultivators', as a reference to Irish emigration is an uncomfortable evasion of grim experience, masked as sardonic irony.)

Butler held tenaciously to his theory that racialist nationalism is a product of displacement and dispersal. In 1963, in a talk entitled 'Wolfe Tone and the Common Name of Irishman', he continued to value a patriotism which 'concerns our country and not our blood'.[23] Indeed, by 1963 he had come to the view that the racialism that had so deleteriously affected the Germans and the Italians in modern times was not nationalism at all, but racialism *pur sang*.

So-called Italian and German nationalists of thirty years ago were racialist and anti-nationalist. Hundreds and thousands of men, who lived for centuries under the same hills, beside the same lakes, were all at once told that they were aliens. In their thousands, Germans were rejected from the Tyrol and Slavs from northern Italy. What had this to do with nationalism, which is comprehensive and based on neighbourliness and shared experiences and common devotion to the land in which you live? It has nothing to do with racial origins.[24]

And the essay expresses a fear of the kind of dispersed society modernity has created, in which a diasporic version of national identity can all too easily replace the patriotism of a Tone:

We can keep in touch with like-minded people by post in disregard of the person next door; we can get all the support for our views by turning a knob on the radio. That is why nationalism as Tone conceived it, that is to say a concentration of affection for the land in which you live and the people with whom you share it, has become in our day a delicate and fragile plant. It implies an intercourse with your neighbours which is direct and personal, whereas nowadays we need not bother with our neighbours, particularly if, as most people do, we live in cities; there are dozens of impersonal, indirect ways of bypassing our neighbours and being adherents of some remote community.[25]

Sixteen years later, Butler returned to his theme in 'Divided Loyalties' (first collected in *Escape from the Anthill*, 1985, where a revised version of the essay is dated 1984). There he compared his own sustained feelings for Ireland with the short-lived, early twentieth-century emotions of a cousin Theo and the young Eric Dodds (subsequently Regius Professor of Greek in the University of Oxford and the editor of Louis MacNeice's *Collected Poems*). Their nationalism, he argues, had been skin-deep, his more deeply engrained, based as it was on his ownership of land: 'If you are heir to some trees and fields and buildings and a river bank, your love for your country can be more enduring'[26] than that of such as cousin Theo and Dodds 'who had not an acre between them'.[27] Yet this essay of old age is touched with a valedictory, pessimistic note too as it records the passing of a way of life, the life of a minor gentry in Ireland, who might have been a bulwark against the forces of international commerce, if enough of them had been able (like Butler himself it can truly be said) to extend their love of place to a dutiful love of country. For Butler, as old as the century in his eighty-fifth year, ownership of a 'few acres of Irish soil' could give 'an unreasoning obstinancy' but only 'the illusion of security'.[28]

There is in those final phrases something of the quintessential Butler spirit – a sure grasp on the precise limits of a situation, whatever sentiment might hope for, which made him so refreshingly clear-eyed a writer. For he certainly knew that in modern conditions, racialism, or ethnic nationalism, which had so besmirched 1930s and 1940s Europe, could be a threat in his own country as the patriotism he so valued, and in fact represented in his good-mannered yet exacting way, faded with the social conditions that had nurtured it in a vital few. His analysis of nationalism, implicit in the vivid essay that stands at the head of his oeuvre, and returned to throughout his career, challenges us to be aware of dangers that may lurk in a nationalism in the early twenty-first century, which can invoke a globalised Irishness, a diaspora of putatively shared identity, but which can also involve willful ignorance of our immediate neighbours in their sometimes difficult human particularity.

NOTES

1 H. Butler, *The Children of Drancy* (Mullingar: Lilliput Press, 1988), p. 3.
2 *Ibid.*, p. 4.
3 *Ibid.*, p. 8.
4 *Ibid.*, p. 11.
5 H. Butler, *In The Land Of Nod* (Dublin: Lilliput Press, 1996), p. 197.
6 *Ibid.*, p. 67.
7 *Ibid.*
8 *Ibid.*, p. 68.
9 *Ibid.*
10 *Ibid.*
11 *Ibid.*, p. 69.
12 *Ibid.*
13 *Ibid.*
14 *Ibid.*, p. 72.
15 *Ibid.*
16 *Ibid.*, p. 73.
17 *Ibid.*, p. 75.
18 *Ibid.*, p. 83.
19 *Ibid.*, p. 72.
20 *Ibid.*, p. 73.
21 *Ibid.*
22 *Ibid.*
23 *Ibid.*, p. 34.

24 *Ibid.*, p. 35.
25 *Ibid.*, pp. 35–6.
26 H. Butler, *Escape From The Anthill* (Mullingar: Lilliput Press, 1985), p. 97.
27 *Ibid.*
28 *Ibid.*

CHAPTER 21

The Irish Dylan Thomas: versions and influences

In 2006 a horse named 'Dylan Thomas' won the Budweiser Irish Derby at the Curragh in County Kildare. One wonders what the ghost of the Irish poet and dedicated follower of racing form, Patrick Kavanagh, made of that turn-up for the books. Did he place a spectral bet on the favourite, named for a Welsh poet he had once admired for 'fresh young attitude and vocabulary',[1] and a poet he had at one time seen as possessed of 'the blood of life as it is lived'.[2] Did he remember that he had also opined: 'As far as I am concerned, Auden and Dylan Thomas, Moravia, Sartre, Pound are all Irish poets. They have all said the thing that delighted me, a man born in Ireland'[3] and put his celestial shirt on Dylan Thomas, whatever the odds (9 to 2, in fact). Or did he recall with bitterness that when he had been introduced to Thomas in London in 1951 (he was hoping for regular work with the BBC, where the Welsh poet was a less than securely ensconced broadcaster, alert one supposes, to a possible rival), Thomas had immediately, to quote Kavanagh's biographer, 'launched into a broad, offensive imitation of his accent'[4] causing considerable hurt? If that came to mind in the afterlife, we may perhaps imagine the Mucker poet betting on any horse but Dylan Thomas, the name of a writer whose life and death as broth-of-a-boy, cadger, showman, backer of horses and drunk so resembled that of Dubliner Brendan Behan, whom Kavanagh loathed. He might well have judged *sub specie aeternitatis* that both men had proven what he himself had observed whilst alive: 'For a man in Ireland to have the label "poet" attached to him is little short of a calamity … He becomes a sort of exhibit, not a man in and of the world … the idea is that he is either an uproarious, drunken clown, an inspired idiot, a silly school girl type, or just plain dull. He is in no way to be taken seriously.'[5] And Kavanagh particularly denounced 'a bourgeois concept of rebelliousness'.[6] Dylan Thomas as an 'Irish poet' had fallen victim to an Irish fate, one that was subsequently to destroy Behan. So back any horse but Dylan Thomas, or God save the mark, Brendan Behan.

After that unfortunate meeting between Kavanagh and Thomas in 1951, the former could, had he been inclined, have made the latter a representative target in a polemic in which he constantly engaged against what he called the 'bucklep'. By this term Kavanagh meant in the local Irish context any trading on a fake version of national identity, usually by way of whimsical, overly coloured phrase-making, ostentatious wildness of manner or literary style. The Ulster poet W. R. ('Bertie') Rodgers was, in Kavanagh's terms, 'a remarkable bucklepper ... a word-weaver, a phrase-maker the equal of any Radio Eireann writer'.[7] Referring to an introduction Rodgers had supplied for a volume of John Millington's Synge's plays (Synge was another notorious 'bucklepper' in Kavanagh's estimation), Kavanagh adduces such Bertie-isms as '"a community as rounded as the belly of a pebble one would pick up on a shore", "the halter of hunger round their necks", "tongue forked for praise or blame"', as evidence against him.[8] This certainly sounds familiar to the reader of Thomas's prose. And the 'bucklepper' supreme for Kavanagh was the Mayo-born County Meath poet F. R. Higgins of whom Kavanagh wrote in 1947 in an essay entitled 'The Gallivanting Poet' ('gallivanting' being a synonym of 'bucklepping'),

Personally Higgins was like his verse. He carried the gallivanting pose into his ordinary life. He pronounced poetry 'poertry' and drawled humorously.

One gets weary of such posing and longs for the reality of simple man. I hate being cruel to his memory, but I cannot get away from the thought that he never became adult and sincere ...

I never thought him a droll and gallivanting fellow for all his acting; and meeting an illusion always tired me.[9]

The Irish poet Louis MacNeice, who was a distinguished producer at the BBC when Kavanagh was hoping for the corporation's patronage, did not share this view of either Rodgers or Higgins. Indeed, in his long poem *Autumn Sequel* (1954), they both appear as exemplary figures among a pantheon of individuals who redeem a debased age from its colourless mediocrity, from the 'murk / And mangle of modernity'.[10] Higgins especially, in the figure of Reilly in the poem, is afforded a peroration that makes him the image of the true poet, whom to know was 'a hailfellow idyl, a ragout / Of lyricism and gossip'. He is represented as the quintessential Gaelic bard: he 'came / from Connaught, and brown bogwater and blue / Hills followed him through Dublin' with an 'Aura of knowing innocence, of earth that is alchemised by light'. Lacking the conventional virtues, he was unreliable but was 'generous and vague', well-able to 'down his beer / With gusto', 'always game / For hours and hours of

Rabelaisian mirth'.[11] This makes Higgins, in MacNeice's poem, an Irish cousin of Dylan Thomas, news of whose death in New York occasions these memories of the Irish poet. Like Thomas had just done, Higgins had died prematurely twelve years earlier. And in various sections of *Autumn Sequel*, Thomas, under the sobriquet of 'Gwilym' is romantically associated with place and honoured as an inspired, rambunctious, yet meticulous 'maker', in terms that recall Kavanagh's excoriation of the 'bucklep'. If Kavanagh thought Higgins a fake, he would surely have thought MacNeice's version of Thomas equally suspect (though we have no record of his actual response to *Autumn Sequel*).

'Gwilym' (as Thomas is named in the poem) turns up early for once, in this work, for in the second canto of the twenty-six canto poem, he 'comes to town' bringing poetry to a drab London city:

> For Gwilym is a poet; analogues
> And double meanings crawl behind his ears
> And his brown eyes were scooped out of the bogs,
> A jester and a bard.[12]

He is a force of nature, a rebel whose enemy is the money he does not have, a planetary god of the irrational:

> And so today, with Gwilym come to town
> Like Saturn swathed in ring on ring of smoke,
> The walls of Albany street came tumbling down
>
> With enough cries of time to point the joke
> While enough ash to fill a funeral urn
> Dropped from his cigarette; a dwarfish folk
>
> Crept out from under the counter and took their turn
> Mumbling and gesturing their pagan lore
> Till dolmens rose and us and a quern
>
> Ground out red herrings and mustard sauce galore
> Which flowed all over the borough of Marleybone
> To prove that two and two do not make four.[13]

Canto V takes MacNeice on holiday to Wales. In a work in which the Irish poet Higgins and the Welsh poet Thomas have been treated as Celtic cousins, it is no surprise that MacNeice considers Wales is 'half-way home'[14] to Ireland, and that in this and the following canto, Wales is made the site of fabled romance and of a quixotic, whimsical climate that suggests the principality itself manifests the poetic spirit. In lively if stereotypically gendered terms, Wales is evoked in 'her moodiness, madness, shrewdness, lewdness, feyness', her variegated weather made to seem 'wilful, not to be pinned / Down to a definite answer'.[15]

Cantos XVII and XX respond to hearing of the death of Dylan Thomas in New York and describe his funeral in Camarthenshire. In a work of tired alienation from a drab post-war world, in *Autumn Sequel* Dylan Thomas's death is treated as if it represented the death of all poetry, the obsequies appropriately being conducted in that half-way Ireland, Wales. In canto XVIII, a lament for the makars, the poet imagines

> Once more and once more Arthur has passed by
> In the slow barge and all who draw their breath
> For the last time in ballad and saga die
>
> Once more and for the last time; in Gwilym's death
> We feel all theirs and ours.[16]

And the poem associates the death of Arthur with the image of Deirdre and Naisi playing chess together in knowledge of their doom, and with the drowned Sir Patrick Spens, as if to summon into imaginative existence a Celtic confederacy against ever-encroaching mediocrity, bureaucracy and mechanisation that are excoriated in the work as a whole. Even Lycidas is allowed his place, drowned in the Irish sea.

The funeral day in Laugharne once again links Dylan Thomas with Irish poetry and with Ireland. The journey to Wales is a journey to 'the misty west' and MacNeice notes that he is wearing the shoes he remembers buying with Thomas, to attend the interment of the remains of W. B. Yeats at Drumcliff five years earlier. The weather, true to Welsh (and Irish) form, is spectacularly changeable. A night in Swansea 'benighted / In black and barren rain' gives way to a day of sunlight as 'Delighted / Morning erupts to bless all Wales'.[17] As the poet recalls the scene at the graveside in Laugharne, he makes of Thomas a poet of place as Yeats is often made the poet of his native Sligo and his own 'misty west'. He suggests 'What he took / From this small corner of Wales survives in what he gave', and his home on a cliff is read as 'an open book / Of sands and waters, of silver and shining brown / His estuary spreads before us and its birds / To which he gave renown, reflect renown / On him'.[18]

All of this is sentimental enough. What raises this canto above the level of skilfully registered sentiment is its sense of how death as shocking absence cannot be made amenable to consolatory illusions and that even poetry is insufficient 'rebuttal of the silence and the cold / Attached to death'.[19] The canto ends with the knowledge that Dylan Thomas 'will keep us waiting'[20] forever, even as we can imagine him walking in the door. After the first death, indeed, there is no other.

Which reminds us that both MacNeice and Thomas had been Second World War poets, whose work had made death itself a theme in the years of the Blitz and of V1 and V2 rockets – Thomas most famously in 'A Refusal to Mourn the Death by Fire of a Child in London', MacNeice in such poems as 'Brother Fire', 'The Trolls' and 'Troll's Courtship'.

In MacNeice's career the turn towards a form of existential humanism couched as a mode of faith, which found expression, as in these poems, in archetypal images, is usually attributed to the influence of Yeats. MacNeice, we remember, had been working on his critical study of Yeats in the early stages of the war. This work appeared in 1941 as *The Poetry of W. B. Yeats*, with a preface dated September 1940 that, in admitting the mystical element in poetry, suggested that Yeats was having a distinct effect on him. 'To both the question of pleasure and to the question of value', he observed, 'the utilitarian has no answer. The faith in the *value* of living is a mystical faith.'[21] By July 1941, in one of his published 'London Letters' written for an American journal, he went further and recognised that what was 'being forced upon people' was 'the religious sense'; for in the circumstances of nightly bombardment (the piece was subtitled 'Reflections from the Dome of St Paul's' and was written after one of the most destructive German attacks on the city), MacNeice concluded, 'we need all the senses we were born with; and one of those is the religious'.[22] About the same time, in an unpublished, unfinished article he also wrote:

Death in its own right – as War does incidentally – sets our lives in perspective. Every man's funeral is his own, just as people are lonely in their lives, but Death as a leveller also writes us in life. & Death not only levels but differentiates – it crystallizes our deeds.[23]

To the Yeatsian influence on MacNeice in the war years I would like to add, arguably, that of Dylan Thomas, whom he would memorialise, as we have seen, in *Autumn Sequel*, in terms of the philosophy of life he had developed in the early years of the war, while reading Yeats intensively in preparation for his published study of that poet. For in *Autumn Sequel* Thomas is seen, in Ivan Phillips's words, as 'co-existing at an interface between art and life, life and death'.[24] Yeats forced MacNeice to ponder the mystical aspects of existence and question how life was to be valued. War brought immediate intimations of death and revived the religious sense, zones of feeling in which Thomas was an habitué.

One of Thomas's biographers notes that Thomas probably met MacNeice in Manchester in October 1938 when he took part in a broadcast entitled 'The Modern Muse'.[25] Given that Thomas was highly jaundiced about 'MacSpaunday' and that the other participants on that day were Auden and Spender, we cannot assume that their friendship began there and then. And Thomas had written earlier that year to Henry Treece that MacNeice was 'thin and conventionally-minded, lacking imagination and not sound in the ear'.[26] So the auspices for friendship between them were not good. How close their artistic friendship would become is evidenced, however, by the fact that MacNeice's widow has recorded that Thomas was one of only two poets with whom he cared to discuss the craft of poetry.[27] That friendship probably had its origins in the early war years when they both were engaged in propaganda work, MacNeice at the BBC and Thomas with Strand films, when they drank in the same pubs and moved in overlapping circles. Indeed, MacNeice himself in 1954 asserted they had first met in 1941, apparently failing to recall the Manchester encounter.[28] By 1946, MacNeice had identified what they shared as poets, for it was in those years that he himself had come to understand that the poet's calling was essentially that of a maker of patterns. He observed in an essay entitled 'The Traditional Aspect of Modern English Poetry', published in 1946 that although Thomas 'might be classed with the latest Romantics, the anti-traditionalists' and although his 'matter may seem at times to approach the Surrealists', he 'remains, when it comes to the *pattern* of his verse, *par excellence* a shaper'.[29] So it is possible, perhaps, to see MacNeice and Thomas in the war years sharing not only a thematic engagement with death, with MacNeice's verse admitting mystical, even religious, dimensions that had never been absent in their various ways from Yeats's and Thomas's writings, but also a preoccupation with form and pattern.

This preoccupation demonstrably reaches its apogee in Thomas's oeuvre in the sequence 'Vision and Prayer', finished August 1944, with its stanzaic shape embodying, as it were, the fullness and emptiness of pregnancy and birth. Thomas completed this work about six months after MacNeice had published his poem 'Prayer Before Birth' in *Penguin New Writing*. The fact that both poems can be seen to have at the very least a source in the poetry of George Herbert increases the sense of the connections between them. Thomas's stanzaic experiment can be seen to emulate Herbert's 'Easter Wings', while as Robyn Marsack has shown in detail,[30] 'Prayer Before Birth' is an intricate reworking of the same poet's 'Sighs and Grones', with an allusion too to 'Providence'.[31] What she does not note, however, is that while MacNeice follows Herbert's rhyme scheme in rhyming the first and last lines of the stanzas and exploits enjambement, as did Herbert in his poem, he also varies the line lengths and employs indendation in a marked way so that on the page, 'Prayer Before Birth' suggests gestation and the coming to term of a pregnancy. She does, however, suggest the oral qualities of the poem, alerting us to how the poet performed it in a recorded version. It possesses, I would argue, as well as a distinctive visual effect on the page, akin to that of Thomas's 'Vision and Prayer', a liturgical intensity and a rhetorical drama that makes it the most Dylanesque of MacNeice's poems. The theme of gestation and birth are obviously Dylanesque, and the focus on a child who wishes to be killed in the womb if the world that awaits it is too terrible to be lived in reminds us that John Goodby and Chris Wigginton have noted the 'centrality of the dead child to the two best known of Thomas's war poems' and to 'a group of themes common to every phase of his writing'.[32]

Following Thomas's death on 9 November 1953, MacNeice was to act as advocate for Thomas's poetic achievement in a decade in which the rhetorical, the bardic, the orphic were under heavy interdiction in England as the Movement's aesthetics took the field. Thomas was the *bête noire* of some of its propagandists, who judged Thomas a charlatan. The tenor of MacNeice's case for the defence is interesting.

He opened with an essay 'Dylan Thomas: Memories and Appreciations' which appeared in January 1954 in *Encounter*. There he identified Thomas as a bard possessed of three of the great bardic virtues, 'faith, joy and craftsmanship'.[33] That last virtue was to be a theme he would return to in subsequent reviews of selected works by his dead friend and in a further piece of memoir, as if he was conscious that this is where the reputation was vulnerable in the decade of the well-made poem. Thomas's poems are very well made indeed, MacNeice insists: 'no writer of our time approached his art with a more reverent spirit or gave it more devoted attention';[34] 'his diction was as closely controlled as his content';[35] 'he was a most painstaking craftsman';[36] he was 'so well versed in his craft, that he could stand the rules on their head';[37] 'so let us get it straight and forget all the wishwash about "neo-romanticism". Thomas would not be pleased to hear he was still being bracketed with Barker and Treece and remember that here was a man who was both craftsman and a mixer'.[38] MacNeice, it can be stated, helped to establish the view that Thomas was a dedicated poetic craftsman deeply committed to form, for all the messiness of the life, which it became easier to argue when the correspondence between Thomas and Vernon Watkins was published in 1957.

To Thomas as craftsman, however, MacNeice adds the Thomas who reached down imaginatively to the depths of things, finding him 'nearer to the folk world than to the bookish world'[39] and one in whom the poet is seen to be 'a maker rather than a piece of litmus paper, who knows that poetry is organic and not mechanical'.[40] Intriguingly, in 'Memories and Appreciations' he celebrates Thomas in terms that associate him with Yeats, for this essay links Thomas with the late Yeatsian theme of gaiety and joy. It echoes, too, MacNeice's preface to his critical study of W. B. Yeats when he affirms: 'Many of his [Thomas's] poems are concerned with death and the darker forces yet they all have the joy of life in them … all the poems (a rare thing in this age of doubt) are suffused both with a sense of value, a faith that is simultaneously physical and spiritual.[41] Thomas and his poetry confirmed MacNeice in a kind of humanistic mysticism that he had begun to establish, as we saw, in the writing of his book on Yeats.

The MacNeice who commemorated Dylan Thomas in *Autumn Sequel* represents himself as a metropolitan for whom London is at the centre of things, despite the visits it records to Oxford, Glastonbury and Norwich, as well as to Wales. Its basic tonal register, despite passages of poster-colour poeticism, is well-bred, educated commentary, suited to BBC third programme broadcasting (the work was in fact broadcast as a serial production). Its references to the poet's Irish background, indeed, make that remembered world a kind of generalised childhood of folklore and Celtic mystery that sets it apart from contemporary reality, and not something that indicates MacNeice's own complex inheritance. In this, *Autumn Sequel* differs markedly from the poet's work of 1939 to which it is a successor, for in *Autumn Journal* Ireland had in its violent atavisms been entered as a defining constituent of MacNeice's adult political consciousness, which coloured his attitudes to Fascism in Spain and to the threat of imminent war in London during the autumn of 1938. By 1954 when *Autumn Sequel* was published, MacNeice's persona was that of the Londoner for whom an Ulster background, and by extension even Dylan Thomas's Wales, were essentially regional phenomena which might add colour to memory and current brooding on a grey, tedious mode of life in the capital but did not really affect the poet's take on the generally depressing state of affairs in post-war, ill-fare-state Britain.

Ironically, it was the fact that Dylan Thomas hailed from a provincial, peripheral part of our islands that made his voice so compelling for the generation of poets which emerged as writers in the north of Ireland in the 1960s, who were themselves grammar-school educated provincials as Thomas had been when he began to commute between Swansea and London (though they all continued their education in universities in Belfast and Dublin after their grammar-school educations). In this way, Thomas was involved in their cultural self-definition as poets from a problematic region of the United Kingdom in which national and socio-political issues conjoined in challenging ways. In his essay on Thomas, 'Thomas the Durable? On Dylan Thomas', Seamus Heaney remembered in fact how for his generation in their teens Dylan was 'The Poet', whose recorded voice spoke to provincials everywhere. 'Those records of Dylan Thomas reading his poems', he avers, 'records which lined up on the shelves of undergraduate flats all over the world, were important cultural events.'[42] He recollects how

They opened a thrilling line between the centre and the edges of the Anglophone world. For all us young provincials, from Belfast to Brisbane, the impact of Thomas's performance meant that we had a gratifying sense of access to something that was acknowledged to be altogether modern, difficult *and* poetry.

Later, of course, there were second thoughts, but Dylan Thomas will always remain part of the initiation of that first 'eleven-plus' generation into literary culture. He was our Swinburne, a poet of immediate spellbinding power.[43]

And in *Tuppenny Stung*, Michael Longley's memoir of undergraduate days in Trinity College, Dublin, in the early 1960s, that poet includes Thomas in an eclectic packet of poets whom he and his fellow northerner Derek Mahon inhaled with their 'untipped Sweet Afton cigarettes'.[44] And he quotes an example of Mahon's juvenilia, in which he suggests that echoes of 'Hart Crane, Robert Graves and Dylan Thomas do not diminish the originality of this writing'.[45]

It is in Seamus Heaney's essay referred to above that the socio-political and national issues that are involved in being a Northern Irish and Irish poet writing in English and being published in London can readily be observed as determining how Heaney read Thomas. He tells us in 'Dylan the Durable' how the first enchantment wore off as the 'buckleppin' element in the Thomas performance became evident to him and as its rhetorical excesses began to grate. He was particularly harsh on Thomas's erotic poem 'A Winter's Tale', which he damns as 'the verbal equivalent of a Disney fantasia'.[46] What is pertinent here too is not just that Heaney is deploying Patrick Kavanagh's term ('the bucklep') in this essay but that the critic is identifying Thomas's failures as a poet within what might, a little preten-tiously perhaps, be called a Kavanaghesque paradigm. For it was Kavanagh who had introduced, in terms that deeply impressed Heaney at an early stage of his development, the binary categories of the provincial (bad) and the parochial (good) to Irish cultural debate. So in Heaney's essay, apart from the early poems, which he sees as a primal state of feeling which approached, if did not quite enter, a 'longed-for prelapsarian wholeness ... where the song of the self was effortlessly choral and its scale was a perfect measure and match for the world it sang in',[47] Thomas can be allowed mature poetic power only when he is open, as in 'Poem in October' and 'Fern Hill' to the 'sweet, uninflated particulars of the world'.[48] 'Fern Hill', is admired because it is 'buoyant upon memories of a sensuouly apprehended world'.[49] That such memories are likely to be the most vital when they are of the home ground, the 'parish' in Kavanagh's terms, is suggested by Heaney in an earlier essay of 1989 when he had indicted Thomas as one who could not consistently escape the provincial's fate, for he could not 'envisage the region as the original point'.[50]

Interestingly, Thomas on death escapes from the provincial/parochial binary in Heaney's critique. Perhaps there are personal reasons for this. The 1980s saw the death of both of Heaney's parents, and their memorialisation in his poetry. And Heaney as a poet who is deeply respectful of familial and communal obligations, of poetry's ritual duties, would, one feels, have been particularly conscious at this time of Thomas's own similar, almost liturgical appreciation of his calling. Accordingly, Heaney writes of 'Do not Go Gentle into That Good Night', sounding a distinctly personal note: 'Through its repetitions, the father's remoteness – and the remoteness of all fathers – is insistently proclaimed, yet we can also hear, in an almost sobbing counterpoint, the protest of the poet's child-self against the separation.'[51] Which calls to mind Heaney's poems for his dead father, 'Stone Verdict' and 'Seeing Things', which recreate him as an uncommunicative, yet fragile, mortal figure, who filled a child's world with awe and premonition.

For Derek Mahon, by contrast, Thomas has been a poet who has registered the powerful energies of human sexuality. The young Belfast poet whom Michael Longley met in Dublin in the early sixties had long been an enthusiast for the poetry of Dylan Thomas. Heather Clark, in her book on the Ulster poetic renaissance, reports that Mahon remembers being 'inspired by Thomas from an early age' and quotes him as claiming that at the age of seventeen he won a school poetry prize 'for an "unabashed" Dylan Thomas pastiche ... which won only because the judge did not recognise the influence'.[52]

It is easy to imagine Mahon reading Thomas in Dublin in the early 1960s where the Rimbaud of Cwmdonkin Drive served as a figure of flagrant disregard of bourgeois proprieties in a university where he was doubly a provincial; first as a Belfastman, from a city instinctively condescended to in Ireland's capital as somehow beyond the cultural pale, and secondly as an Irishman among the many English public-school-educated Oxbridge rejects who then made up a significant part of the student body. And Mahon's early celebration of insouciant bohemianism ('The Poets Lie Where They Fell') in his first volume *Night Crossing* (1968) surely owes something to Thomas's inspiring example of genius combined with free-loading. Yet what is more telling is that Mahon's regard for Thomas as a poet has lasted the distance, as it were. This was made evident when he chose to contribute a selection of his work to the Faber and Faber 'Poet to Poet' series, in which a contemporary poet 'selects and introduces a poet of the past' (to the series Heaney contributes selections from Wordsworth and Yeats, Longley from MacNeice, Paulin from Hardy; Mahon's other contribution is a selection from Swift). In his introduction to this 2004 volume, Mahon makes his continued esteem for Thomas unambiguously clear. Despite the 'recurrent and strangely vindictive … attacks on his reputation', he remains persuaded: 'he was the real thing, the true vatic voice, if slightly overdone from time to time'.[53] And not only does he respond to the visceral, somatic early work and to the war poems, in which Mahon sees Thomas as developing 'to tremendous effect'[54] the theme of linguistic inadequacy before the fact of death, already present in the early work, but also to the later poems of love and marriage and of sexual celebration. Contra Heaney, he relishes 'A Winter's Tale', finding it 'largely disregarded … perhaps for its too obviously picturesque and sentimental touches, perhaps for its calm mystery, its uncharacteristic quietude, its absence of verbal games'.[55] He quotes, as expressive of mature sexuality, the lines

> Burning in the bride bed of love, in the whirl-
> Pool at the wanting centre, in the folds
> Of paradise, in the spun bud of the world.
> And she rose with him flowering in her melting snow.

And he concludes his selection from Thomas's poetry with the three poems, 'In Country Sleep', Over St John's Hill' and 'In The White Giant's Thigh', which he declares 'represent his crowning achievement'.[56] Of the last of these he reports 'Feminist critics generally praise this poem for its affirmation of female sexuality, quoting Julia Kristeva on "biological" thought',[57] and he quotes admiringly from the poem without in any way demurring from that view. Indeed, one is tempted to read Mahon's response to this set of poems, which he reads as a sequence beginning as a prayer for his daughter and moving through a poem of dark premonition to 'an ecstasy of rhapsodic resolution and celebration',[58] as a liberating force in his own aesthetic, which in 'The Cloud Ceiling', a poem for a new daughter in a recent volume *Harbour Lights* (2005), opens itself to indeterminancy, and the shared intimacies of nurture.

NOTES

1 A. Quinn, *Patrick Kavanagh: Born-Again Romantic* (Dublin: Gill and Macmillan, 1991), p. 145.
2 *Ibid.*
3 Cited A. Quinn, *Patrick Kavanagh: A Biography* (Dublin: Gill and Macmillan, 2001), p. 294.
4 *Ibid.*, p. 307.
5 P. Kavanagh, 'A Goat Tethered Outside the Bailey', in A. Quinn (ed.), *Patrick Kavanagh: A Poet's Country* (Dublin: Lilliput Press, 2003), p. 238.
6 *Ibid.*, p. 241.
7 P. Kavanagh, 'Paris in Aran', in Quinn (ed.), *Patrick Kavanagh*, p. 189.
8 *Ibid.*
9 *Ibid.*
10 P. McDonald (ed.), *Collected Poems of Louis MacNeice* (London: Faber and Faber, 2007), p. 399.
11 *Ibid.*, p. 455.
12 *Ibid.*, p. 380.
13 *Ibid.*, pp. 381–2.
14 *Ibid.*, p. 394.
15 *Ibid.*, p. 397.
16 *Ibid.*, p. 456.
17 *Ibid.*, p. 462.
18 *Ibid.*, p. 463.
19 *Ibid.*, p. 462.
20 *Ibid.*, p. 464.
21 L. MacNeice, *The Poetry of W.B. Yeats* (London, New York and Toronto: Oxford University Press, 1941), p. xviii.
22 A. Heuser (ed.), *Selected Prose of Louis MacNeice* (Oxford: Clarendon Press, 1990), p. 136.
23 *Ibid.*, p. 142.
24 Ivan Phillips, '"Death Is All Metaphor": Dylan Thomas' Radical Morbidity', in J. Goodby and C. Wigginton (eds.), *Dylan Thomas: New Casebooks* (London: Palgrave, 2001), p. 125.
25 P. Ferris, *Dylan Thomas: The Biography*, new edn. (Washington, DC: Counterpoint, 2000), p. 156.
26 P. Ferris (ed.), *Dylan Thomas: The Collected Letters*, new edn. (London: J. M. Dent, 2000), p. 328.
27 See H. MacNeice, 'The Story of the House That Louis Built', in J. Genet and W. Hellegouarc'h (eds.), *Studies on Louis MacNeice* (Caen: Publications de l'Université de Caen, 1988), pp. 9–10. The other poet was W. R. Rodgers.

28 See L. MacNeice, 'I Remember Dylan Thomas', in A. Heuser (ed.), *Selected Literary Criticism of Louis MacNeice* (Oxford: Clarendon Press, 1987), p. 195.

29 *Ibid.*, p. 140.

30 See Robyn Marsack, *The Cave of Making: The Poetry of Louis MacNeice* (Oxford: Clarendon Press, 1982), pp. 113–14.

31 Herbert's poem 'Providence' speaks of the man who withholds praise of God as one who 'doth commit a world of sin in one'. MacNeice's poem prays 'forgive me / For the sins that in me the world shall commit' (McDonald (ed.), *Collected Poems*, p, 193).

32 Goodby and Wigginton (eds.), 'Introduction', *Dylan Thomas*, p. 16.

33 Heuser (ed.), *Selected Literary Criticism*, p. 183.

34 *Ibid.*, p. 183.

35 *Ibid.*, p. 184.

36 *Ibid.*, p. 185.

37 *Ibid.*, p. 187.

38 *Ibid.*, p. 199.

39 *Ibid.*, p. 202.

40 *Ibid.*

41 *Ibid.*, p. 183.

42 S. Heaney, 'Dylan the Durable? On Dylan Thomas', in *The Redress of Poetry* (London and Boston: Faber and Faber, 1995), p. 124.

43 *Ibid.*, pp. 34–5.

44 M. Longley, *Tuppeny Stung: Autobiographical Chapters* (Belfast: Lagan Press, 1994), p. 36.

45 *Ibid.*

46 Heaney, *Redress of Poetry*, p. 135.

47 *Ibid.*, p. 133.

48 *Ibid.*, p. 142.

49 *Ibid.*

50 Cited by Goodby in Goodby and Wigginton (eds.), *Dylan Thomas*, p. 198.

51 Heaney, *Redress of Poetry*, p. 137.

52 See H. Clark, *The Ulster Renaissance: Poetry In Belfast 1962–1972* (Oxford University Press, 2006), pp. 20–1.

53 D. Mahon, 'Introduction', in *Dylan Thomas: Poems Selected by Derek Mahon* (London: Faber and Faber, 2004), p. vii.

54 *Ibid.*, p. xii

55 *Ibid.*, p. xiv.

56 *Ibid.*, p. xv.

57 *Ibid.*, p. xvii.

58 *Ibid.*, p. xvi.

Index